Kosovo and International Society

Kosovo and International Society

Alex J. Bellamy

School of Political Science and International Studies
The University of Queensland
Australia

First published 2002 by
PALGRAVE MACMILLAN
Houndmills, Basingstoke, Hampshire RG21 6XS and
175 Fifth Avenue, New York, N.Y. 10010
Companies and representatives throughout the world

PALGRAVE MACMILLAN is the global academic imprint of the Palgrave Macmillan division of St. Martin's Press, LLC and of Palgrave Macmillan Ltd. Macmillan® is a registered trademark in the United States, United Kingdom and other countries. Palgrave is a registered trademark in the European Union and other countries.

ISBN 0–333–99260–1

This book is printed on paper suitable for recycling and made from fully managed and sustained forest sources.

A catalogue record for this book is available from the British Library.

Library of Congress Cataloging-in-Publication Data

Bellamy, Alex J., 1975–
    Kosovo and international society / Alex J. Bellamy.
        p. cm. – (Cormorant security studies series)
    Includes bibliographical references and index.
    ISBN 0–333–99260–1
        1. Kosovo (Serbia) – History – 1980– 2. Kosovo (Serbia) – Ethnic relations. 3. Kosovo (Serbia) – History – Civil War, 1998 – Diplomatic history. 4. Europe – Politics and government – 1989– 5. North Atlantic Treaty Organization – Yugoslavia. I. Title. II. Cormorant security studies.

DR2086 .B45 2002
949.7103–dc21   2002022006

10   9   8   7   6   5   4   3   2   1
11   10   09   08   07   06   05   04   03   02

Printed and bound in Great Britain by
Antony Rowe Ltd, Chippenham and Eastbourne

For Ann and Robert Jude

Contents

Preface and Acknowledgements

It is now a truism to say that the dissolution of Yugoslavia began in Kosovo. It is also a truism to say that international society did not engage with the Kosovo conflict until 1998. In fact, international attempts to manage the break-up of Yugoslavia also began in Kosovo though the province's troubled human rights situation was soon forgotten as the West attempted to bring the wars in Croatia and Bosnia to an end. The decision to exclude Kosovo from the peace process shaped the province's destiny and led ultimately to war. Many myths remain despite the dearth of literature that has been produced on the subject since NATO launched Operation Allied Force. One myth is that international society did not engage with Kosovo before 1998. That myth lets many Western policy-makers off the hook by brushing over their choice to ignore the province's problems.

The main aim of this book is to show that international engagement after 1998 did not start from a blank sheet of paper. In fact, the starting point was broad agreement with Serbia's claim to sovereignty over the province. I want to show that it was not by chance that Kosovar politics turned violent or that international society failed to prevent the conflict. In the early 1990s those who argued for a proactive international engagement with conflict resolution in the province were actively silenced. The UN's Special Rapporteur on Human Rights in the region, Tadeusz Maziowiecki, was only once invited to brief the Security Council. A special working group created to investigate the national minorities issue in the province was disbanded. This marginalisation of Kosovo was a largely British creation. It was Lord Carrington who allowed international society to consult the Bosnian Serbs but not the Kosovar Albanians. It was Lord Owen who insisted that the working group be wound up.

The international activism of 1998 and after had Anglo-American roots. Tony Blair and Madeleine Albright were responsible for forging an international coalition against ethnic cleansing. The second aim of the book, then, is to chart the background to that coalition, highlighting the constant debates and the many tools that statesmen used to pursue their goals. In doing so, it exposes many other myths along the way. Whilst I wrote this book I was surprised by how many myths and conspiracy theories are part of the popular discourse about Kosovo. According to some of these myths the Racak massacre was faked, the Kosovo Verification Mission was designed to fail as were the Rambouillet negotiations, the Chinese Embassy in Belgrade was bombed deliberately, and the ethnic cleansing and mass murder that was witnessed in 1999 were at least provoked, if not caused, by NATO. My final aim, therefore, was to expose these myths and explain as accurately as possible how NATO came to launch Operation Allied Force and discuss some of the things that happened when it did.

This book has decidedly Welsh roots. A week or so before NATO launched Allied Force I gave a paper in a meeting above a pub in Aberystwyth. Under questioning from Nick Wheeler I confidently called for NATO to launch air strikes and predicted that they would last less than one week. I spent the next two-and-a-half months trying to understand why I had got my prediction so very wrong. Much of the research and writing was completed during my time with King's College London at the UK's Joint Services Command and Staff College. The finishing touches were added in Brisbane.

This is a well-travelled book and I owe many debts of gratitude. First, I would like to thank Lord Carrington, Lord Owen, Nicholas Rostow, Michael Libal, Geert Ahrens, Thomas Niles, Ben Farrell, Rohit Sawhney and Ivor Roberts for taking the time to answer my questions so thoughtfully and providing so much information. I was also greatly helped by many other people who wished not to be named. They know who they are and I am deeply grateful.

Nick Wheeler, Marc Weller, Stuart Griffin, James Gow, Christopher Greenwood, Paul Williams, Ken Booth, David Jordan, Bill Park, and Ann Lane all provided useful and constructive comments on earlier drafts or other works that led directly into this one. I am deeply grateful to Violeta Hamidi (Becky), who was a wonderful host in Pristina and to Agim Çeku, Sulejman Selimi, Hydajet Hyseni, Mustapha Remy, and 'Lata', for their hospitality and useful insights.

Most of the research was conducted from open sources, though often not sources that are easily traceable. I am therefore extremely grateful to Mary Bone at the Royal Institute of International Affairs library for all her excellent help. I would also like to thank Alison Howson at Palgrave Macmillan and Geoff Till for their help and support, and also Ann Marangos for successfully and patiently navigating the work through its final stages despite the many obstacles I created. Thanks go to NATO photos for permission to use the photo on the front cover and the UN for permission to reproduce the maps. Finally, I owe a large debt of gratitude to Sara Davies for both compiling an excellent index and providing friendly support during the final stages of putting this book together.

All errors of fact and interpretation are, of course, my own.

Brisbane
May 2002

List of Maps

List of Abbreviations

ACTORD	Activation Order
ACTWARN	Activation Warning
CIA	Central Intelligence Agency
CSCE	Conference for Security and Co-operation in Europe
CSO	Committee of Senior Officials (CSCE)
ECCY	European Community Conference on Yugoslavia
EUKDOM	European Union Kosovo Diplomatic Observer Mission
FRY	Federal Republic of Yugoslavia
FYROM	Former Yugoslav Republic of Macedonia
G-7	Group of Seven States (United States, United Kingdom, Canada, France, Italy, Germany, Japan)
G-8	Group of Eight States (G-7 plus Russia)
ICFY	International Conference on Former Yugoslavia
ICRC	International Committee of the Red Cross
ICTY	International Criminal Tribunal for Former Yugoslavia
IFOR	Implementation Force
JAT	Yugoslav Airlines
JNA	Yugoslav People's Army
KDOM	Kosovo Diplomatic Observer Mission
KFOR	Kosovo Force
KVM	Kosovo Verification Mission
LBD	United Democratic Movement
LCY	Yugoslav League of Communists
LDK	Democratic League of Kosovo
MPRI	Military Professional Resources Incorporated
MUP	Serbian Ministry of Interior
NGO	Non-Governmental Organisation
ONUC	United Nations Operation in the Congo
OSCE	Organisation for Security and Co-operation in Europe
SACEUR	Supreme Allied Commander Europe
SANU	Serbian Academy of Arts and Sciences
SFOR	Stabilisation Force
SFRY	Socialist Federative Republic of Yugoslavia
SHAPE	Supreme Headquarters Allied Powers Europe
UÇK	Kosovo Liberation Army

UDBa	Socialist Yugoslav secret police
UKDOM	United Kingdom Kosovo Diplomatic Observer Mission
UN	United Nations
UNESCO	United Nations Educational, Scientific and Cultural Organisation
UNHCR	Office of the United Nations High Commissioner for Refugees
UNPREDEP	United Nations Preventive Deployment
UNPROFOR	United Nations Protection Force
UNTAES	United Nations Transitional Authority in Eastern Slavonia
USKDOM	United States Kosovo Diplomatic Observer Mission
VJ	Yugoslav Army
WEU	Western European Union

Chronology of Events

1912–13	The two Balkan Wars see Kosovo pass from the Ottoman Empire to the Kingdom of Serbia.
1918	Kingdom of Serbs, Croats and Slovenes established.
1945	Socialist Federal Republic of Yugoslavia (SFRY) established. Kosovo becomes part of the Republic of Serbia.
1974	New Yugoslav Constitution promulgated giving Kosovo the status of an autonomous province of Serbia and a high degree of autonomy.
1976	Adem Demaçi and eighteen others imprisoned for 'distributing hostile propaganda'.
1977	Serbian League of Communists publishes the 'Blue book' demanding greater Serbian control over Kosovo.
1981	Student protests in Pristina.
1985	The Martinović case raises the profile of Serb nationalism in Kosovo.
1986	The Serbian Academy of Arts and Sciences leaks a draft memorandum condemning what it describes as genocide against Serbs in Kosovo.
1987	Slobodan Milošević becomes President of Serbia.
23 March 1989	Milošević deposes the Kosovar Albanian Communist leadership. Its leader, Azem Vllasi, is imprisoned.
28 March 1989	The Serb Assembly pass constitutional amendments bringing Kosovo under direct rule from Belgrade.
June 1989	European Parliament delegation visits Kosovo.
24 January 1990	Mass demonstrations in Pristina.
22 March 1990	Serb Assembly passes legislation designed to promote the position of Serbs in Kosovo.
April 1990	US Congressional visit to Kosovo.
November 1990	US Congress passes the 'Nickles amendment'.
May/June 1991	Slovenia and Croatia declare independence.

August 1991	Badinter Arbitration Commission created.
7 September 1991	European Community Conference on Yugoslavia (ECCY) convened at The Hague.
25 September 1991	UN Security Council 713 passed imposing an arms embargo on the whole of collapsing Yugoslavia.
30 September 1991	Unofficial referendum in Kosovo delivers a 99.8 per cent vote in favour of independence.
January 1992	Slovenia, Croatia, Bosnia and Hercegovina and Macedonia are recognised as states.
June 1992	Milan Panić is appointed Prime Minister of Serbia.
August 1992	The International Conference on the former Yugoslavia (ICFY) is created at the London Conference. Special Working Group on Minorities created.
September 1992	CSCE Mission of Long Duration despatched to Yugoslavia.
December 1992	The US issues its 'Christmas Ultimatum' to Milošević. Milošević defeats Panić in Serbia's Presidential election.
June 1993	CSCE Mission of Long Duration ordered to withdraw from Yugoslavia by Milošević.
July 1993	David Owen instructs the ICFY Working Group to cease investigating human rights in Kosovo.
June 1994	Secret negotiations begin between the Serbs and Kosovar Albanians.
November 1994	The UN Human Rights Rapporteur notes that the situation in Kosovo is deteriorating.
December 1995	The Dayton agreement brings peace to Croatia and Bosnia and Hercegovina.
January 1996	Many Western states normalise relations with Yugoslavia and the EU eases the sanctions regime.
February 1996	The UÇK launches its first attacks.
May 1996	The EU recognises Yugoslavia.
September 1996	Serbs and Kosovar Albanians reach an agreement on education.
March–June 1997	The collapse of 'pyramid schemes' in Albania provokes general anarchy.

February 1998	The US eases sanctions against Yugoslavia.
2 March 1998	US officials describe the UÇK as a terrorist organisation.
5 March 1998	Serb forces massacre 58 people in Donji Prekaz.
9 March 1998	The Contact Group condemns the massacre. The US and EU impose sanctions on Yugoslavia.
31 March 1998	UN Security Council passes Resolution 1160.
April 1998	Serbs reject international involvement in the conflict in a referendum.
May 1998	Richard Holbrooke becomes the US Special Envoy to the Balkans and travels to Belgrade.
12 June 1998	The Contact Group issues four demands to Milošević.
16 June 1998	Yeltsin–Milošević agreement.
July 1998	Christopher Hill completes the first draft of a political settlement and invites comments from the parties.
6 July 1998	KDOM deployed in Kosovo.
22 September 1998	NATO issues an Activation Warning for a phased air campaign against Yugoslavia.
23 September 1998	UN Security Council passes Resolution 1199.
1 October 1998	First draft of the Hill plan is formally presented and rejected by both parties.
8 October 1998	Ministerial meeting at Heathrow Airport.
9 October 1998	NATO issues an Activation Order for a phased air campaign against Yugoslavia.
15 October 1998	Holbrooke–Milošević agreement calls for the deployment of an OSCE Kosovo Verification Mission (KVM).
24 October 1998	UN Security Council passes Resolution 1203.
November 1998– March 1999	KVM personnel verify a ceasefire and troop withdrawal.
2 November 1998	NATO deadline for political progress passes unnoticed.
15 January 1999	Racak massacre.
22 January 1999	Contact Group meeting ends inconclusively.
29 January 1999	The Contact Group demands that the Serbs and Kosovar Albanians send high level

	delegation to Rambouillet to agree to an interim settlement based on the Hill plan.
6 February 1999	The Rambouillet conference begins.
20 February 1999	The original deadline passes with neither side accepting the proposals.
23 February 1999	The Kosovar Albanians agree in principle to the settlement and agree to return to Paris in two weeks time to conclude negotiations and sign the agreement.
8 March 1999	Fischer and Van Den Broek visit Belgrade.
13 March 1999	The negotiations begin again in Paris.
18 March 1999	Serbian President Milutinović rejects the proposed agreement.
20 March 1999	The KVM withdraws from Kosovo.
22 March 1999	Holbrooke makes his final visit to Belgrade for talks with Milošević. Serb forces in Kosovo begin a campaign of ethnic cleansing.
24 March 1999	NATO launches Operation Allied Force.
26 March 1999	NATO approves moving to Phase Two of the operation.
27 March	American 'stealth' bomber shot down over Serbia.
12 April 1999	NATO announces its five war aims.
14 April 1999	NATO aircraft mistakenly attack a refugee convoy on the Djakovica road.
23 April 1999	NATO attacks the RTS television studio.
23–25 April 1999	The Washington summit: NATO celebrates its fiftieth anniversary.
26 April 1999	Strobe Talbott opens negotiations with Ivanov and Chernomyrdin in Moscow.
6 May 1999	G-8 meeting in Bonn agrees to appoint an EU mediator to work with Chernomyrdin and NATO and Russia agree common aims.
7 May 1999	The Chinese Embassy is attacked by NATO.
19 May 1999	G-8 process reconvened in a series of meetings in Bonn, Helsinki, and Moscow.
24 May 1999	The ICTY indicts Milošević and his key allies for war crimes.
26 May 1999	UÇK launches a major offensive. Talbott and Chernomyrdin come close to agreement.

27 May 1999	NATO defence ministers meet in Bonn and come close to agreeing to a ground invasion. The UK pledges 50,000 troops for the operation.
1 June 1999	Talbott, Chernomyrdin and Ahtisaari meet in Bonn to discuss a form of words to deliver to Milošević.
3 June 1999	The three negotiators meet in Petersberg and reach an agreement. Ahtisaari and Chernomyrdin deliver the terms to Milošević, who accepts them.
9 June 1999	NATO and the VJ agree a 'military–technical' agreement.
10 June 1999	UN Security Council passes Resolution 1244 and KFOR begins its deployment.

Map 1 The Former Yugoslavia

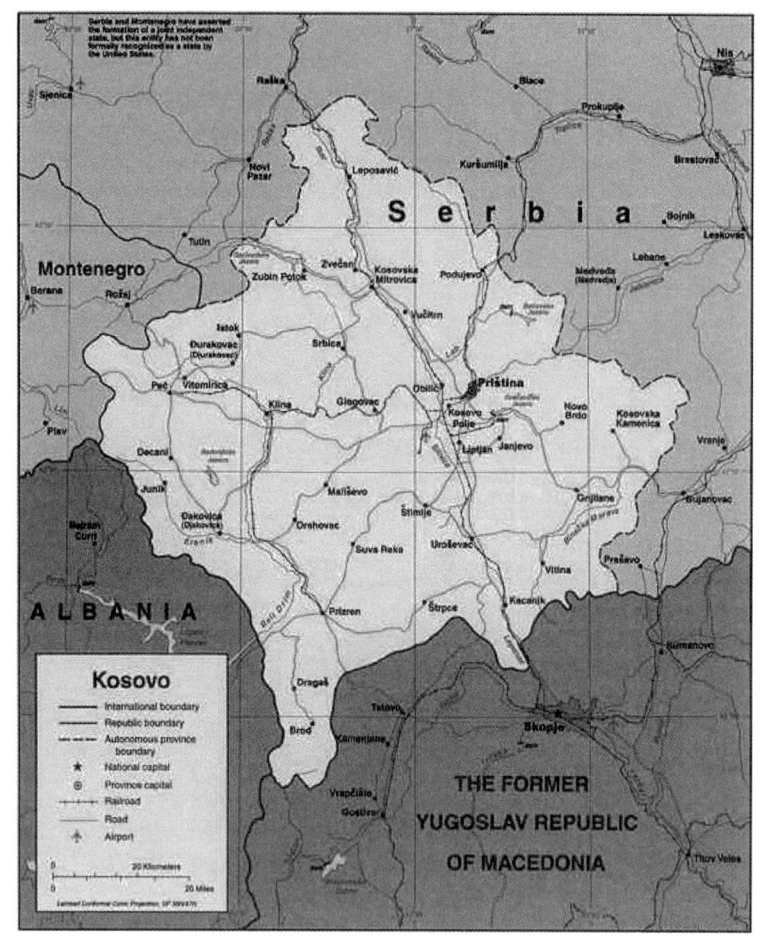

Map 2 Kosovo and Region

Introduction

On 24 March 1999, NATO went to war for the first time. Created in Washington DC in April 1949, NATO was originally designed as a military alliance whose primary purpose was to defend Western Europe against the communist threat in the East. Article 5 of its founding treaty effectively declared that an attack on one member was an attack on all. However, its first war was not a war against the Soviet Union or one of its allies, in fact it occurred almost a decade after the collapse of communism. Nor was it a war of collective self-defence. No NATO members were attacked or even threatened. Instead, NATO's first war was a 'humanitarian war'.[1] It was a war ostensibly aimed at preventing a humanitarian catastrophe in the southern Balkans, a catastrophe caused by a decade of Serbian oppression in Kosovo. Once NATO failed to prevent that catastrophe it chose instead to reverse its consequences and was undoubtedly successful in doing so.

This book asks how NATO came to launch its first war. It argues that international society's engagement with the Kosovo conflict spanned a decade and traversed many different phases, from ambivalence to war. It attempts to explain the complex international diplomacy that enabled NATO to go to war in 1999. It points out that simplistic explanations about American hegemony in Europe are misplaced and that there was nothing inevitable about international responses to the conflict.[2] In answering this question two recurring themes come to the fore: The plurality of international opinion about what to do in Kosovo and the complicated relationships between states, international organisations, and non-governmental organisations (NGOs) that shaped the response. Throughout the 1990s events across the globe influenced the depth and tone of international interest in Kosovo. Events such as the 1992 American presidential election, the 1995 Dayton agreement

1

for Bosnia–Hercegovina, the 1997 British general elections, Albania's descent into anarchy in the same year, and the Russian Duma's attempt to impeach Boris Yeltsin in 1999 all had a profound effect on the situation in Kosovo. The interrelationship between internal and external politics was also vital. Not only is it impossible to explain the activities of particular states without considering internal debates it is also impossible to explain the descent into violence in Kosovo without understanding the conflict's international dimensions. While I argue that NATO was right to launch Operation Allied Force when it did, the central argument of the opening chapters is that not only did the West fail to prevent the conflict it failed to even attempt to prevent the conflict. Although the Kosovo issue was at the fore of the Yugoslav problem more generally in 1990 it was soon relegated to the status of a 'minorities issue' once war broke out in Slovenia and Croatia. From that point on, Kosovo's fate was intimately tied to Serbia's until violence erupted in Kosovo too. Once violence broke out, dominant states in international society embarked on nearly a year of debate about how to respond, ultimately leading to NATO's decision to use force without explicit UN Security Council authorisation.

International engagement with Kosovo was shaped by changing international perceptions of political necessity. For almost seven years the prevailing international perception was that Kosovo was an internal Serbian problem that should not be allowed to threaten the search for peace in Croatia and Bosnia and its subsequent implementation. This was based on a mistaken understanding of the Yugoslav constitution, the belief that the Kosovar Albanians could not stake a claim to sovereignty because they did not control territory, and the insistence that it was not an issue that international society should address because war had not erupted there. This explains why, prior to March 1998, most actors in international society accepted Serbia's claims to sovereignty over Kosovo. What it does not explain is why there was no attempt to mediate or prevent the conflict. Chapter 2 points out that the absence of conflict prevention efforts resulted from an untested and flawed assumption that Serbian President Slobodan Milošević would have jeopardised peace efforts in Bosnia had he been put under pressure to address the human rights problem in Kosovo.

The increase in violence in 1998 began to change prevalent perceptions of political necessity in the West and hence the policies that could potentially be applied to attempt to remedy the situation. I identify three 'syndromes' in particular that persuaded Western policy makers to take a more proactive stance:

- The 'Srebrenica syndrome' (the fear of a repeat of the 1995 massacre in Srebrenica in which Serb forces butchered over 7,500 Bosnian Muslims).
- The 'refugees syndrome' (the fear that conflict in the southern Balkans would inspire a flood of Albanian refugees into the West).
- The 'Balkan wars syndrome', a belief that violent conflict in Kosovo, left unchecked, would spread throughout the region, destabilising Macedonia[3] and Albania and threatening to draw in Bulgaria, Greece, and Turkey.

Consequently, 1998 saw a series of debates between hawks and doves within NATO, Russia, the UN Security Council, the G-7 and G-8 groups of states, and international organisations around the world. The result was a broad, if uneasy, consensus on the use of force within NATO and Russian acquiescence. This proved to be instrumental in persuading China to allow the UN to create a protectorate in Kosovo after the war. The frequent disagreements, alternative proposals and numerous diplomatic processes are charted here but the overall picture that emerges is not one of conflict and instability but one of entrenched institutional affiliation and emerging shared norms. Such affiliation and shared norms prompted some states to place their actions before the 'court of world opinion' and others to accept that they continue to have international responsibilities even when they disagree fundamentally with what others are doing.[4]

The Kosovo conflict

Histories of Serb–Albanian relations in Kosovo tend to focus on a series of bloody encounters. In recent times, the first of these came during the first Balkan War of 1912–13, during which the Serbs conquered Kosovo from the Ottoman Turks. Following their victory, the Serbs embarked on a campaign of mass murder and ethnic cleansing, not unlike the campaign in 1999. Leon Trotsky covered events for a Ukrainian newspaper and reported that, '[t]he Serbs in old Serbia, in their national endeavour to correct data in the ethnographical statistics that are not quite favourable to them, are engaged quite simply in the systematic extermination of the Muslim population'.[5] It is estimated that 25,000 Kosovar Albanians were killed.[6] A revenge of sorts was exacted on the Serbs as they retreated from the advancing Austrians during the First World War.

Although there were relatively few cases of Kosovar Albanians actually attacking the retreating Serbs, most did nothing the help the thousands of Serbs who perished whilst exposed to the harsh Kosovan winter. The tide turned again, however, with the formation of the Kingdom of Serbs, Croats and Slovenes in 1918, which was a manifestation of the Greater Serbia ideology in many respects. Albanians were subjected to colonial rule by Belgrade, thousands were killed and imprisoned, and still more were deported to Turkey. Despite this, the Second World War in Kosovo did not witness the scale of blood-letting that occurred in the rest of (by then renamed) Yugoslavia, though in the war's immediate aftermath the Communist Party cracked down severely on what it saw as irredentist Albanian nationalism. In particular, Aleksander Ranković, head of the Socialist Yugoslav secret police (UDBa), pursued his own vision of a united Serbia by carrying out harsh repression in Kosovo before he was deposed by Tito in 1963.[7]

The 1974 Yugoslav constitution attempted to resolve the 'national question' and end this cycle of violence. The new constitution, which was an enormous tome, provided each republic and province with theoretical statehood. This effectively created a semi-confederal system in which decision-making at the centre was dependent on consensus between political leaders in the republics and provinces.[8] Members of the different national communities in Kosovo were entitled to freely express, 'their national specificities',[9] which included the right to fly their national flag.[10] The Albanian language was given an equal footing with Serbo-Croatian and all school pupils were entitled to receive an education in 'the mother language', be it Albanian, Serbo-Croat or Turkish.[11] Kosovo was awarded economic autonomy through the establishment of a provincial bank, and the province was granted a degree of political autonomy virtually identical to that of the republics. Most significantly, the Kosovan Communist Party was represented in all Yugoslavia's central organs and had identical voting rights to the Communist Party's of the republics. After Tito's death this meant that decisions could not be reached by the central government without the consent of the Party in Kosovo.[12]

According to Gazmed Zajmi, the 1974 Constitution had a calming effect on Serb–Albanian relations by balancing their demands.[13] By keeping Kosovo within Serbia but granting it a significant degree of autonomy, Tito was able to chart a third way through the competing demands of the national groups. An alternative perspective views the 1974 Constitution as an ambiguous compromise that, whilst trying the halt atavistic nationalisms, actually fuelled them by situating political power at the level of the national groups, promoting the further ethnic stratification of Yugoslav politics.[14] While providing a greater voice for Kosovar Albanian communists, the new order did not ease the suppression of those outside the Party who advocated change. In 1976, Adem Demaçi and eighteen other Kosovar Albanians were sentenced to prison for allegedly 'distributing hostile propaganda'.[15] The accusations concerned leaflets distributed around the University of Pristina that criticised the central Party. Because none of the accused had advocated violence, Amnesty International described Demaçi and his 'co-conspirators' as 'prisoners of conscience' in 1985.[16]

The 1974 constitution provoked insecurity among the Serbian community in Kosovo who feared that a surrogate Albanian state was being formed.[17] For the Serbs, the establishment of an Albanian university in Pristina and the relaxation of restrictions on communication and travel between Kosovo and Albania were indicative of the Albaniansation of Kosovo. The Serbs argued that they were subjected to discrimination. Thus, many Kosovan Serbs perceived the 1974 Constitution as a threat to their economic and social status, one that rendered them a minority in their own homeland.[18] In 1977, a working commission of the Serbian League of Communists prepared what became known as the 'Blue Book', which demanded that control of the judiciary, police force and economic policy be returned to Belgrade.[19]

The constitution did nothing to alleviate Kosovo's economic problems. The unemployment rate was the highest in all Yugoslavia: 27 per cent, compared to a mere 2 per cent in the richest republic, Slovenia. The per capita income declined from 48 per cent of the Yugoslav average in 1954, to 33 per cent by 1975, and 27 per cent by 1980.[20] It is true that the reforms ushered in a period of unprecedented freedom for the Kosovar Albanians and that this encouraged their political leaders to make further demands. The Serbian community believed that they were being discriminated against as more Kosovar Albanians entered the Party, the police and the judiciary. In reality, the Serbs remained financially better off (every major state enterprise in Kosovo was run by Serbs) and proportionally better represented than their Kosovar Albanian neighbours.[21] Fred Singleton astutely observed that the structure of the Kosovan economy resembled that of many newly independent Third World states with the minority group (Serbs) holding a high proportion of senior positions.[22]

In 1981 it became clear that the 1974 compromise had failed. Political and cultural freedoms for Kosovar Albanians had not produced a higher standard of living for either the Kosovar Albanians or the Kosovar Serbs.

In addition, 1981 also saw a return to Aleksander Ranković's internal policing methods. This was in stark contrast to what was happening in the rest of Yugoslavia, which continued along a liberalising and decentralising path. Unemployment in Kosovo remained high, a problem enhanced by the high birth rate amongst Kosovar Albanians that meant that an unusually large proportion of the population was less than 21 years of age. One of the tactics employed to alleviate this problem was to recruit huge numbers of young Albanians into the recently founded University of Pristina.

Partly as a result of this, conditions in the University deteriorated and in April 1981 students took to the streets to protest at having to share dormitory beds and at the poor quality of cafeteria food.[23] Protests swept through six towns in Kosovo giving voice to an array of demands. For the majority, the rallying call was 'Kosovo – Republic!' Some demanded Demaçi's release while others insisted that the province be allowed to form a union with Albania.[24] Although the weight of evidence suggests that the protests were spontaneous and disorganised, the authorities in Belgrade insisted that they were provoked by anti-Yugoslav secessionist movements that were in league with Enver Hoxha's Albania. The Party newspaper in Croatia proclaimed that the demonstrations were a manifestation of the 'organised work of internal and external enemies'.[25] Although most writers are agreed that the number of Kosovar Albanians demanding union with Albania was relatively small, the communist press insisted that the unrest was planned by Tirana and executed by fanatical Albanian nationalists.[26] The Albanian government gave verbal support to the protesters but there was no evidence to support the claim that it had orchestrated the demonstrations.[27]

The Yugoslav League of Communists (LCY) singled out two institutions for blame in the immediate aftermath. The Kosovan League of Communists was denounced for being 'permeated with counterrevolutionaries and irredentists'[28] by *Tanjug*, the state news agency. The University of Pristina was found to be a hotbed of nationalist fervour and the Belgrade newspaper, *Borba*, launched a campaign against it claiming that Kosovo was not wealthy enough to support such a large number of students.[29] The most significant immediate effect of the protests was the response of the security forces. Several protesters reported that after the marches had been brought to a violent end the police broke into houses and physically attacked those suspected of participating.[30] According to Pajazit Nushi, a professor at Pristina University, the result of the 1981 violence was that '120 Albanians were killed by firearms and died as a result of physical and psychic tortures of the army and police'.[31] The Yugoslav authorities admitted that as many as 11 may have died in the fighting but Amnesty International reported that the number of dead in Kosovo was as high as 300.[32]

The police clampdown in Kosovo continued throughout the 1980s. In 1983 the proportion of Yugoslav political prisoners that were Kosovar Albanians was 41.8 per cent. Between 1981 and 1983 alone, 688 Kosovar Albanians were convicted for writing 'hostile slogans'. As Christine von Kohl and Wolfgang Libal point out, what was particularly interesting about the numerous show trials of Kosovar Albanians that were held in this period was that 'none of the "hostile groups" had actually committed an act of violence. At the most, they had simply planned actions. No stores of weapons were ever discovered. Despite this, there was talk of "plots to threaten the security of Yugoslavia"'.[33] The sentences passed down were severe. Writing the slogan 'Kosovo – Republic', for example, earned its author five years in prison.[34] In 1982, Amnesty International's list of prisoners of conscience included fourteen new names of young Kosovar Albanians including a school pupil.[35]

In 1984, Atanasije Jevtić, the Orthodox Archimandrite, publicly complained about 'the rape of girls and old women in villages and nunneries' committed by Kosovar Albanians. According to one Albanian writer many Serb publications gave the impression 'that Albanians rape anyone they can get hold of, old women, children, married women, teenagers, and that they rape them in the houses, in public places, in the street'.[36] Noel Malcolm points out that a detailed study of the incidence of rape in Yugoslavia carried out in Belgrade in 1989 showed that not only did Kosovo have the lowest incidence of rape but also that of the rapes committed in Kosovo, 71 per cent were same nationality.[37]

One case gripped popular imagination in Serbia and prompted comparisons between perceived Kosovar Albanian crimes and torture methods used by the Ottoman Turks.[38] In May 1985, Djordje Martinović, a Kosovan Serb farmer, was rushed to hospital to have a beer-bottle removed from his anus. Martinović claimed that he had been attacked by two Albanians who wanted to drive him from his home. However, an investigation in Pristina found no evidence of an attack and doctors at Pristina hospital concluded that the wound was probably 'self-inflicted'. Whatever the truth of the incident the 'Martinović case' came to dominate political discourse in Serbia. According to Vuk Drasković, the voice of the Serbian nationalist renewal in 1986:

> Can we remove the knowledge that one whole nation, the Serbian nation in Kosovo and Metohija, are being subjected to a campaign of

organised terror by their Albanian neighbours and the government in that area, which is now only formally considered part of Serbia? Can we remove the knowledge of the soothing words and the promises of consolation that have been offered to Kosovo Serbs so that we can tolerate the most brutal and most primitive outpouring of hatred and fascism?[39]

This view was echoed by the now infamous draft memorandum written by the Serbian Academy of Arts and Sciences (SANU), which portrayed the Serbs as victims of 'neo-fascist aggression in Kosovo'.[40]

By breaking with the communist mantra of 'brotherhood and unity' and the idea that compromise could be charted through the competing demands of different national groups, Slobodan Milošević ousted his political patron, Ivan Stambolić, and assumed control of the Party in Serbia. After rising to power, Milošević moved swiftly to consolidate his position by deposing the Party leaderships in Montenegro, Kosovo and Vojvodina, and installing puppet regimes. This gave him four votes in the federal decision-making bodies. While the coups were relatively swift and easy in Vojvodina and Montenegro, largely because the majority of the population there were Serbs who supported Milošević's anti-bureaucratic revolution, the coup in Kosovo required a military clampdown against Kosovar Albanian opposition and the removal of their political and cultural rights. This initiated more than two decades of intense conflict.

Milošević deposed the Party leadership in Kosovo in the first few months of 1989. Azem Vllasi, Kosovo's Party leader, was arrested on the charge of 'counter revolutionary endangering of the social order', an offence that carried the death penalty. On 23 March, the Kosovo Assembly voted itself out of existence by accepting a new constitution proclaimed in Serbia.[41] That decision was taken against a backdrop of hundreds of political arrests and the stationing of tanks and armoured cars throughout Pristina and at the assembly itself. The essence of the constitutional change was that 'the authority of the state in all its forms and at both local and provincial levels was overthrown and handed over to Serbia'.[42]

Almost overnight Kosovo was transformed from a self-governing entity into one that was entirely controlled by Belgrade. Kosovar Albanians were reduced to non-citizens and excluded from the decision-making processes. In response they demanded independence and set up their own parallel state organisations.[43] Ibrahim Rugova, the unofficially elected President of Kosovo, argued that non-violent resistance would attract international support for the Kosovar Albanian cause, insisting that 'we will continue this strategy because to do otherwise would have disastrous consequences for our people'.[44]

In August 1990, the Serbian administration demanded that Albanian schools teach a Serbian curriculum in the Serbian language. Hundreds of Albanian headteachers were replaced with Serbs and thousands of Albanian teachers were deemed to be incompetent in the Serbian language and were removed from their posts.[45] The official justification for these measures was that educational institutions in Kosovo were bastions of counter-revolution and resistance and that Kosovar Albanian pupils were being indoctrinated by their teachers.[46] Furthermore, it seemed only logical that a unitary Serbian state should have a unitary Serbian school curriculum. These reforms came on top of an earlier reform that segregated Kosovar Albanian and Serb school pupils, providing finance, teachers and facilities for the Serb pupils whilst providing Albanian pupils with very little.[47] Not surprisingly, most Kosovar Albanians refused to cooperate with these reforms and were forcibly barred from attending school by riot police and the armed forces. Some schools were even surrounded by tanks to prevent pupils from attending.[48] Similar reforms were initiated in Pristina's university. Kosovar Albanian protests only led to further reprisals and dismissals. In the winter of 1991 a parallel education system was formed in which dismissed teachers delivered lessons in private homes.[49]

In 1991, the Serbian regime began a campaign of Serbianising all public discourse in Kosovo. This rendered public signs and the organs of government utterly alien to many Kosovar Albanians who spoke only Albanian. As Pristina journalist Behlull Beqaj describes:

> The law on the official use of the language and names [27 July 1991] practically cancels the use of language. ... Resolutions concerning names of streets, boulevards, schools and other social and cultural institutions have the same intent. Based upon these resolutions, the former names were changed and the new names from the history, culture and mythology of the Serbs were introduced. All the names ... are officially written in the Serbian language and Cyrillic alphabet.[50]

The Serbianisation of public life extended to the media. Television was directly controlled by Belgrade and became a crucial propaganda tool for Milošević. The most widely distributed newspapers were brought under de facto state control. In 1990, *Rilindja*, the only Albanian language daily newspaper in Yugoslavia, was closed down with the loss of 1,300 jobs.[51] Those independent newspapers that were allowed to continue publication became subject to intense state pressure. On 2 March 1998, for example, Veton Surroi the editor-in-chief of the free-thinking Pristina based newspaper *Koha Ditore*, was beaten by the Serbian police.[52]

On 11 January 1995, the Serbian Parliament decreed that Serbs wishing to move to Kosovo were eligible for loans to erect houses and buy apartments and could obtain plots of land free of charge.[53] Very few Serbs from Serbia took up the government's offer because of the dire economic and political situation in Kosovo. As a result, many Serbian refugees from Croatia were forcibly resettled in Kosovo in 1995 and although many of these left soon afterwards those that stayed – radicalised as they were by war – created greater tension and risk of violence.[54] The government also made it illegal for Serbs to sell property to Albanians; imposed hefty sentences on any Kosovar Albanian who avoided national armed service in Croatia or Bosnia; made it very difficult for Kosovar Albanians abroad to return to Kosovo; and penalised Albanian families that had more than one child, while rewarding Kosovar Serbs for having large families.[55]

The imposed constitutional changes provided ample scope for Serb enterprise owners to remove Kosovar Albanians from the formal economy. According to an Amnesty International report in 1998, 'following large-scale dismissals from state enterprises, most Albanians are dependent on income from small businesses, or, often, money from relatives working abroad'.[56] The authorities often cut off this form of income as well.[57] It was estimated that as a result of the mass dismissals, by the beginning of 1998 unemployment in the Kosovar Albanian community was higher than 70 per cent. Whatever work was available was most often in the service sector, small-scale commerce or the more lucrative black market. According to the Pristina Economic Institute in 1996, money earned by Kosovar Albanians through regular paid work amounted to just ten per cent of total earnings whilst the black economy accounted for up to 60 per cent of total economic activity.[58] The economic apartheid imposed by Belgrade was directly aimed at impoverishing the already poor (by Yugoslav standards) Kosovar Albanians. New factories were only built in areas predominantly inhabited by Serbs and recruitment opportunities in new state supported enterprises were only offered to Serbs. Shortly before the completion of the Dayton negotiations, *Rilindja*, which had relocated in Tirana, reported that between 1991 and 1995 more than 300,000 Albanians had left Kosovo to escape Serbian oppression and find work abroad.[59]

Apartheid extended to the healthcare system. The seeds of distrust were sown in March and April 1990 when thousands of school children were taken to hospital suffering from stomach pains, headaches and nausea. Although the Serbian medical authorities claimed that the children were suffering from mass delusion caused by Albanian irredentist propaganda, a UN toxicology report five years later revealed that blood samples contained traces of chemicals used by the Yugoslav People's Army (JNA) to produce Sarin.[60] Whatever the truth of the matter, this case was enough to produce mass mistrust of the Serbian healthcare system and provided a pretext for the dismissal of Kosovar Albanian doctors. This produced an 'ethnically pure' state healthcare system in which prescriptions could only be written in the Cyrillic script.[61] Between 1992 and 1996 the incidence of preventable disease increased dramatically among the Kosovar Albanian community. In this period there were over 5,000 cases each of measles and tuberculosis.[62] In 1996 it was left to the United Nations Children's Fund (UNICEF), the World Health Organisation and a Kosovar humanitarian organisation, 'Mother Teresa', to provide polio vaccinations for Kosovar Albanian children – a vaccination offered to Serbs free by the state.[63] The Kosovar Albanians created a parallel healthcare system, but this lacked both funds and facilities.

In 1994, the head of the highest court in Kosovo bluntly stated that 'when an Albanian is accused of violating the territorial integrity of Yugoslavia, we can beat them and even kill them'.[64] State violence against the Kosovar Albanian community increased dramatically after the Dayton agreement at the end of 1995. The newly self-confident Serbian government was able to pour more coercive resources into Kosovo and paramilitary leaders made notorious by their exploits in Bosnia began turning their attention southwards. However, even before Dayton, Amnesty International reported in 1994 that the police used violence with impunity on a daily basis. The report continued by stating that 'thousands of ethnic Albanians have witnessed police violence or experienced it at first hand'. This violence usually consisted of, 'brutal beatings with truncheons, punching and kicking ... [and] electric shocks are sometimes used'. Finally, Amnesty International reported that, 'police officers express their ethnic hatred towards their victims. A particularly savage instance involved a police officer slashing a Serbian symbol on the chest of an 18-year-old ethnic Albanian'.[65] Other incidents detailed in the report were the murder of a six-year-old boy by police and the severe beating of a 90-year-old man in one of their daily raids on Kosovar Albanian homes. At the same time as this report was released, the Helsinki Human

Rights Watch produced a report that described Kosovo as a 'police state' run by 'brute force and intimidation'.[66]

The Kosovar Albanians responded by establishing a parallel state. In 1991 they elected a shadow parliament with the Democratic League of Kosovo (LDK) led by the Sorbonne educated intellectual, Ibrahim Rugova, forming the government. They held a referendum that recorded over 95 per cent support for independence, from an electoral turn out of over 75 per cent. Rugova adopted a twin strategy for independence. He created the parallel state and tried to internationalise the Kosovo issue. He justified the policy of non-violent resistance by pointing to their own military weakness compared with the might available to the Serbs. As he put it, 'we would have no chance of successfully resisting the army. In fact, the Serbs only wait for a pretext to attack the Albanian population and wipe it out. We believe that it is better to do nothing than to be massacred'.[67] Rugova's strategy therefore depended on international support for Kosovan independence.

Rugova failed in his attempt to internationalise the conflict, leading to the rise of the more radical Kosovo Liberation Army (UÇK). Although having origins in the early 1990s it was not until 1998 that the UÇK became involved in combating the Serbian armed forces. In spring 1998, guerrillas seized almost a quarter of Kosovo's territory in the Drenica Valley region to the north of Pristina. The Serbs responded with ethnic cleansing and mass murder. The various institutions of international society began to reap the consequences of their failure of prevention and to debate how they should respond.

The seven phases of engagement

The international response was shaped by shifting perceptions of political necessity. It can be divided into seven phases of engagement. The periods of transition between the phases are crucial. Each of these transitional periods saw either a dramatic event in Kosovo (such as the Donji Prekaz massacre in March 1998 and Racak massacre in January 1999), important shifts in Serbia (such as the rise of Milan Panić in 1992), or the failure of a particular international initiative (the expulsion of the Conference for Security and Co-operation in Europe [CSCE] in 1993 and the withdrawal of the Organisation for Security and Co-operation in Europe [OSCE] six years later). What becomes evident is that there was an interdependent relationship between international responses to the conflict and events in Kosovo themselves.

The prevalent international perception between 1991 and 1998 was that Kosovo was an internal matter for Serbia. This limited the scope of the international engagement, particularly the relationship between resolving Kosovo's conflict and resolving the conflicts in Croatia and Bosnia. It suggested particular ways of responding, based upon limited policy tools and an often non-existent diplomacy, whose silence was only infrequently broken. This, in turn, directly affected both Serb and Kosovar Albanian political life. As their arguments were accepted by international society, the Serbs became more self-confident and oppressive particularly after the Dayton agreement made Milošević the guarantor of regional stability. By contrast, the international engagement delegitimised Rugova's strategy in the eyes of his constituents, contributing directly to the rise of the UÇK. In turn, this prompted new problems for international society causing key actors to reassess what they understood by political necessity. This reshaped the political scenery in Kosovo once again. Thus, the international engagement was shaped by perceptions about the situation in Kosovo, a situation that the engagement itself contributed significantly to creating. The pace at which this happened quickened as conflict became more violent and the need to respond was perceived to be more urgent by the West.

The seven periods of engagement identified here are:

1. *Non-engagement (January 1991–August 1992)*. International society attempted to decipher the meaning of Yugoslavia's dissolution in political and legal terms. Although Kosovar Albanian political actors pressed Kosovo's claim to be accorded the same status as the Yugoslav republics, these claims were rejected without the reasons why ever being made explicit. It was in this period that international society tied Kosovo's fate to that of Serbia's.

2. *Limited engagement (August 1992–June 1993)*. The linking of Kosovo and Serbia did allow for some degree of engagement. Based on the presumption that Kosovo was legitimately part of Serbia, the CSCE included it in its Mission of Long Duration to Yugoslavia, the International Conference on Former Yugoslavia (ICFY) mandated a 'minorities rights' working group to include Kosovo in its studies, and the United States warned Serbia that it would be held responsible for violence in Kosovo and would face military action if that happened. This engagement was facilitated by the premiership of the Milan Panić in Serbia, but came to an end once Milošević ousted him.

3. *Malign non-engagement (June 1993–March 1998)*. Panić's removal allowed the expulsion of the CSCE and removal of Kosovo from the

ICFY working group's mandate. This ushered in another period of non-engagement. I describe this period as malign because the fate of Kosovo was explicitly subordinated to the perceived need to make Milošević a peace broker with the Bosnian Serbs. For five years international society refused to engage constructively. Sanctions were lifted, trade resumed and the new Federal Republic of Yugoslavia (FRY) was widely recognised, despite the deteriorating situation in Kosovo. There were sporadic attempts at mediation but they all failed in the face of Serb intransigence.

4. *Debating intervention (March 1998–October 1998)*. In response to the increasingly open activities of the UÇK, the Serbs launched a military crackdown in 1998. In Donji Prekaz, an attack on the UÇK led to the massacre of around 60 Kosovar Albanian civilians including women, children and the elderly. As violence increased, international society argued about the best way to respond. Some states, such as the UK and the US State Department argued that NATO should be prepared to use force but most states were reluctant to do so. Hawks argued that failure to act would lead to an escalation of conflict in the region and the possibility of a Bosnia-style bloodbath in Kosovo. This became a debate about whether NATO could act without the sanction of the Security Council, which would require Russian and Chinese acquiescence. When a Russian peace initiative failed, Yeltsin modified his stance suggesting that Russia would tolerate a NATO attack on Serbia. With the number of refugees moving into the hundreds of thousands the North Atlantic Council authorised NATO to launch airstrikes against Yugoslavia. Milošević backed down and accepted a ceasefire, promised to withdraw his forces from Kosovo, and host an OSCE Verification Mission in Kosovo.

5. *Unarmed intervention (October 1998–January 1999)*. The OSCE mission was flawed from the start. Firstly, the Kosovar Albanians were not consulted about the deal and the UÇK used the opportunity to occupy former Serb positions. Secondly, the deal did not explicitly link airstrikes with a political settlement and Milošević showed no intention of coming to such a settlement. With the threat of airstrikes receding, Serb forces began to launch 'counter-terrorist' operations throughout the province. On 15 January they massacred 45 Kosovar Albanian civilians in the village of Racak. This prompted international fears about escalation and persuaded reluctant NATO allies that the use of force might be necessary.

6. *Coercive diplomacy (January 1999–March 1999)*. The Racak massacre encouraged NATO, with Russian acquiescence, to adopt a strategy of

coercive diplomacy. Using the threat of NATO bombardment the Contact Group summoned the Serbs and Kosovar Albanians to Rambouillet to accept a political settlement based on a plan developed over the previous ten months. Although the Kosovar Albanians were asked to postpone their claims for independence and disband the UÇK, they accepted the peace agreement. The Serbs, however, rejected it outright having failed to enter into serious negotiation.

7. *Limited war (March 1999–June 1999)*. In the immediate aftermath of the failure of Rambouillet, the Serbs launched a new wave of ethnic cleansing in Kosovo. This provided the trigger for NATO to launch airstrikes, amidst international fears of an escalation of the unfolding humanitarian catastrophe. The campaign, Operation Allied Force, was characterised by continuing disagreement amongst allies manifested most publicly in the debate about the deployment of ground forces. Nevertheless, NATO retained a remarkable degree of cohesion and after a three-week period of denouncing the Alliance and threatening retribution the Russian government came to play a vital role in the search of peace.

Throughout these seven phases the relationship between events in Kosovo and international engagement with those events was mutually constitutive. What this book traces, therefore, are the debates and initiatives that prompted international society to engage with Kosovo in particular ways, charting the transition from one phase to another. In doing so, I not only show how international consensus was repeatedly forged and then broken but also the impact that international events and decisions had in Kosovo. What this means for International Relations is discussed in the Conclusion. For now, it is important to bear in mind that the decision not to intervene was itself a form of intervention.

1
Kosovo and the Dissolution of Yugoslavia

International society was made aware of the human rights problem in Kosovo in 1981, when the student riots in Pristina featured in Western newspapers. The riots also sparked some intellectual interest in the province though this was short-lived.[1] In the space of less than two years, between 1990 and late 1991, Kosovo's international resonance markedly increased. Internationally, Kosovo was viewed as a fundamental issue as Yugoslavia began to dissolve. By the time the European Community (EC) decided to recognise Slovenia, Croatia, Bosnia and Macedonia, Kosovo was not even on the agenda. Its leaders were not invited to participate in peace negotiations and the province's fate was linked to that of Serbia's. Indeed, Kosovar Albanian leaders did not properly participate in any international peace process until the Rambouillet summit early in 1999. However, Kosovo was subject to all the punitive measures that international society imposed on Serbia in response to its support to rebel Serbs in Croatia and Bosnia, and its abuse of human rights in Kosovo.

This chapter focuses on the changing importance of Kosovo within the dissolution of Yugoslavia. I argue that finding a constitutional settlement for Kosovo was considered to be an important litmus test by international mediators for as long as the maintenance of a united Yugoslav state remained a priority for the US and EC. However, once violence broke out in Slovenia and Croatia the international involvement with Kosovo entered a phase of 'non-engagement' whereby Kosovo was systematically excluded from the peace process and its fate tied to Serbia's. There appears to have been little thought as to why Kosovo should be excluded from the process among those given the job of finding a peaceful solution to the crisis. I argue that the institutional processes developed to facilitate the dissolution would have been able to respond to the dilemmas posed by Kosovo. However, the processes that were put in place removed the issue of Kosovo's status from the agenda by assuming its resolution in favour of Serbia. This created an opening for a second phase of involvement, which I describe as *limited engagement*. This phase was manifested by the creation of an international working group to consider the Kosovo conflict and deployment of the CSCE Mission of Long Duration. Although there was institutional engagement on the ground in Kosovo the tools available to the interveners and the degree of flexibility that policy-makers had in dealing with the crisis were heavily circumscribed. This predicament continued to restrict international activity throughout the 1990s.

Human rights and international society

The first indication that the conflict in Kosovo could embroil the rest of Europe came in Brussels, in February 1990. Enver Hadri, a Kosovar Albanian who attempted to raise international awareness of the situation in Kosovo was shot in an incident that looked to many like a professional killing. This led commentators to conclude that the perpetrators were Yugoslav secret police.[2] Ten days before his death, Hadri had organised a silent protest outside the Yugoslav Embassy in Brussels that had caused great embarrassment to the government. Later on that year, four human rights officials who worked for the Helsinki Federation were expelled from the province. They had accused the Belgrade government in March of a 'massive purge' of ethnic Albanians.[3]

Two of the most proactive foreign institutions in the early stages of the international engagement with the Kosovo question – the European Parliament and United States Congress – began to express concern a year before Hadri's murder. In June 1989, the European Parliament dispatched a delegation to explore the situation. The visit was less than successful, however, because the Serbian authorities refused to grant the parliamentarians access to 'ordinary' Kosovars, restricting them to meetings with government officials. As a result, the visit was terminated earlier than scheduled though it had an enduring impact as the European Parliament became vocal on the plight of the Kosovar Albanians, condemning human rights abuse and passing a resolution which insisted that Kosovo be part of the international peace process.[4] In March 1991, it passed a resolution calling for a new Yugoslav constitution that would facilitate respect for democratic self-determination. It also specifically condemned human rights violations against the Albanian community in Kosovo.[5] Towards the end of that year it awarded the Sakharov prize for human rights to Adem Demaçi, who remained incarcerated.[6]

At around the same time as the European parliamentary delegation to Kosovo, the US House of Representatives began stating its concern with the deteriorating situation in the province. An amendment on 'human rights in Yugoslavia' was added to the 'International Cooperation Act of 1989'. The amendment demanded that 'the human rights of all ethnic groups in Kosovo be preserved' and noted that 'those human rights violations, in addition to recent actions taken to limit the social and political autonomy of Kosovo, have precipitated a crisis in the region'.[7] The wording here is significant because Congress recognised a direct correlation between the constitutional and human rights issues in Kosovo and the danger of a wider regional conflagration. It is statements like this and the fact that most books on the dissolution of Yugoslavia begin their story in Kosovo[8] that shows the centrality of this issue at the outset of the dissolution, though Zivorad Kovačević, the Yugoslav Ambassador to the United States at the time insisted that the amendment gave 'a mistaken impression of Yugoslavia'.[9]

These Congressional initiatives spurred further activity by American congressmen. In April 1990, Senator Dennis DeConcini led a four-man delegation on behalf of the CSCE. DeConcini reported that human rights violations were taking place in the province because of 'heavy handed behaviour by the Serb authorities'. Another member of the delegation complained that, as the European parliamentarians had experienced, 'we have been given less information about political prisoners in Kosovo than we get from the Soviet Union'.[10] Five months later, Republican Senate leader, Robert Dole, led a group of seven Senators to Kosovo. The Senators 'expressed deep concern with the latest proof that the Serbian government is destroying the human rights of Albanians in a systematic way'.[11] Dole himself became convinced that American economic aid to Yugoslavia should be closely tied to Kosovo's fate, a policy that appeared in the so-called 'Nickles Amendment' discussed later. The American ambassador in Belgrade, Warren Zimmermann, was outspoken in his criticism of the Milošević regime's actions in Kosovo, so much so that the Serbian President refused to see him for nine months.[12]

These apparently positive early American and European initiatives were built on the assumption that Yugoslavia could be held together and that Kosovo would remain an integral part of the federation. However, in autumn 1990 the American Central Intelligence Agency (CIA) estimated that Yugoslavia would break apart within 18 months and that armed conflict was very likely. The authors of the report went so far as to identify Milošević's crackdown in Kosovo as the primary potential cause of the dissolution.[13] If anything, however, talk of dissolution limited the scope of imaginative thought applied to Kosovo, though it was eight months before the report's findings began to be believed and taken seriously.

The Nickles Amendment

The experience of various American representatives in Kosovo prompted Congress to pass the so-called 'Nickles Amendment' in November 1990. The amendment gave Yugoslavia six months (until 6 May 1991) to cease the repression of Kosovar Albanians otherwise it would lose its US$5 million of aid. In many ways the amendment was more symbolic than practical. Given the conditionality attached to the aid and the size of the economic deficit that confronted Ante Marković's federal government, the suspension of this aid did not have a huge consequence though it did indicate diplomatic support to a federal regime that was battling with nationalists from every republic whilst trying to revive the ailing economy. Importantly, the amendment singled out Serbian oppression of Kosovar Albanians as a particularly important litmus test.[14]

On the deadline set by the amendment, the State Department concluded that 'we have not reached a final decision on Yugoslavia's status under this legislation...however, continued Serbian blockage of constitutional authority will have a direct influence on our decision'.[15] The 'blockage of constitutional authority' that was referred to was Milošević's stonewalling of the rotation of the federal presidency to the Croatian member of the presidency, Stipe Mesić. The decision over whether to implement the amendment posed a dilemma for American policy-makers. On the one hand, Bob Dole submitted a further resolution to the Senate that called upon Milošević to cease all repressive measures against the Kosovar Albanians.[16] Nevertheless, the Secretary of State, James Baker, was working along an altogether different tangent. Baker was aware that implementing the Nickles Amendment would have had an adverse effect on the federal government and Marković's programme of economic reform in particular. As the Marković programme was widely viewed as the only chance of keeping Yugoslavia together, Baker calculated that the US should make support for Marković a regional priority. George Bush even went so far as to accuse Serbia and Franjo Tuđman's Croatia of plotting together to destroy the Marković government and thereby disband Yugoslavia.[17] Baker also wanted to remain in step with the EC, which was putting together an aid package for Marković at the time. He suspended the cut in aid to reiterate American support for Yugoslavia.

It was at the point at which Kosovo began to ask questions of American policy that it began to get sidelined. The desire to support the Marković government (despite warnings from the CIA that it would be a futile gesture) and remain in step with EC meant that the work and recommendations of senior politicians such as Dole went unheeded. Kosovo's fate was fully subsumed into Serbia's in the international debate about imposing sanctions on Yugoslavia. As the Kosovo conflict became more prescient, so international thought on the issue became more limited.

The sanctions debate

American debates about whether to implement the Nickles Amendment were intimately linked with wider international debates about imposing sanctions against Yugoslavia. At the end of 1991, the US and EC adopted different approaches. At the beginning of December, the Bush administration decided that it would use economic sanctions to halt the war in Croatia and keep Yugoslavia together.[18] In order to achieve these twin aims, it imposed economic sanctions against the entire territory of dissolving Yugoslavia. The American strategy adopted the region-wide perspective taken by the UN Security Council when it passed Resolution 713 on 25 September 1991.[19] This controversial resolution imposed an arms embargo over the whole territory of Yugoslavia, empowering the Serbs (who had most of the JNA's weapons and personnel under their control) whilst removing the soon-to-be new states' supposedly inherent right to self-defence.[20] The rationale behind this resolution and the US sanctions policy was that all sides were equally to blame for the violence (primarily in Croatia at this stage) and that coercive inducements should be imposed on all the 'factions' to encourage them to agree to a political settlement.

The US suspended Yugoslavia's membership of the Generalised System of Preferences, a programme of duty-free tariff preferences that the US and 27 other states granted to developing states. According to the State Department, the sanctions were intended to persuade the 'various factions engaged in conflict there to cease hostilities and resolve their differences through peaceful means'.[21] The Department's spokesman, Margaret Tutwiler, emphasised the point that the sanctions applied to the entire territory of Yugoslavia. She stated that, 'these sanctions are intended to exert pressure on parties to participate mean-ingfully in the EC-sponsored Conference on Yugoslavia'.[22] Hawks such as Robert Dole opposed this indiscriminate application of sanctions. In an open letter he argued that he wanted to direct 'the administration to channel aid to republics that are on the road to democracy, and simultaneously deny aid to the Communist central government ... in Belgrade'.[23] However, members of the administration such as Ralph Johnson, the Principal Deputy Assistant Secretary of State for European and Canadian Affairs, insisted that Dole's proposals were flawed. Johnson argued that the United States needed to maintain flexible options, remain in concert with the EC, and withhold from the urge to offer support to secessionists.[24] The key issue was that even in late 1991, the US still supported the maintenance of a unified Yugoslavia and, more importantly, continued to believe that this was a viable option.[25] This was in contrast to emerging Western European thinking at the time.

Prompted principally by the German government, but with substan-tial vocal support from the Austrian and Hungarian governments, the EC moved considerably quicker than the US to envisaging the break-up of Yugoslavia.[26] This was due in part to the work of the international arbitration commission chaired by the French constitutional jurist, Robert Badinter. The realisation that Yugoslavia could not be held together was manifested in European sanctions policy, which by the end of 1991 was more discriminating than American policy. One of the effects of this, however was that Kosovo was punished for the deeds of the Serbs in Croatia and the Kosovo question was viewed as an internal Serbian matter by the EC.

EC trade policy with regards to Yugoslavia altered radically as a result of the violence initiated by the JNA and armed Serbian irregulars in Slovenia and Croatia that resulted in the destruction of cities like Vukovar and Dubrovnik. Throughout 1990, the EC had attempted to support efforts to revive the Yugoslav federation by providing loans to the federal government and encouraging others to do likewise. The European Commission proposed an investment package of £648 mil-lion over a period of five years, which was made dependant on progress towards democracy (though the Commission did not specifically men-tion Kosovo).[27] At around the same time, the International Monetary Fund (IMF) approved a loan worth US$600 million on top of Yugoslavia's outstanding US$860 million debt to the IMF.[28] This policy attempted to support Marković's economic reform plan and was endorsed by many commentators. Mary Kaldor and Sonja Light, for example, argued that, 'the governments of Western countries and European institutions should provide substantial economic assistance to Yugoslavia on the condition that all human rights are respected and political conflicts solved in a peaceful and democratic way'.[29] However, it was the problem of encouraging respect for human rights that enthused those such as Dole who argued for a discriminating sanctions regime and could see little progress towards compliance with international demands on human rights, particularly in Kosovo. Furthermore, a package of loans to Marković's increasingly impotent federal government was hardly likely to persuade Milošević's republican government in Serbia to alter its course of action in Croatia, Bosnia and Kosovo.

The Marković reforms failed to halt the slide into war and EC trade policy changed in 1991.[30] The EC took the lead in trying to secure a negotiated settlement to the conflict and sanctions were linked to Milošević's acceptance of a plan to reconfigure Yugoslavia on confederal lines. The EC imposed sanctions when the negotiations floundered. First of all sanctions were imposed on the whole of Yugoslavia. A month later, however, they were lifted from all except Serbia, Montenegro, Vojvodina and Kosovo.[31] For the purposes of EC sanctions, Kosovo was considered to be part of Serbia. This lack of differentiation derived from the decision not to include Kosovo in the EC Conference on Yugoslavia (ECCY), which later became the International Conference on Yugoslavia (ICFY) chaired by Lord Carrington and, after August 1992, by David Owen and Cyrus Vance.

The ECCY

The so-called Badinter Arbitration Commission had its genesis with the convening of the ECCY in The Hague on 7 September 1991, though provision for such a Commission was made two weeks earlier. Negotiations at The Hague were based upon three key principles: There could be no unilateral changes of borders and there must be full respect for the rights of minorities and respect for all legitimate interests and aspirations.[32] The talks were chaired by Lord Carrington, a former British Foreign Secretary and NATO Secretary-General. The wording 'all legitimate interests and aspirations' is of particular interest.[33] The primary aim of the ECCY was to find, 'new relationships and structures' for Yugoslavia that could facilitate peaceful coexistence.[34] This meant constitutional reform. As Kosovo was a constitutionally recognised part of the Socialist Federative Republic of Yugoslavia (SFRY), whose autonomy had been unconstitutionally rescinded by Serbia in 1989, one would in all probability have expected it to be invited to send delegates to The Hague. It was not.

Paragraph Four of the 1974 Constitution of the Socialist Autonomous Province of Kosovo stated that:

> The working peoples, nations and nationalities of Kosovo shall make decisions on the federal level according to the principles of agreement between Republics and Autonomous Provinces, solidarity and reciprocity, [and] *equal participation between Republics and Autonomous Provinces*...[35]

Furthermore, Article 4 of the 1974 Constitution stated that internal borders that included the autonomous provinces (Kosovo and Vojvodina) could not be changed without the agreement of the province concerned. Finally, the same article declared that the SFRY's external borders could not be changed without the agreement of all republics and autonomous provinces. Given this constitutional context and the fact that both the quality of Kosovo's borders and those of the SFRY were being discussed, and in view of the conference's terms of reference, the chairman of the ECCY should have invited the Kosovar Albanians to the negotiations. One might argue that Kosovo was represented at the talks because under the Milošević directed constitutional reforms of 1989 the responsibility for representation passed to Belgrade or the Serb leadership in Pristina. Two points need making though. First, it is generally accepted among constitutional lawyers that Milošević's decision to revoke Kosovo's autonomy was unconstitutional because it did not have the agreement of the other republics. Secondly, while the other republics could be represented by democratically elected leaders, the Serbian government denied Kosovo such privileges.

The European Parliament, which had supported the creation of the ECCY, called upon Western leaders to allow the full participation of Kosovo and Vojvodina in the talks.[36] In a parliamentary resolution it explicitly endorsed the claims of the republics and autonomous provinces to a right of democratic self-determination, which could be reached only through negotiation and voluntary co-operation.[37] This resolution rightly suggests to Steve Terrett that the EC still envisaged a solution in which either Yugoslavia remained together or else a separation could be negotiated, as subsequently happened in Czechoslovakia. Given this belief, it seemed obvious to the European Parliament that as a constitutional entity, Kosovo should have been able to participate in the peace process.

Outside the institutional framework created by the EC, a debate raged in the chancelleries of Europe about the merits of recognising the breakaway republics. This debate shaped the legal procedures for dissolution and effectively barred Kosovo from the peace process. What is remarkable though is how little thought went into the decision to exclude Kosovo. There were no sound legal grounds for the exclusion and it appears that only German foreign ministry officials gave serious consideration to the dilemmas posed by Kosovo's status. It is also important to bear in mind that whilst the American legislature had been proactive on the issue, the American administration maintained its opposition to the dissolution of Yugoslavia until it was presented with a *fait accompli* by the EC's recognition of Slovenia, Croatia, Bosnia and Macedonia in early 1992. The decision to exclude Kosovo from the peace process was influenced by three considerations.

First, and apparently most importantly, there was no armed conflict in Kosovo. We saw in the introduction that the Kosovar Albanians opted for passive resistance to Serb oppression rather than armed rebellion because Rugova feared that an armed rebellion would provoke terrible reprisals by the Serbs.[38] According to Lord Carrington, his mandate had been to halt the armed conflict in Croatia and then (in 1992) in Bosnia. As there was no armed conflict in Kosovo there was no reason to raise the issue. Placing Kosovo on the agenda would have been politically imprudent, he thought. Moreover, Carrington gave the impression that he believed that the issue was outside his jurisdiction as chair of the ECCY, particularly by the time of the London conference in 1992.[39] By 1992, he suggested, Kosovo was an internal issue for Serbia and not part of the problem he was trying to solve. This was a view shared by his successor, Lord Owen.[40] This position was based on the view that Kosovo was a particularly sensitive issue for the Serbs and that placing it on the international agenda would have therefore unduly antagonised them, making a peaceful resolution more elusive. As the Slovene Foreign Minister, Dimitrij Rupel, later recalled about the Hague conference:

> The only question that really bothered the Serbs in The Hague was the question of Kosovo. In one of the commissions they started to talk about how to regulate the question of minorities, the Serbian minority in Croatia – at that time it was only Croatia that was under discussion – and how painful it was for them, the Serbs, to live under Croatian rule. Then I said we should design in this new arrangement equal rights for all minorities, including Albanians, ha. [Vladislav] Jovanović [the Serbian Foreign Minister] really got mad, that was something I shouldn't have said, it was the end of our relationship.[41]

The second reason for the exclusion of Kosovo from the peace process, which the German foreign ministry was alone in considering at the time but which is still raised today, is the idea that recognition of Kosovo would have legitimised the claims of the Croatian and Bosnian Serbs. As Zarko Korac put it in 2001, 'if Serbs in Croatia or Bosnia could not make new states, why should Kosovo Albanians be able to – especially since Albanians have a "mother state" in Albania?'.[42] Michael Libal, head of the German foreign ministry's department dealing with the Yugoslav crisis, shared a similar – if somewhat more sophisticated – train of thought. Libal believed that the Croatian Krajina and Kosovo problems were interrelated. Given his view that the Krajina crisis could only be resolved on the basis of the territorial integrity of Croatia, he envisaged a similar solution for Kosovo based upon the territorial integrity of Serbia but involving a commensurate level of rights for Croatian Serbs and Kosovar Albanians within new Croatian and Serbian states.[43] The perceived interrelationship of Kosovo and Krajina manifested itself in the second draft provision for a convention, presented by Carrington on 1 November 1991. This provision identified areas that had a 'special status of autonomy' that warranted particular concern for human rights.[44] A crucial point was overlooked however. Kosovo was a constitutionally constituent part of the SFRY with legally defined borders drawn up in exactly the same way as the republic's borders and given precisely the same status in Yugoslav law as inter-republic boundaries. Furthermore, the Kosovan claim to sovereignty was couched in terms of the Yugoslav constitution and the international legal principle of *uti posseditis*.[45] These claims were identical to those put forward by the republics. It is important to note that Kosovo's claim to independence was not based on arguments about the ethnic rights and ancient history that formed the substance of the Bosnian and Croatian Serb claim.[46]

The third and final reason for Kosovo's exclusion from consideration for independence and hence from participation in the peace process (the two went hand in hand) was that the Kosovar Albanians who were pursuing the claim were not in control of the province's territory.[47] At the time, British newspapers erroneously reported that control of territory was one of the conditions for recognition stipulated by the ECCY.[48] In fact, although it is a traditional prerequisite of statehood,[49] control of territory was not mentioned by the EC when, on 16 December 1991, it invited all Yugoslav *republics* to apply for recognition.[50] The Kosovar Albanians would have been in a similar position to the Croats and Bosnians with regards to controlling territory well enough to enforce respect for human rights laws and the will of the UN. Indeed, given that Kosovar Serbs constituted a considerably smaller section of the Kosovan population than did Serbs in either Croatia or Bosnia and that the

Kosovar Albanians had begun organising a parallel state and had a political leadership that genuinely advocated human rights for all citizens, it could be argued that Kosovo was better placed to survive that Croatia and Bosnia, at least in the absence of armed intervention by Belgrade.

On 19 October 1991, the underground Assembly of the Republic of Kosova announced that a referendum held in the province between 26 and 30 September had delivered a 99.87 per cent vote in favour of sovereignty and independence for Kosovo.[51] Three days later, Ibrahim Rugova wrote to Lord Carrington urging him to grant his 'full and immediate consideration' to the request that the Republic of Kosova be recognised as a sovereign and independent state.[52] Carrington never replied to this letter nor did Robert Badinter's arbitration commission. What is more, the Chairman gave no indication to this author that he had given the letter any consideration at all.[53]

The Badinter Arbitration Commission

Badinter's request was heeded on 28 August 1991, when an EC declaration stated that the 'relevant authorities' were to 'submit their differences to an arbitration commission' that would submit its opinions within two months.[54] Steve Terrett points out that this declaration immediately raised two key questions that had a direct pertinence for Kosovo, the resolution of which facilitated the province's disappearance from the international agenda. The first question was *what issues was the commission supposed to rule upon?* The EC statement made reference only to 'differences', leading Terrett to conclude that this meant differences about the constitutional make-up of Yugoslavia.[55] Given that one of the primary constitutional 'differences' was the absorption of Kosovo into Serbia in 1989, it is fair to argue that the Kosovo question was precisely the sort of problem that should have been addressed by the commission.

The second question Terrett identified was, *who was entitled to refer differences to the Commission?* The EC declaration stated only that the 'differences' be submitted by 'relevant authorities'. As they were primarily differences over the structure of the Yugoslav constitution, Terrett concluded that:

> Any entity affected by the outcome of the Commission's findings would be allowed access to the Commission to ascertain its legal rights in any constitutional resettlement. Accordingly, a case may be made for including Kosovo and Vojvodina as such 'relevant authorities'.[56]

Craven argued that the Krajina Serbs should have been recognised as relevant authorities. In doing so he makes the same mistake as Korac because Serbian Krajina had no personality in the Yugoslav constitution whereas Kosovo and Vojvodina were territorially defined constituent elements.[57] Terrett correctly points out that despite Kosovo's constitutional status, the Bosnian Serbs enjoyed a much greater level of participation in the Commission's work than either Kosovo or Vojvodina.[58]

The commission's first opinion was released on 20 November 1991, in response to a letter from Lord Carrington. Carrington noted that:

> Serbia considers that those republics which have declared or would declare themselves independent or sovereign have seceded or would secede from the SFRY which would continue to exist. Other republics on the contrary indicate that there is no question of secession, but the question is one of disintegration or breaking-up of the SFRY as the result of the concurring will of a number of republics.[59]

Carrington went on to enquire about the nature of self-determination by asking whether the Serbian populations in Croatia and Bosnia held a right to self-determination because of their status as one of Yugoslavia's constituent peoples. There are two important points to be drawn from this letter. Firstly, despite the letter he received from Rugova, Carrington only enquired about the status of Serbs in Croatia and Bosnia and not about the Albanians in Kosovo. This policy appears to be coherent with Carrington's belief that Kosovo should not have been included in the process because there was no armed conflict there, no imminent possibility of armed conflict, and because of Serb sensitivities on the matter. The second interesting thing to note is the reference to the Serbs in Croatia and Bosnia as 'constituent peoples'. This seems to imply a reference to the distinction between 'nations' and 'nationalities' in the Yugoslav constitution, a distinction that provided the rationale for withholding republic status from Kosovo. According to the constitution, the SFRY consisted of six constituent 'nations' (Serbs, Croats, Slovenes, Montenegrins, Macedonians and Bosnian Muslims) and assorted other 'nationalities' (including Albanians, Italians and Hungarians). The 'nationalities' were not considered to be constituent because they had home states outside the borders of Yugoslavia (Albania, Italy, Hungary).

The commission responded to these questions by issuing three opinions. It noted that Slovenia, Croatia, and Macedonia had held referenda that resulted in votes in favour of independence and that the sovereign parliament of Bosnia had decided to hold its own referendum. It also noted that 'the authorities of the Federation and the Republics have shown themselves to be powerless to enforce respect for the succeeding ceasefire agreements'.[60] As such, the commission issued a landmark judgment that, 'the Socialist Federal Republic of Yugoslavia is in a process of dissolution'.[61]

The commission's second opinion dealt with the question of self-determination that was raised by Carrington's letter. In delivering its opinion, the commission gave a list of bodies that it had consulted. These included the governments of the republics and the self-appointed 'Assembly of the Serbian People of Bosnia–Hercegovina'. While one would not have expected the commission to have considered information garnered from the Kosova Assembly because the question addressed in its second opinion specifically enquired about the Serb communities in Croatia and Bosnia, the inclusion of the Bosnian Serb assembly as an institution that the commission could consult should surely have meant that – legally at least – the Kosova Assembly ought also to have had the opportunity to forge such relations.

Two aspects from of the second opinion are of importance here. First, the commission resolved that 'whatever the circumstances, the right to self-determination must not involve changes to existing frontiers at the time of independence (*uti possidetis juris*) except where the states concerned agree otherwise'.[62] Secondly, it noted that international law demanded that states respect the rights of minorities and that 'this requirement applies to all the republics *vis-à-vis* their minorities'.[63] Given the aspects of Yugoslavia's 1974 constitution that I discussed earlier, it would be fair to assume that changes in the legal quality of frontiers required Kosovo's acquiescence. After all, Kosovo's border with Macedonia was given the status of an international frontier. It is also worth noting that unlike the claims of the Croatian and Bosnian Serbs, Kosovo's unheeded request did comply with the *uti possidetis* rule as Kosovo was a territorially defined constituent entity within the SFRY. As for the second part of the opinion, when Serbia's new Yugoslavia (FRY) was admitted to the UN in 2000 it could hardly be said that Belgrade had established a track record of according full minority rights to the Kosovar Albanians.

With regards to Kosovo, therefore, the Badinter arbitration commission raised more questions than it provided answers. In both its terms of reference and in its first two opinions it intimated ways in which the Kosova Assembly could participate in the peace process and suggested that, in accordance with European Parliament resolutions, Kosovo could be considered for recognition. Yet, despite this, its rulings were concerned solely with *republics* and issues concerning specific communities raised by Lord Carrington. It was deeply unfortunate that Rugova's request to Carrington was never forwarded to the commission, both because we will never precisely know on what legal grounds the Kosovo question was excluded and because it condemned Kosovar Albanians to a further decade of Serb oppression, halted only by military action in 1999.

The London conference

According to Tim Judah, the London conference, held in August 1992, provided a 'grotesque' expression of the international sidelining of Kosovo.[64] The significance of the London conference laid not in its neglect of the situation in Kosovo – that had already been manifest in Carrington's failure to respond to Rugova's letter of 22 December 1991 – but in the institutionalisation of a particular set of responses to that situation. In a back handed way this institutionalisation reinforced Kosovo's integration into Serbia. Herein lies the transition to the second phase of international involvement with the Kosovo crisis, a phase of 'limited engagement'.

Prior to the London conference, Carrington responded to an earlier request from Rugova that Kosovo be allowed to participate in the talks. Carrington wrote:

> If you are in London at the time of the Conference (from 26– 28 August) then I am pleased to inform you that it will be possible for you and your delegation to have access to the Queen Elizabeth II Conference Centre for meetings, for example with me, Secretary Vance and other participants. As it will not, for practical and other reasons, be possible to grant your delegation access to the Conference chamber itself, the organisers will set up a 'Salle d'ecoute' to which the formal Conference proceedings will be relayed live.[65]

What this effectively meant, Judah points out, was that Kosovo was being invited to watch the other republics sort out their own problems while leaving Kosovo's untouched. Nonetheless, the Kosovar Albanian delegation arrived at London and presented the conference chair with a lengthy memorandum that conveyed a persuasive case to support the claim that Kosovo should be treated as an equal to the other participants in the conference. However, the conference's chairman staunchly refused to allow Kosovar Albanian participation in the talks.

The London conference was dominated by a power-struggle between the Serbian President, Slobodan Milošević and the Federal Prime Minister, an eccentric American-Serb called Milan Panić. As part of Milošević's attempt to broaden his appeal within Serbia, Panić had been invited to take over the post on 15 June. Born in Belgrade, Panić had defected to the Netherlands in 1956 when representing Yugoslavia at a cycling competition. He had gone on to build a highly profitable pharmaceuticals company in California. According to Robert Thomas, Milošević believed that Panić would present a more acceptable moderate image at home and abroad, whilst being easy to control.[66] However, by the time of the London conference, just over two months later, Panić was showing that he could be his own man and a significant thorn in Milošević's side.

The prospect of international mediation in Kosovo (a long standing Kosovar Albanian request) was raised at the conference. Silber and Little insist that Milošević refused to contemplate 'the despatch of international mediators to negotiate the future status of the ethnic Albanians in Kosovo'. Instead, the Serbian president argued that this was an internal matter for Serbia.[67] It was Milan Panić, Silber and Little point out, who augmented Serbian acceptance of the deployment of CSCE monitors in Kosovo and the creation of a working group on minorities issues that would consider the Kosovo question (as well as Krajina, Sandžak, Vojvodina, and Macedonia). The widely respected German diplomat, Geert Ahrens, would chair this working group. The CSCE Mission of Long Duration was despatched on 8 September 1992 and remained in place until Milošević expelled it in June 1993.[68] Furthermore, a by-product of the London conference was an agreement between Rugova and Panić. The Federal Prime Minister promised to restore Kosovo's autonomy, re-admit Kosovar Albanians into Pristina University, and guarantee the freedom of the press.[69]

On the issue of working groups, Milošević insisted that Kosovo could only be included within a group on 'national minorities' that also included the Krajina Serbs, reinforcing the interrelationship between these two issues that I discussed earlier. The 'Ethnic and National Communities Working Group' was therefore tasked to 'recommend initiatives for resolving ethnic questions in the former Yugoslavia', and a special sub-group was formed to work on Kosovo related issues.[70] The working group opted to avoid the difficult issue of Kosovo's status – an international strategy that persists today – and focused instead on the practical improvement of life in the province.[71] It immediately set to work trying to facilitate an agreement between Serbs and Albanians on the provision of education, at the behest of Rugova.

Rugova hoped to persuade the working group to expand its work and to act as a conduit for the Kosovar Albanians to become involved in the ICFY. The merits of this line of thinking were echoed by Ahrens when he concluded his first report in November 1992 by arguing that, 'I believe that it is essential for the Peace Conference to be involved in seeking a settlement between the Kosovans and the Serbian government'.[72] Though Ahrens went on to state that such a settlement should be based on 'real autonomy' for Kosovo, Rugova believed that by becoming a participant in the conference process the province could have its status raised to a level footing with the republics, which had been recognised as states by the EC in January 1992.

The London conference marked the beginning of the second phase of international involvement with the Kosovo conflict. Lord Carrington stood down as Chair and was replaced by Lord Owen. By deploying CSCE monitors and establishing a working group to consider minority rights issues, international society had chosen to become institutionally involved on the ground in Kosovo. The price for this was that the question of Kosovo's legal status was formally dismissed and any hope that the Kosovar Albanians could have a voice in the peace process was dashed. There is no evidence from the papers and statements connected with the conference that international mediation over Kosovo was on the agenda nor do Kosovar Albanians close to Rugova at the time suggest that this was the case.[73] However, it was not until after the Dayton agreement in 1995 that the leadership and people of Kosovo were finally made aware of the fact that international concern with minority rights would not lead to negotiations about independence.

The CSCE Mission of Long Duration

The CSCE was one of the first international organisations to deal specifically with the Kosovo conflict. In July 1991, Serbia was heavily criticised for its actions in Kosovo by a CSCE meeting of experts on national minorities. The Belgrade government rejected the criticism in the strongest possible terms.[74] In May 1992, a rapporteur mission lead by the Swiss legal expert, Thomas Fleiner-Gerster, visited Serbia and recommended the despatch of human rights monitors to Kosovo, Sandžak and Vojvodina.[75] Reporting on the visit, the Committee of Senior Officials (CSO) noted 'the grave situation of ethnic Albanians in Kosovo', and decided to continue work in 'determining the military situation in Kosovo', an observation that the Yugoslav delegation considered to be an unacceptable 'one-sided declaration'.[76] The Fleiner-Gerster mission was followed by another fact-finding mission led by the Canadian Ambassador, Robert Peel. The Peel mission concluded that there was no immediate threat of armed conflict in Kosovo but that the political situation there constituted a major problem.[77] The CSO created a task group to evaluate undertaking an observer mission of either short or long duration to Kosovo, Vojvodina, and Sandžak. The Yugoslav delegation initially opposed the idea, arguing that the CSO wanted the task group to liase with appropriate regional authorities but that these authorities did not have the jurisdiction to authorise CSCE monitors.[78]

In July 1992, the CSCE held a summit in Helsinki and adopted a resolution on the Yugoslav crisis that specifically mentioned Kosovo. The declaration called for 'immediate preventive action' in Kosovo and urged Belgrade to halt its repression of Kosovar Albanians and to engage in serious dialogue in talks chaired by international mediators.[79] The CSCE also temporarily suspended Yugoslavia's membership, ostensibly because the SFRY no longer existed and the new FRY had not yet been recognised. A subsidiary reason was Yugoslavia's failure to adhere to the 'third basket' of Helsinki principles concerning human rights and humanitarian cooperation.[80]

On 14 August 1992 the CSO decided to despatch a Mission of Long Duration to Kosovo, Vojvodina and Sandžak. The Mission had four primary tasks:

- To promote dialogue between the central authorities and the communities in these regions.
- Monitor and collect information on human rights abuse and promote solutions to these problems.
- Establish contact points for solving problems that are identified.
- Assist in providing information on relevant legislation on human rights, free media and democratic elections.[81]

It is widely thought that Milošević opposed the very idea of an international presence within Serbia and that Yugoslavia's decision to accept the mission came from Panić. In his initial report, Ambassador Bøgh observed that whilst there was some willingness on the part of the Serbs to accept a degree of international scrutiny of negotiations, this only extended to allowing silent observation.[82] This was the limit to the concessions that Panić could extract from Milošević. Milošević undoubtedly preferred working with Ambassador Ahrens' working group because it came under the auspices of the ICFY, of which he was a key player. Milan Panić's intervention created a window of opportunity for dialogue between Belgrade, Pristina and the CSCE, a point Bøgh recognised. In his first interim report, the Head of Mission observed that 'both sides expressed a willingness to engage in dialogue'. Whilst he noted that 'they [the Serbs and Albanians] are entrenched in diametrically opposed positions on the fundamental question of the status of Kosovo in Serbia', he believed that progress could be made, particularly in the field of education, which was also the chief concern of Ahrens' group at this time.[83]

Chapter 2 will deal with the findings and fate of the mission in more detail. The mission tells us important things about international thinking about Kosovo in summer 1992. It established a permanent institutional presence in Pristina and a formal international relationship with the Kosovar Albanians. Its permanence gave it a distinctly different character to that of Ahrens' working group and contributed to the belief among Kosovar Albanian politicians that they were enhancing their international standing. However, in terms of the sort of standing desired, the mission represented a sideways step. In many of the CSCE documents discussed above, Kosovo is described – along with Vojvodina and Sandžak – as a 'region' of Serbia, a wholly different status to that sought by the Kosovar Albanians. Indeed, the fact that Kosovo and Sandžak shared the same mission should have given cause for concern among the Kosovar Albanian leadership because Sandžak is a region of Serbia in the normal sense of the word and was not a constitutionally recognised entity. A comparison between Sandžak and Krajina would have been more appropriate.

If the international engagement from the beginning of 1990 to August 1992 can be described as one of 'non-engagement' one can discern a shift with the creation of the ICFY working groups and the despatch of the CSCE Mission of Long Duration. This new phase could be described as one of 'limited engagement'. While there was a perceptible increase in international institutional commitment that was given physical form by the establishment of a CSCE office in Pristina, the type of engagement was limited by the assumptions that either the status of Kosovo had been resolved in favour of Serbia or that that it was effectively irresolvable and should therefore by bypassed. In practical terms both assumptions had the same outcome: a working assumption that Kosovo was part of Serbia and would/should continue to be so.

In December 1992, though, George Bush made a dramatic gesture that appears to challenge my categorisation of this period as one of limited engagement but, as we shall see, did in fact correspond with dominant Western thinking at the time.

The Christmas ultimatum

On 24 December 1992, George Bush instructed Acting Secretary of State
Lawrence Eagleburger (a personal friend of Milošević) to send a classi-
fied cable to the American embassy in Belgrade. Attached to the cable
were instructions that the acting ambassador should personally read the
message to Milošević, verbatim and without elaboration.[84] The one sen-
tence message stated that, 'in the event of conflict in Kosovo caused by
Serbian action, the US will be prepared to employ military force against
Serbians in Kosovo and in Serbia proper'.[85] Given that the Americans
had failed to react decisively to the bloody wars in Croatia and Bosnia
and that the Europeans led the international engagement on the
Kosovo issue, the ultimatum not only appeared to be out of step with
American policy in the region it also appeared inconceivable that
the threat could have had any credibility in Belgrade. This raises the
question of why it was issued in the first place.

According to Thomas Niles, who was Assistant Secretary in the Bureau
of European and Canadian Affairs at the time, the American administration had intelligence information, which they considered to be credible,
that Milošević was planning a major onslaught against the Kosovar
Albanians. This attack would aim to provoke a massive exodus from
Kosovo into Albania, similar to that which happened in 1999.[86] The
credibility of this intelligence is supported by the fact that Sylejman
Selimi, one of the founding members of the UÇK, recalled that in the
winter of 1992–93 there was a Serbian crackdown on Kosovar Albanians
and in particular an attempt to confiscate arms.[87] Given that Albanian
society as a whole is traditionally an armed society, such a forcible con-
fiscation programme would have provoked conflict, particularly given
the political, social and economic conditions at the time.[88] As for why
Milošević should have chosen winter 1992 to conduct this operation,
American intelligence pointed to two factors. Firstly, Milošević calculated that the US would be preoccupied with the transition from
the Bush administration to the new administration under President
Clinton. The out-going president would be reluctant to act and Clinton
would take time to settle in at the White House. Secondly, during the
election campaign Governor Clinton had talked vaguely about using
force in former Yugoslavia and had criticised Bush for being too timid in
this respect. American intelligence therefore suggested that Milošević
wanted to present the incoming administration with the *fait accompli*
of an ethnically cleansed Kosovo.[89] There was an inter-agency debate
about how the US should respond to these reports and the telegraphed

ultimatum emerged as the preferred course of action. This was the basis of a recommendation put to President Bush, which he accepted.[90]

Thomas Niles makes two points on the question of how credible the threat was. Firstly, he argues that although the US had been far from proactive in response to the wars in Croatia and Bosnia, 'given the fact we had not previously promised more than we had delivered, despite Milošević's provocations … we believed that the warning would be taken seriously'.[91] This was the first time that the US, or NATO, or – for that matter – any other state or organisation had made such a threat. Nicholas Rostow, a member of the National Security Committee at the time, concurs with Niles' second point. He argues that if we consider the intelligence reports to have been credible (and the very nature of preventive action means that it is always impossible to ascertain because it is impossible to know whether the act would have been carried out had there not been intervention) then the threat succeeded because there was no significant violent crackdown against Kosovar Albanians at this time.[92]

The Christmas telegram appears to have been a half-hearted gesture by an out-going administration that had allowed its European allies to take the lead in dealing with the dissolution of Yugoslavia. This is Tim Judah's view, among others.[93] The problem is that there is no clear evidence that it had an impact on policymaking in Belgrade, leaving us to speculate with counterfactual debates. On the other hand, there is evidence that the Serbs were increasing their pressure on the Kosovar Albanians and that while Serb oppression did increase steadily throughout the 1990s, progress towards easing tension was made by Ambassadors Ahrens and Bøgh in the first half of 1993. The Christmas ultimatum should be seen, therefore, as an American contribution to the limited engagement of this second phase of international involvement. This strategy, spearheaded by the ICFY and CSCE would have been seriously compromised had there been an increase of violence in Kosovo. The American threat persuaded Milošević that it remained in Serbia's best interest to continue co-operating to some extent with the West over Kosovo and to refrain from ethnic cleansing. This was particularly so, because he had been successful in the debate about Kosovo's future status, unrest in the province was not of the significant armed variety, and Milan Panić had the power to create political problems.

Summary

International society viewed the Kosovo problem as fundamental to the wider Yugoslav problem before the outbreak of armed conflict in

Yugoslavia. As the entity with the most obvious schism with the federal authorities, Kosovo provided a litmus test for the redesigning of Yugoslavia. However, Kosovo was sidelined once Croatia and Slovenia declared their independence in the summer of 1991. Although there was never an explicit legal explanation as to why this happened, three key reasons are discernable:

1. There was no armed conflict in Kosovo, nor was armed conflict likely in the near future.
2. The Kosovo problem was viewed as being interrelated with the Krajina problem in Croatia despite the very different constitutional status of the two. It was feared in some quarters that independence for Kosovo would legitimise Serb claims in Croatia. As such, a solution based upon minority rights was seen as being best for both.
3. The Kosovar Albanians did not control Kosovo's territory.

These concerns dominated thinking during this first phase of 'non-engagement'. In particular, the Chairman of the ECCY and later ICFY, Lord Carrington, believed that his mandate did not extend to engaging with Kosovar Albanian leaders or allowing their participation in the peace process.

The period of non-engagement effectively removed the issue of Kosovo's final status from the international agenda. This created the policy space for the second phase of international involvement that began in earnest in August 1992. This was a phase of 'limited engagement' in which international society became institutionally involved in Kosovo. The level of engagement was restricted, however, by the working assumption that Kosovo's future status had been resolved in favour of Serbia, although no such resolution had actually occurred given the lack of a legal ruling on Kosovo's claim to independence. Indeed, Kosovo was the only entity that asked for an opinion but did not receive one – the commission's affirmation of *uti posseditis* ruling out Serbian claims in Croatia and Bosnia.

2
The Absence of Prevention

In spring 1993, Madeleine Albright, the American Ambassador to the UN who later became Secretary of State, told the Security Council that, 'we are coming to the day when countries in need will call the global 911 and get a busy signal'.[1] Unwittingly, in doing so she summed up the forthcoming half decade of international engagement with the Kosovo conflict. During this period Kosovar Albanian leaders such as Ibrahim Rugova and Bujar Bukoshi repeatedly raised the province's plight in the international arena but attracted little attention. Detailed reports by organisations such as Amnesty International, Human Rights Watch, the UN and C/OSCE (in December 1994, the CSCE became the OSCE) supported their case. Nevertheless, once the Serbian government removed its consent to an international presence in Kosovo the limited institutional engagement that had been made possible by the Panić interlude came to a rapid end. Moreover, the prioritisation of the quest for peace in Bosnia meant that accepting a 'Serb-led' solution to the Kosovo conundrum was widely viewed in international society as a price worth paying.

This chapter begins by outlining the work of the CSCE Mission of Long Duration and tracing its demise, which was intimately linked with the Bosnian war. It goes on to show that between the summer of 1993 and the end of 1997 international society failed to offer a preventive strategy for Kosovo similar to that offered to Macedonia.[2] Indeed, the original title of this chapter had been, 'the failure of prevention', but there were in fact only scant attempts to prevent the conflict. It is not surprising that international diplomats placed a premium on ending the Bosnian war and on ensuring peace there. After all, that conflict claimed over 200,000 lives. What is surprising is how few people in the intellectual and NGO communities publicly raised the Kosovo issue. As

1995 drew to a close, Julie Mertus was almost alone in pointing out that the Dayton agreement was flawed because it did not address the Kosovo Issue. Although many subsequent books and articles have correctly pointed out that this absence struck a decisive blow against Rugova's strategy of non-violent resistance because that strategy depended upon the internationalisation of the conflict, it needs to be borne in mind that Dayton was never intended to provide a comprehensive settlement to the wars of Yugoslav dissolution. Its sole aim was to bring an end to the Bosnian war. The work that the negotiators did on the Croatian Eastern Slavonian and Prevlaka peninsular problems came about because of the vital role that Croatia and Serbia played as guarantors of the peace. In the immediate aftermath of Dayton, Milošević was widely viewed as crucial to the success of the agreement by foreign statesmen. As a result, Yugoslavia enjoyed dramatically improved relations with other states even though its treatment of the Kosovar Albanians continued to deteriorate.

The end of the CSCE mission

Although it provided the spearhead of the international engagement with Kosovo, the CSCE Mission of Long Duration was limited to only 12 members by the Memorandum of Understanding that the organisation signed with the Serb government. The Committee of Senior Officials[3] agreed to enlarge the mission to 20 in November 1992, and again to 40 the following January. However, like its much larger successor in 1998 the mission never got up to full strength and never had more than 20 members. Those 20 members and their local support staff were spread across four different offices, in Belgrade, Pristina, Novi Pazar (Sandžak), and Subotica (Vojvodina). Within Kosovo, the mission also attempted to maintain a permanent presence in Prizren and Pec. The mission was also poorly financed. For example, Daniel Plesch pointed out at the time that the CSCE High Commissioner for Minorities had only four staff and US$250,000 to cover the entire region.[4] Although the Mission of Long Duration received supplemental funding and voluntary donations from member states it had neither the money nor logistical support to carry out anything other than the most rudimentary of monitoring.

The mission to Kosovo initially consisted of only three members, Philipp Hahn, Daniel Droulers and Veniamin Karacostanoglu. Although local staff supported them, the CSCE observers were unable to carry out their assignments proactively. They contributed little to human rights reporting, doing less than NGOs such as Amnesty International. Nor did they actively promote dialogue between the national communities, primarily because they lacked the resources and presence to do so. One thing it did do reasonably successfully was assist the CSCE's monitoring of the Yugoslav elections that were held at the end of 1992. As an indication of the scale of the problems confronting the Mission of Long Duration, however, it is worth noting that whilst over 100 observers were temporarily despatched to Yugoslavia to monitor the elections, they managed a report of only seven pages. That report concluded that the December elections were 'neither free nor fair'. It continued, 'on election day, virtually every delegation that visited polling sites in Serbia witnessed irregularities in electoral administration'.[5] The CSCE itself came in for what it described as 'media manipulation' by the Yugoslav state new agency, *Tanjug*. The agency reported that the senior official running the election monitoring operation had 'expressed satisfaction' with the way that the elections had been run. The CSCE election report retorted that 'such unreserved praise simply did not take place'.[6] Interestingly, although the Kosovar Albanians boycotted the elections *en masse* they did not warrant a mention in the report. Kosovar Albanian plans to hold shadow elections and the general human rights situation in the province were not discussed either.

The CSCE mission did not have as wide a mandate as its successor in 1998. Its main aim was to promote dialogue and this could only take place within the assumed limit proscribed by international society: That Kosovo was an internal Serbian problem. The Kosovar Albanian leadership was therefore reluctant to cooperate with the mission. This point was duly noted by Tore Bøgh, the Head of Mission, who observed in his final report that, 'Albanian leaders have not been greatly concerned about CSCE efforts to promote dialogue with Serbia. In drawn-out educational talks and more recently in the negotiations to retain an independent press, they have been less flexible that their Serbian counterparts'.[7]

This concern directly touched on a debate that recurred throughout Kosovar Albanian politics in the 1990s. On the one hand there were moderates around Ibrahim Rugova who argued that dialogue with Belgrade was needed to improve living conditions in Kosovo. On the other hand, an ever-growing group of radicals based around Adem Demaçi argued that such dialogue legitimised Serb rule over the province and undermined the twin strategies of passive resistance that the Kosovar Albanian community had embarked upon. The first strategy was to create a functioning parallel state, a *de facto* set of institutions that could show themselves to be capable of democratically governing Kosovo. They argued that negotiating with Belgrade about the school curriculum, for example, was an implicit admission that the parallel state did not function in practise. The second strategy was the internationalisation of the conflict. This strategy was particularly problematic after Rugova's failure to get a seat at the main table of the London Conference. Political dispute emerged about how to internationalise the conflict. Rugova preferred a strategy of cooperation. In order to participate in the talks Rugova had to implicitly accept the basic rule of the game, that Kosovo was part of Serbia. Bøgh understood this dilemma and commented that, 'the [Kosovar Albanian leadership] rejected all conditions that in the narrow and at times inconsistent perception of their people could be interpreted as acceptance of Serbian sovereignty over Kosovo'. He continued, 'they perceive their benefit from the CSCE presence in terms of exposing and ameliorating human rights violations by the Serbian administration'.[8]

Although the CSCE mission did not contribute much in itself towards reducing the level of human rights abuse and mistrust in Kosovo, it did serve two important functions.[9] First, it provided a symbol of international society's interest in the province and offered the potential for further engagement through its proposed enlargement. Secondly, by doing so the mission provided an impetus for international NGOs to become more involved. Save the Children, Oxfam, and the Soros Foundation began their involvement in Kosovo during this period.[10]

What is interesting about this early NGO engagement is that much of it focused on providing support to indigenous Kosovar Albanian projects, many of which were directly linked to the parallel state system. Save the Children was initially active in Kosovo in 1993, providing assistance and advice to institutions working with children. The Soros Foundation also became involved in 1993, providing both material and pedagogical assistance to educators in the province. Oxfam was present from 1993 and set up an office in Pristina in 1995. At the outset, Oxfam concentrated on infrastructure programmes that provided clean water and sanitation to many of the rural communities that lacked it after the Serb authorities stopped providing services for Kosovar Albanians in many regions.[11]

Serbia's decision to accept a CSCE mission on its soil had been brought about by Milan Panić, who forced Milošević's hand in the matter. Although it was proving to be ineffective owing to its limited capability and restricted mandate the mission remained an irritant to the Serb leader and a symbol of Panić's resistance. The crunch came in the December 1992 elections. Panić decided to stand against Milošević for the presidency of Serbia. Both Lord Owen and Geert Ahrens attempted to persuade the Kosovar Albanians to participate in the elections to oust Milošević and replace him with Panić, something that Rugova refused to countenance.[12] Both the international mediators believed that Panić was willing to contemplate improving the rights of Kosovar Albanians, and Ahrens made significant progress in persuading Panić and Rugova to begin negotiations about the education system. The key problem, though, was that these requests were not accompanied by promises of international assistance to Kosovo if Panić were elected. Although such promises were outside the mandate of Ahrens' working group, Owen could have offered Rugova greater participation in the peace process in return for Kosovar Albanian votes.

Because Milošević controlled the media, could manipulate the ballot, and because over a million Albanian voters decided to take no part in the election, he was able to prevail, securing 53 per cent of the vote compared to Panić's 32 per cent.[13] Panić remained in position as Yugoslav Prime Minister, preventing any immediate move against the CSCE. The mission's Memorandum of Understanding with Yugoslavia had given it a six-month mandate from 28 September 1992, which was subsequently extended by the federal government until the end of July. However, at the beginning of the new year Milošević began a crackdown on all forms of opposition including the media and universities. He also forged an alliance with the ultra-nationalist Radical Party leader, Vojislav Šešelj, which allowed him to force a vote of no confidence through the federal parliament. Panić had faced, and survived, two such Milošević inspired votes before but on this occasion he also lost the support of Montenegrin deputies who reasoned that his decision to stand for the post of President of Serbia was incompatible with his current position as Prime Minister of Yugoslavia. The no confidence motion was carried and Milan Panić was forced to resign, closing the brief window of opportunity that his rise to prominence had created.[14] With Panić out of the way, Milošević set about ridding himself of the CSCE mission, a move that would allow a crackdown on Kosovo and appease Vojislav Šešelj, the president's new ally.

Shortly before the mandate came up for renewal once again, Milošević announced that it would not be extended though the Montenegrin government indicated that it opposed the expulsion. The Serb government argued that the decision was motivated by the failure of the organisation to reinstate Yugoslavia's membership, which had been revoked the previous summer (prior to the deployment of the

Mission of Long Duration) in response to the violence in Croatia and Bosnia. Announcing the decision, Margit Savović, the Federal Minister for Human Rights, argued that, 'Yugoslavia is interested in renewing its rights and membership in the organisation, and the fact that the mandate of the CSCE mission has not been extended cannot be regarded as refusing to cooperate, because Yugoslavia has been all the time willing to but was hindered'.[15] The Belgrade daily, *Verčenje Novosti*, which was close to Milošević's ruling Socialist Party, put the point more bluntly, stating that, 'since Yugoslavia does not have access in the CSCE, and no right to introduce its views about events in its own country, why should it then have any obligations towards this organisation?'.[16] The Head of Mission, Tore Bøgh shared the view that the decision not to extend the mandate had little to do with what the mission itself was doing.[17]

Although the CSCE membership issue was an irritant to the Serb leadership it was not the principal reason for the decision not to extend the mission's mandate. After all, the mandate had been accepted in the first place and then extended after Yugoslavia's expulsion from the organisation. Instead, the explusion was based on three key factors. First, the mission was a product of the 'Panić interlude' and its expulsion a symbol of Milošević's reassertion of power in Belgrade. Second, the Serb leadership was concerned that the mission could be used as a vehicle for internationalising the Kosovo conflict. Finally, although small in scale, the mission did inhibit Serbian 'security operations' in the province. Political arrests, show trials and police brutality were reported back to CSCE headquarters in Vienna and on to foreign ministries in Europe and North America. The CSCE's Committee of Senior Officials repeatedly authorised the mission's enlargement, from the original 12 to a possible 40. This would have increased its capabilities and further hampered Serbian policing.

CSCE members responded to the exclusion by insisted that the mission's mandate be renewed and refusing to offer the Serb government any inducements to do so, though they also failed to threaten any punitive measures. The Serb government offered to extend the mandate for a few weeks to allow discussion of Yugoslavia's status within the organisation but the CSO rebuffed the offer when it met in Prague at the end of June.[18] The CSO decided that although its international personnel would have to be withdrawn it would not terminate the mission. The mission's reporting role would be formally carried out on a temporary basis by the Belgrade ambassadors of member states. The ambassadors created a working group tasked to send weekly reports about the situation in Yugoslavia to the organisation's headquarters in Vienna.[19] This had little effect on the Serbs as the committee disseminated very little information to the wider international audience about what was going on inside Kosovo.

The decision to expel the CSCE from Kosovo brought with it a renewed crackdown against the Kosovar Albanians. The Human Rights Committee, a monitoring NGO based in Pristina, reported that within two months of the CSCE's withdrawal more than 90 political activists had been arrested.[20] Ibrahim Rugova was in no doubt that the crackdown was related to the expulsion of the handful of monitors. He told journalists that 'since the CSCE left, villages have been surrounded and searched with brutality'[21] and, 'the situation is very grave indeed, very tense. Since the expulsion of the CSCE mission there have been large-scale arrests and thousands of families have been mistreated'.[22] There were also indications that the Serbs were trying to hide their actions from the outside world, as the authorities refused to grant Amnesty International access to the province. Further concern was prompted by the announcement that Željko Raznatović, otherwise known as Arkan, a gangster whose paramilitary organisation, the 'Tigers', were responsible for some of the worst atrocities in Croatia and Bosnia, was setting up base in the Grand Hotel in central Pristina.[23]

After its withdrawal, the CSCE became principally concerned about the fate of local staff that had been recruited to provide administrative and linguistic support to the mission. These Kosovar Albanians were specifically targeted by the Serbs. In Prizren, the authorities arrested around 100 people who had had contact with the CSCE. As well as people who had actually worked for the organisation, this figure included intellectuals, journalists, local politicians and members of other NGOs who had cooperated with the international monitors. Testimony from those arrested in this crackdown revealed that it was provoked by a concern with the CSCE's activities. Kadri Kryeziu, president of the Human Rights Council in Prizren, recalled that he was beaten during his time in jail and had the bruises to prove it. Speaking of the police brutality he said:

> There was no bread or water for seven days, they interrogated me for forty-eight hours in one stretch. They kept asking me 'what did you tell the CSCE?' and said that the CSCE mission was only here to start war and make trouble. My family thought I was dead. It took five days for them to know I was in jail.[24]

Kryeziu went on to observe that even though the CSCE mission had been small in size and limited in mandate it had a positive impact, particularly by reducing the number of politically motivated arrests. The problem was recognised by Margaretha af Ugglas who reported that there were alarming reports of mounting repression in Kosovo and deliberate harassment of the CSCE's local staff there.[25] Events elsewhere, however, revealed that international society was not much interested in dealing with these matters.

Although the UN, CSCE and Western leaders repeatedly called for the reinstatement of the CSCE mission they did not wield any political carrots or sticks to support their demands. Instead, just as Rugova visited London to call for more international pressure to be applied on the Serbs, the French and German governments launched a new initiative aimed at bringing peace to Bosnia. The plan proposed the suspension of the economic sanctions imposed against Serbia in return for concessions over Bosnia, emphatically removing Kosovo from the international agenda.[26] It was not implemented however, largely because the Bosnian Serb leadership was unwilling to compromise, but it created a precedent whereby the removal of punitive measures originally put in place partly because of Serb activities in Kosovo (sanctions and expulsion from the CSCE) was linked solely to Serb acquiescence in places other than Kosovo.

This linkage, between sanctions on Serbia and Serb activities in Croatia and Bosnia remained throughout the rest of the wars there. The initial impact of sanctions was undermined because the Western states that were keen to create a sanctions regime often had trouble persuading other members of the Security Council. In April 1993, for example, Yuli Voronstov, the Russian Ambassador to the UN threatened to use Russia's veto for the first time since the end of the Cold War to block a resolution tightening the sanctions regime. The Russian government requested a delay to a resolution aimed at closing the loopholes in the already existing sanctions regime to allow Boris Yeltsin's special envoy, Vitali Churkin, time to pursue his peace effort with the Bosnian Serbs.[27] The US and others agreed and offered to delay the Security Council vote. In return, they insisted on explicit linkage between the sanctions imposed against Yugoslavia and Bosnian Serb acceptance of the Vance–Owen peace plan for Bosnia.[28]

In October, the UN linked the lifting of sanctions to the reintegration of Serb held territories in Croatia (Krajina) into Croatia proper. Yugoslav Foreign Minister, Vladislav Jovanović complained that, 'singling out Yugoslavia is a roundabout way to enable Croatia to continue undermining the [peace] plan and its aggressive behaviour towards the UN protected areas'.[29] A month later, the Belgrade leadership began to make its own demands, insisting that they would not take part in any peace negotiations until the sanctions were lifted.[30] They continued to maintain this demand until 1995 when Richard Holbrooke persuaded Milošević that the sanctions would be lifted once an agreement was reached rather than before negotiations were begun.[31] By 1995, the need to have the sanctions lifted was an overriding concern for the Serb leader, to the extent that he effectively abandoned his 'greater Serbia' policy.[32] This opens the possibility that contrary to what many international diplomats have said, there may well have been scope to persuade Milošević to include a settlement for Kosovo in the negotiations. However, although the UN Security Council, General Assembly, and its Economic and Social Council repeatedly called for the reinstatement of the CSCE mission there was never any suggestion that this be linked to lifting sanctions. As a result, it was 1998 before the (by then) OSCE returned to Kosovo.

The institutional involvement with the Kosovo conflict during this period of limited engagement was not limited to the CSCE mission. In the previous chapter, I explained how the ICFY created a special working group to look at minority rights issues across the former Yugoslavia. The group, headed by the German diplomat Geert Ahrens, who is widely considered to be an expert on Balkan politics, began its work in 1992. Ahrens immediately identified a problem with his terms of reference. He observed that the Serbs opposed the very idea of an international working group because it internationalised the Kosovo conflict. The Kosovar Albanians were also unhappy with the group because they did not believe themselves to be a national minority. After all, they told Ahrens, Albanians made up 90 per cent of Kosovo's population.[33]

Writing in September 1993, Ahrens noted that the Kosovo question presented him with 'the most dangerous and by far the most difficult problem'.[34] To meet this challenge, the ICFY steering committee created a special group dealing specifically with Kosovo. Between its creation and the expulsion of the CSCE mission, this special group (which was also chaired by Ahrens) met on only three occasions. Nevertheless, their work on Kosovo took on greater significance after the expulsion of the CSCE. They focused on the education issue and hoped to bring the two sides together to reach an accord on sharing state schools and the incorporation of the parallel Kosovar Albanian schooling system into the mainstream. Bilateral talks, sponsored by the UN Educational, Scientific and Cultural Organisation (UNESCO), were scheduled for the beginning of September 1993 but failed to materialise because the Serb government raised a number of spurious technical objections. These objections included a refusal to hold the talks in Geneva. The government argued that because education in Kosovo was an internal Serbian matter the talks should be held in Belgrade.[35] Nevertheless, the mediators held talks with the Kosovar Albanian delegation fronted by Fehmi Agani, the Vice-President of Rugova's party. Agani told the mediators that the Serbs would have to meet three preconditions before meaningful talks could begin:

- The unconditional release of school and university buildings for use by the Kosovar Albanians.
- A readiness to address other (non-education) issues on an equal footing.
- A readiness to have a further meeting provided it was in Geneva.[36]

Ahrens was not impressed by these demands and saw in them a hardening of the Kosovar Albanian position. He observed in the autumn of 1993 that, 'no progress has been achieved' and that, 'the situation appears more tense'.[37] Ahrens noted that the human rights situation in the province had markedly deteriorated after the expulsion of the CSCE and that social trends in the province suggested only a worsening of inter-community relations there.

The retreat from limited engagement involved both the expulsion of the CSCE Mission of Long Duration and the redrafting of the ICFY working group's terms of reference. Milošević repeatedly insisted in his negotiations with the ICFY co-chairs, David Owen and Thorvald Stoltenberg, that the minorities working group not consider Sandžak and Kosovo because these were internal matters. David Owen's clear priority at this time was to win the Serb leader's approval for his Bosnian peace plan and so the co-chairs accepted Milošević's argument, believing that an insistence that the working group should continue its work on Kosovo would act as a barrier to a breakthrough on Bosnia. The co-chairs therefore proposed that Ahren's working group be limited to dealing with Macedonia and the Serb held Krajina region of Croatia. These proposals were accepted by the ICFY's steering committee at the beginning of July, despite the strong objections from Turkey, Austria, Portugal, Germany and even Russia, who argued that the Kosovo conflict remained a fundamental problem that the working group could play a vital role in mediating.[38]

Lord Owen argues that these reports were mistaken and that in fact the group continued to address the Kosovo question until the ICFY was wound up in the aftermath of Dayton.[39] Geert Ahrens, the working group's chair, remembers differently and holds documentary evidence to support his view. Ahrens recalled that on 1 July 1993, Owen proposed that the working group stop addressing the Kosovo question, arguing that its six members could not deal with all the minorities issues in the former Yugoslavia. Ahrens objected, arguing in the presence of subsequent Norwegian Foreign Minister and OSCE Chairman-in-Office Knut Vollebaek, that the removal of Kosovo from the working group's mandate would remove the last vestiges of international engagement. Several members of the steering committee agreed, including the Russian representative, but Owen won out and Kosovo was removed from the minorities working group's mandate.

The expulsion of the CSCE Mission of Long Duration and the failure of the ICFY working group to bring the parties together brought about the end of the period of *limited engagement*. During this period, international society established a small institutional presence in Kosovo, which in turn attracted NGOs such as Save the Children and Oxfam to the province. The CSCE's departure prompted many of the smaller NGOs to leave. The limited engagement was framed by the idea that the constitutional issue had been resolved in favour of the Serbian government and that engagement should be concerned with finding solutions to practical problems such as education. Because the engagement was based on an assumption that accepted Serbia's claim to Kosovo it was dependent on the consent of the Serbian government and had its agenda set by the need to obtain and preserve that consent. Milošević withdrew his consent after he ousted Milan Panić, forcing a reduction of the level of international engagement even though those engaged observed that conditions in the province were worsening. International society's response to the conflict thus reverted to one of non-engagement inasmuch as there was little or no permanent international presence and that although there were sporadic attempts to mediate and improve inter-community confidence there was no systematic attempt to prevent violent conflict that was anywhere near comparable to what happened in Macedonia. This new period of non-engagement was, from Kosovo's point of view, one of *malign non-engagement* because international society viewed resolution of the province's problems as secondary to finding an end to the Bosnian war. As a result, the relaxing of sanctions that were originally imposed partly because of Serbian policies in Kosovo came to be linked solely with Serb activities in Croatia and Bosnia. Because Milošević came to be seen as vital to the search for peace and because he insisted that there could be no negotiations about the future of Kosovo, the province's troubles were marginalised. Turning a blind eye to the fate of Kosovo was seen as a price worth paying for peace elsewhere. It was only once the province itself erupted into war in 1998 that international society began to treat it as a distinct problem.

Kosovo and the search for peace in Bosnia

Throughout this period (summer 1993 to March 1998) there was limited UN human rights reporting in Kosovo. The UN attempted to take on the monitoring function that many Kosovar Albanians had hoped the CSCE would have emphasised in its mission. Although the UN's Special Rapporteurs took on an important function after the CSCE's withdrawal the reports and comments they produced were not widely disseminated outside the immediate recipients (UN committees). The reports referred to, 'police brutality against ethnic Albanians', 'the discriminatory removal of ethnic Albanian officials' from public service and the, 'arbitrary imprisonment of ethnic Albanian journalists'. They also demanded that Yugoslavia respect the human rights and fundamental freedoms of the Kosovar Albanians.

These reports prompted the Security Council to address Kosovo for the first time. Resolution 855 passed on 9 August 1993, with 14 votes in favour and one abstention, called upon the Yugoslav government to 'reconsider' its refusal to allow the continuation of the CSCE mission, to cooperate with the CSCE, assure the monitor's safety and allow them unimpeded access throughout the country.[40] In debates preceding the vote, the Chinese Ambassador emphasised the importance of the principle of non-interference in the internal affairs of sovereign states and insisted that 'the issue of Kosovo is an internal affair of the Federal Republic of Yugoslavia'.[41] There was little dispute that Kosovo was an internal issue for Serbia, but Madeleine Albright, the US Ambassador, argued that the Serbs should fulfil their responsibilities to the CSCE and noted that the conflict in Bosnia could spread to Kosovo. This argument, coupled with the fact that CSCE missions are dependent on host nation consent, persuaded the Russian Ambassador to vote in favour of the resolution and the Chinese Ambassador abstained rather than use his veto. The Resolution stopped a long way short of authorising political, economic, or military measures to persuade Yugoslavia to comply, primarily because most of the Council's members accepted China's view that the Kosovo conflict was primarily an internal matter.

That the US did not take a stronger position in the Security Council is particularly interesting given George Bush's 'Christmas ultimatum' and new president Bill Clinton's apparently robust line on the Balkans. Almost immediately on taking office, the Clinton administration restated Bush's ultimatum. Announcing that Warren Christopher would act as the new President's special envoy to the Balkans, State Department spokesman Richard Boucher told journalists that Christopher was, 'going to reiterate to the Serbian leadership the fact that we would respond as appropriate if there were violence in Kosovo'.[42] When Christopher came to do so, the precise wording he used fell some way short of specifically mentioning the use of force by the US, as Bush's message to Milošević had done. Instead, speaking about the Balkans more generally, he promised that the US would:

> Increase political pressure on Serbia and deter Serbia from widening the war. We've informed the Serbians that we plan to raise the economic and political price for aggression. We will work with our allies, the Russians and others to achieve that result. *We remain prepared to respond against the Serbians in the event of conflict in Kosovo caused by Serbian action.*[43]

A few months later, after discussing the conflict prevention effort in Macedonia, Christopher told the North Atlantic Council that, 'neither can we permit a crackdown in Kosovo that could lead to an expansion of the conflict. The US has made it clear to the Serb authorities that such a move will not be tolerated. NATO should also support an increase in the CSCE long duration missions'.[44] Thus, although the American envoy reiterated the previous administration's rhetorical determination to prevent the escalation of conflict in Kosovo he chose only to single out the 'economic and political' costs to Serbia and deliberately omitted any mention of military costs.

These aims were reiterated by Stephen Oxman, the Assistant Secretary of State for European and Canadian Affairs (a position later held by Richard Holbrooke). Oxman underscored the idea that the American administration's key concern in the southern Balkans was the prevention of violent conflict and he went into more detail about the specific nature of American policy in the region. Oxman told a special congressional CSCE committee that the new administration was pursuing four policy avenues:

- Demanding the cessation of human rights abuse in Kosovo while simultaneously confirming American opposition to the idea of Kosovan independence in a meeting with Rugova.
- Providing US$5 million worth of humanitarian aid for the province, mostly for the provision of foodstuffs and other basic commodities.

- Warning Milošević that the US was prepared to 'respond' to conflict in Kosovo caused by Serbian action.
- Supporting the reinstatement of the CSCE Mission of Long Duration.[45]

Although most accounts simply point out that Clinton reiterated his predecessors' 'Christmas ultimatum', if we look at the new administration's policy in more detail we find a marked withdrawal from the threat of active military engagement with Kosovo. This mirrored the wider transition in international society's engagement from a period of *limited engagement* to one of *malign non-engagement*. It also marked a decisive shift in Clinton's own thinking on the Balkans. During the 1992 election campaign, candidate Clinton had lambasted the administration for not being more proactive and interventionist towards the Balkans.[46] On coming to power, however, the new administration adopted many of its predecessors' policies. Clinton's initial optimism about the potential for bringing peace to the Balkans was dashed largely as a result of policy advice from 'Balkan experts' such as Robert Kaplan.

It is well known that Clinton was an avid reader of Kaplan, who argued that the conflict in the Balkans was fuelled by 'ancient ethnic hatreds'.[47] Learning from Kaplan, the President argued that, 'it's no accident that the First World War started in this area. There are ancient ethnic hatreds that have consumed people and led to the horrible abuses'.[48] Leaving aside the fact that the causes of the First World War had very little to do with the Balkans, the policy prescription Clinton drew from this analysis was that the conflict could not be resolved and should therefore be contained instead. Containment meant looking for peace in Bosnia and Croatia and ensuring that violence did not spread to Kosovo. On this latter point the Americans developed a two-pronged policy. They called for restraint from the Serbs while both turning a blind eye to human rights abuse and accepting Belgrade's constitutional claims. To the Kosovar Albanians they began to offer a small amount of humanitarian assistance whilst encouraging them to give up their claims for independence. What the US, along with the ICFY mediators failed to do was offer proactive mediation or conflict prevention measures.

As 1993 came to a close an almost lone voice on the international scene was the UN's Special Rapporteur on human rights in former Yugoslavia, Tadeusz Mazowiecki. Mazowiecki had been a founding member of Poland's 'Solidarity' movement and was the first premier of post-communist Poland. Throughout his time in office, until his resignation in 1995 in protest at the UN's failure in Srebrenica, Mazowiecki distinguished himself by his proactive stance on Kosovo. Although his mandate included human rights problems throughout former Yugoslavia, a mandate that he ably fulfilled, Mazowiecki's reports and comments repeatedly highlighted the situation in Kosovo. At the end of 1993, for example, he produced a report that exposed the high level of discrimination against Kosovar Albanians in the province.[49] Unfortunately, no one was listening.

Just how isolated Mazowiecki was, was revealed in an interview he gave shortly after his resignation. His mandate was to analyse and report on all abuses of human rights and humanitarian law. However, only the UN's Human Rights Commission was obliged to take notice of his reports and this was a consent-based body that came under the auspices of the General Assembly and therefore lacked enforcement powers. Although the Security Council could draw on his reports it was not obliged to heed them and Mazowiecki lamented that after nearly four years in his post he was only once invited to a Council meeting.[50] He received less and less cooperation from Belgrade because he frequently wrote what he described as, 'full and harsh reports about the position of Albanians in Kosovo',[51] and felt that he did not get adequate help from the UN. Mazowiecki argued that this made his job almost impossible.

Under pressure from the Albanian government, in June 1994 a senior Kosovar Albanian delegation led by Fehmi Agani travelled to Belgrade for 'secret' negotiations with the Serb government. Milošević's Socialist Party viewed the talks as a major triumph because they implied that the Kosovar Albanians accepted the principle Serb of sovereignty.[52] As Mihailo Marković, a close associate of Milošević, explained, 'the Albanians want to discuss concrete issues of everyday life, such as health and education but not the final status of Kosovo, which is a big step forward'.[53] The precise nature and scope of the talks remains a controversial issue among Kosovar Albanian politicians. Given that the West had ruled out independence and that Albania had added qualifications to its support many moderates in the LDK, centred around Rugova himself, favoured negotiation and compromise with Belgrade on substantive issues that could improve living conditions in the province. More radical LDK members, such as Bujar Bukoshi and Hyjadet Hyseni, rejected this view, arguing that only independence could resolve the conflict and that negotiating with Belgrade would compromise their cause. It is unsurprising therefore that the Kosovar Albanian representatives at the Belgrade talks were sensitive to public attention. It is also unsurprising that the talks failed to bring about any movement whatsoever from either side.

In the continuing absence of international interest in Kosovo and the continuing failure to bring peace to Bosnia, the trickle of sporadic human rights reports from Mazowiecki and the CSCE mission in absentia were all that brought the problem to a wider international audience. Because the Western media only seldom mentioned the reports they had virtually no impact. In June 1994, a delegation from the CSCE Parliamentary Assembly displayed typical understatement when it noted an, 'alarming amount of mistrust and even hatred between the Serbian authorities and the Albanian population'.[54] The delegation went on to insist that the territorial integrity of Serbia be respected and although it did note in passing that another group had claimed that there was extensive police brutality it suggested only that the matter be 'raised' with the Serbian government. In contrast, Mazowiecki continued to clearly highlight the deteriorating human rights situation in the province. In November 1994, he reported to the General Assembly that, 'during the past month there has reportedly been a drastic increase in the number of violent house searches, raids and arbitrary arrests by the law enforcement agencies', before recording cases of discrimination – often violent – within the education system.[55]

Although Mazowiecki continued to point out that the human rights situation in the province was deteriorating, the US and its Contact Group partners of six states[56] announced that they planned a two-month suspension of the sanctions against Serbia to help persuade the government in Belgrade to put pressure on the Bosnian Serbs in Pale.[57] Meanwhile, the CSCE, whose human rights reporting had failed to highlight the ongoing discrimination in Kosovo, added to this air of complacency about Kosovo. Tore Bøgh, who remained head of the long duration mission, publicly argued that the Bosnian war would not spread south to Kosovo.[58] This both reflected and contributed to the predominant view in the West and supported the widespread belief that as there was no violent conflict in Kosovo (nor likelihood of one emerging) it would be irresponsible to jeopardise the prospects for peace in Bosnia by insisting that the Serbs improve the human rights situation in the province.

At the beginning of 1995, the UN's Special Rapporteur reported once again to the General Assembly that conditions in the province had deteriorated and won a vote condemning the on-going discrimination.[59] The Assembly, however, decided not to refer the matter to the Security Council, which as we noted earlier paid little attention to Mazowiecki's work. Sadly, he resigned in the aftermath of the UN's failure that led to the massacre of over 7,000 Bosnian Muslims in the so-called safe area at Srebrenica. He argued that the lack of support he received from the organisation he was working for made it impossible to fulfil his mandate.[60] Although his replacement, the Swedish politician Elisabeth Rehn, took up the mandate the UN's subsequent human rights reports lacked the clarity and incisiveness that Mazowiecki brought to the job.

When, in 1995, the Serbs decided to change the ethnic balance in their favour by relocating refugees from Croatia in Kosovo[61] the Albanian government wrote to the Security Council condemning what it saw as Serb colonisation. It insisted that contrary to Tore Bøgh's assessment, there was a very real chance of violence there and called on the Security Council to take preventive measures.[62] The Yugoslav representative retorted by arguing that the Albanian government was peddling falsehoods and breaching the UN Charter by interfering in its internal affairs and encouraging secessionists.[63] This debate failed to have much impression on any of the UN's decision-making bodies.

Meanwhile, efforts to resolve the wars in Croatia and Bosnia were gathering pace. Richard Holbrooke was shuttling around Western and Balkan capitals, NATO's Operation Deliberate Force employed air strikes to force the Bosnian Serbs to halt their attacks on Sarajevo, and a Croat-Muslim alliance was retaking land seized by the Serbs in both countries in 1991–92. Kosovo saw precious little of this frenetic international activity. In September, Warren Christopher travelled to Tirana for talks with Berisha but did little other than support the Albanian President's internal reform programme and emphasise the need for conciliation and compromise in Kosovo. For his part, Holbrooke's own account of the pre-Dayton shuttle diplomacy that brought the Croatian, Bosnian and Serbian leaders together reveals that the Kosovo issue played no part whatsoever in his negotiations with Milošević. Nevertheless, Rugova continued to believe that a final settlement for Bosnia would include a resolution to the Kosovo conflict. It is now well known that the omission of Kosovo from the Dayton proceedings came as quite a shock to the Kosovar Albanian leadership and to the Kosovar Albanian people more generally. As Noel Malcolm put it:

> The ending of war in Bosnia brought no end to the crisis in Kosovo. This fact alone was a blow to Rugova's prestige: he had spent four years telling his people, in effect, that they must be patient until the international community imposed a final settlement on ex-Yugoslavia, in which their interests would also be respected.[64]

It is still not fully understood why Rugova thought that international society would address the Kosovo issue decisively despite the lack of interest shown by Richard Holbrooke, his British predecessors, and the assorted international organisations that had shown a limited interest in Kosovo but had never been prepared to force the issue with the Serb President? Moreover, Kosovo was considered to be part of Serbia by everyone other than the Albanians. As the Dutch Foreign Minister, Peter Koijmans put it a year earlier:

> I should like to make it quite clear that I believe that the ethnic Albanians in Kosovo should realise that the province is – and will almost certainly be – part of Serbia. Any attempt to achieve full independence would not have the support of the European Union and ... would encounter fierce opposition from Serbia.[65]

Rugova has never been clear about where his belief that internationalisation would come once international society forced a resolution to the Bosnian war came from, though Tim Judah suggests that his own sense of self-importance persuaded him that Kosovo was more important to the West than it really was.[66]

The Dayton conference tried to secure a peace deal for Bosnia and resolve the remaining issues in Croatia. Only three Balkan delegations were invited, led by the Presidents of Serbia, Croatia, and Bosnia. Rugova was not invited to attend despite his protests. There is little indication that Kosovo was mentioned during the discussions at Wright-Patterson air force base, though with hindsight key negotiators such as Holbrooke are keen to insist that they tried to raise the issue but to no avail. Speaking afterwards he observed that Croatian President Franjo Tudman and Bosnian President Alija Izetbegović had no interest whatsoever in the issue and speculated that had the international mediators placed Kosovo on the agenda the two presidents would in all likelihood have said 'screw you'.[67] Holbrooke told Judah that, 'Kosovo would have happened anyway, and it is part of the mythology that Dayton was responsible and I don't believe it. What really drove this thing was Rugova's failure to produce results and the Serb crackdown'.[68] Holbrooke is right to an extent. The reason why Dayton directly contributed to Rugova's demise and the rise to prominence of the UÇK was because the LDK President had been so public in his belief that international society would address Kosovo, when in fact all the indications suggested that it would not. It was the failure to internationalise the conflict over a period of years – rather than a specific disappointment at Dayton – that caused the shift in Kosovar Albanian politics. And this was as much a failure of international society as a failure on the part of Rugova.

Because Dayton has been singled out by many critics as a missed opportunity for conflict prevention due to its symbolic value, the main architect of the negotiations, Richard Holbrooke, not only argues that the Croats and Bosnians were disinterested but also that Kosovo's inclusion would have made it impossible to win an agreement from Milošević. This echoed the presumption of the international mediators that had preceded him, including Carrington and Owen. Holbrooke offers a single account of an occasion where he did raise the Kosovo issue with Milošević:

> Once, as Milošević and I were taking a walk, about one hundred Albanian Americans came to the outer fence of Wright-Patterson with megaphones to plead the case for Kosovo. I suggested we walk over to chat with them, but he refused, saying testily that they were obviously being paid by a foreign power, and that Kosovo was an 'internal' problem, a position with which I strongly disagreed.[69]

Two points are evident from this account. First, on the one occasion where Kosovo was raised in the negotiations it was not the international mediators who were responsible for raising it. Instead it was a group of Albanian Americans. Secondly, with hindsight, Holbrooke tells us that he disagreed with the proposition that Kosovo was an internal matter though he provides no evidence to suggest that this influenced his approach. More than four years of international engagement actually suggested broad international agreement with the Serb leader on this point.

The Kosovo conflict merited a single mention when the parties at Dayton finally reached an agreement. Towards the end of the final annex the lifting of the so-called outer-wall of sanctions against Yugoslavia was linked to an improvement of the human rights situation in the province. This 'outer-wall' consisted of the selective denial of travel visas for Yugoslav government officials and access to international financial institutions such as the World Bank. Shortly after the formal signing of the Dayton agreement in Paris, the US announced that it would suspend its sanctions against Serbia and Montenegro.[70] The relaxation of sanctions was linked directly to compliance with the Dayton accords and particularly with the military aspects. The suspension was widely seen as strengthening the peace agreement by binding the Serb government in Belgrade to the peacebuilding process.[71] What is more, it revealed once again the importance that international society attached to Milošević as a guarantor of the Bosnian peace. This became a key aspect of the international engagement with the region in the two years following Dayton.

Between 1993 and the end of the Dayton summit, international society subordinated conflict prevention in Kosovo to the perceived greater need to halt the Bosnian war. A failure of prevention would have been bad enough. International society did not even try to prevent the conflict because it accepted Serbian claims over Kosovo and rejected the arguments put forward by Rugova and the Albanian government. This was despite the strenuous efforts of people like Mazowiecki who resolutely tried to bring attention to the deteriorating human rights situation. However, the UN refused to act on his Bosnian reports let alone his observations on Kosovo. Very few people at the time noted Kosovo's omission from the Dayton talks. Bob Dole, who had been instrumental in bringing Kosovo to the fore in the early 1990s, backed the Dayton agreement wholeheartedly. Only Julie Mertus, an academic and human rights activist made the point:

> To be sure, giving the Albanians of Kosovo a place at the table might infuriate Mr. Milošević. But to try to reach peace in the Balkans without addressing the Kosovo issue is to try putting out a fire while leaving the coals burning.[72]

Kosovo after Dayton

At the beginning of 1996, the Parliamentary Assembly of the Council of Europe turned its attention to the province. The main concern for European parliamentarians was not the human rights situation directly but the fact that conditions there were generating an increased number of Kosovar Albanian asylum seekers trying to enter the West. To reduce the number of asylum seekers, the parliamentarians argued, the Peace Implementation Council created by Dayton should create confidence-building measures and facilitate a 'just political settlement' for Kosovo.[73]

Governments throughout Europe chose not to link the so-called asylum problem with the human rights situation in Kosovo. Both Germany and Switzerland, the most popular destinations for Kosovar Albanian asylum seekers, adopted a repatriation policy in agreement with the Belgrade government.[74] Although the US remained sceptical about reincorporating the Yugoslavia into European and global institutions, European states argued that the need to prevent and contain potential conflict demanded Yugoslavia's rapid international rehabilitation. Switzerland called for Yugoslavia to be readmitted into the OSCE even though it still refused to allow the deployment of the long duration mission. France normalised its relations with Yugoslavia by increasing its diplomatic representation in Belgrade to chargé d'affaires level, rapidly followed by Belgium and the UK.[75] The incoming British Ambassador, Ivor Roberts, underscored the point by arguing that Serbia was the centre of gravity in the Balkans, which had a pivotal economic and political role in the region.[76] Finally, the impact of the so-called 'outer wall' of sanctions, which was ostensibly linked to human rights conditions in Kosovo, was undermined when Vuk Ognajonović revealed that Yugoslavia had begun to normalise its relations with the 'London Club' of international lenders, giving it access to large amounts of credit irrespective of its policy towards Kosovo.[77] These measures effectively removed the final non-violent avenue for internationalising the Kosovo conflict.

International negotiations were convened in Geneva in February 1996. Although the primary aim was to assess progress in Bosnia, the Kosovo issue was placed on the agenda for two reasons. The Albanian Prime Minister, Aleksander Meksi, used a World Economic Forum meeting in Davos to urge Western states to adopt a mediation role between Serbia and the Kosovar Albanians. In a meeting with Carl Bildt, the UN's Special Representative in Bosnia, Meksi called upon the West to act, warning that 'the situation in Kosovo is imbued with dangers for peace in the Balkans'.[78] Geert Ahrens used a conference of the Muslim Council of Sandžak to call on international society to intensify its mediation efforts on behalf of all national minorities in 'rump Yugoslavia'.[79] Although Ahrens' own mandate no longer included Kosovo, he argued that lasting peace in the region was dependent on resolving the many potential conflicts that existed in the present and former Yugoslavia. At the behest of the Serb and Kosovar Albanian leaderships, Ahrens began shuttle diplomacy between Belgrade and Pristina. However, he received no support whatsoever from any state or international organisation, bringing this final attempt to find a peaceful resolution to an end. No one was even prepared to pay for Ahrens' flights.[80]

The Geneva meeting achieved very little. Yugoslav Interior Minister, Vukasin Jokanović, insisted that there could be no negotiations with Kosovar Albanian leaders until they accepted Serbia's sovereignty over the province. He also argued that even if they did so, the 'talks' that could take place would only be on substantive issues such as health and education and not on constitutional or legal issues.[81] Because most Western states agreed with the Serbs basic premise about Belgrade's sovereignty over Kosovo their representatives found it very difficult to challenge Jokanović's argument. The result was cosmetic bureaucratic readjustment. Ahrens' working group was formally wound-up and placed under the ambit of the EU and Carl Bildt's Peace Implementation Council. Importantly, Kosovo was restored to the group's terms of reference but this produced very little in the way of international activity.

In spring 1996 International NGOs suggested that the atmosphere in Kosovo was changing and that the conditions for a mediated settlement were falling into place. 'Peacebridges', an American NGO specialising in conflict prevention and resolution reported that:

> Pictures from the state media became light and optimistic. April was a month of calls for dialogue, negotiations and reconciliation. Policemen got new uniforms and were not allowed to carry heavy weapons. Albanians were starting to work in state firms.[82]

The report also pointed towards numerous Serb Government and Socialist Party officials who echoed Jokanović's position but emphasised the point that negotiations could be held on substantive issues so long as the Kosovar Albanians accepted Serbia's sovereignty. For example, Ivica Dačić, the Socialist Party spokesman, called for dialogue on what he called 'concrete questions' pertaining to human rights and the participation of Kosovar Albanians in Serbian democracy.[83] This newfound Serbian self-confidence emanated from the central role they were being given in the Bosnian peace process and the fact that most Western states explicitly supported their political and legal claims over Kosovo. As well as persuading the Serbs that it could use charitable political language on the question of international mediation this new self-confidence also prompted it to tighten their oppression of Kosovar Albanians. The International Helsinki Federation for Human Rights reported an increase of police brutality against peaceful Kosovar Albanian protestors. They registered 2,666 cases of torture and maltreatment by the Serb police and argued that Yugoslavia was falling well short of its international responsibilities. The authorities also temporarily closed the Albanian language newspaper *Koha Ditore*, arrested Ljutvi Zilivoda, owner of an independent publishing house called *Feniks*, and forbade it from publishing without first going through a process of police censorship.[84]

The new Serbian self-confidence, brought about by international society's shift from seeing Serbia as a pariah to seeing it as a pivotal player in the Balkans, was mirrored by the withering away of confidence in the Kosovar Albanian community about the ability of non-violent resistance to secure internationalisation and change. Dayton taught many Kosovar Albanians that passive resistance did not work. This perception was not only held by radicals such as Demaçi but also by people who had worked alongside Rugova for many years, such as Bujar Bukoshi. Passive resistance had failed prevent their exclusion from all forms of public life. It had failed to prevent economic apartheid, impoverishment, and systematic police violence and intimidation. While most Kosovar Albanians continued to support Rugova, the popular belief after Dayton was that his methods had achieved nothing.[85] This provoked a radicalisation of the Kosovar Albanian strategy. On the evenings of 14 and 15 February 1996 a series of well-coordinated bomb attacks against Serb targets announced the explosion of the UÇK onto the political scene.[86]

One by one international society divested itself of policies that could have been used to persuade the Serbian government to improve human rights conditions in Kosovo. Carl Bildt's renamed Regional Issues Working Group reported that 'the question of Kosovo has to be solved on the basis of both the granting of a large degree of autonomy and respect for the internationally recognised borders of Yugoslavia'.[87] Given that minority rights issues could only be settled within existing borders the EU moved to solidify those borders by mediating a mutual recognition agreement between Yugoslavia and Macedonia. As a reward for its cooperation here, the EU formally recognised the FRY, including Kosovo, even though it had failed to meet the political conditions for recognition that the other new states in the region had had to meet before recognition. Nevertheless, EU–Yugoslav relations continued to improve through the summer of 1996. While Prime Minister Radoje Kontić told an economic conference in Salzburg that the federation would not permit any internationalisation of the Kosovo conflict, he indicated to Franchetti Pardo, the incoming head of the EU monitoring mission for the former Yugoslavia, that his government would consider intensifying contacts and cooperation with the mission.[88] In return, EU leaders were forthcoming in their support for Serbia's position. A joint statement issued by the chair of the EU Council of Ministers, Dick Spring, and the Foreign Affairs Commissioner, Hans van den Broeck, insisted that whilst the EU supported dialogue between Serbs and Albanians it would not accept Kosovar Albanian separatism.[89] Carl Bildt also publicly endorsed this view.

The Serb reaction to this supportive atmosphere was twin tracked. On the one hand, it responded to the emergence of the UÇK by becoming more robust in its policing techniques. More soldiers were deployed in the province and the number of politically motivated arrests rose sharply. Milošević ended his cooperation with the UN Special

Rapporteur, Elisabeth Rehn, to prevent her reporting and publicising the abuses. He steadfastly refused to see her and instructed government officials to be less than forthcoming in providing her with the information she needed to carry out her job.[90] On the other hand, Milošević was more than happy to allow international mediators to become involved in finding solutions to Kosovo's everyday problems. This not only helped reinforce the image of Milošević as peacemaker but also helped to further legitimise Serbia's claim over the province, because acceptance of that claim was an agreed prerequisite for political progress.

The first concrete result of this new Serbian approach was the establishment of a US Information Centre in Pristina.[91] Although largely symbolic in nature, the centre provided the first permanent foreign representation in Kosovo since the withdrawal of the CSCE long duration mission. It was warmly welcomed by Kosovar Prime Minister Bujar Bukoshi and provided succour to those who continued to argue that internationalisation could still come about through non-violent means. The centre also acted as a cover for the establishment of an American intelligence network in the province, giving the West a much-enhanced intelligence picture of the situation there and providing an opportunity for greater human rights monitoring.[92]

A second initiative that was facilitated by this apparently more cooperative and certainly more self-confident government in Belgrade was an agreement to reform Kosovo's education system, opening it up to Kosovar Albanians. On 1 September 1996, *Comunità di Saint'Egidio*, a Rome based Catholic laymen's organisation brokered a Memorandum of Understanding that was signed simultaneously in Belgrade by Milošević and Pristina by Rugova, though the two never actually met. International journalists hailed the agreement as the 'first breakthrough in Kosovo since 1989'.[93] An English translation distributed in Belgrade called for the 'normalisation of the educational system of Kosovo for the Albanian children and youth'.[94] It also established a '3+3 commission', consisting of three delegates from either side, to work on the implementation of the agreement. According to sources in Belgrade, there was also an unpublished annex that outlined the specific school facilities that would be made available to Kosovar Albanian students. It was clear from the outset however that although the international media applauded the agreement and suggested that it would expedite Serbia's efforts to end its international isolation, the agreement was seriously flawed.

The first problem emerged from a linguistic difficulty. According to the Albanian version of the memorandum, the agreement covered both school pupils and university students. The Serbian version, however, referred only to school pupils and although one of the mediators, Mario Marazziti, suggested that the Serbs accepted the idea that the agreement should include university students, the prevailing view in Belgrade was that the University of Pristina was a hotbed of secessionism and that key subject areas (such as 'Albanian Studies' and other courses in the Albanian language) should not be allowed to go back to work. This issue was never resolved. The second major problem was that the agreement stipulated that 'because of its social and humanitarian value the present agreement is above any political debate.' There was concern within the Kosovar Albanian community about what else Rugova considered 'above political debate'. Finally, although Rugova hoped that participation in such agreements would enhance his international standing, pave the way to internationalisation, and improve the quality of life in Kosovo, it actually only marginalised him further. Having so publicly failed to get a seat at the table at Dayton, Rugova was widely viewed as selling out to the Serbs and turning his back on the independence movement. His case was not helped when his education advisor, Xhavit Ahmeti, was killed in a car accident as he and two others travelled to the first meeting of the 3+3 commission. This allowed the Serbs to first delay implementation of the agreement and then prevent it altogether. The 3+3 group did meet sporadically into 1997 but no progress was made on implementation and Kosovo's education facilities remained out of bounds to Kosovar Albanians who refused to accept the Serb curriculum taught in the Serbian language.

As 1996 drew to a close, violent conflict in Kosovo drew nearer. As Miranda Vickers put it at the time:

> Mr. Rugova, now a tired and withdrawn man, is fast losing credibility amongst his increasingly frustrated followers. Realising that their passive stance has been ignored by the international community, many Albanians are now demanding more aggressive action to achieve their goal of an independent Kosovo.[95]

Vickers pointed out that the situation on the ground was becoming increasingly dangerous. The UN and Western European Union (WEU) shared these concerns but both lacked the ability to act. Elisabeth Rehn visited Kosovo to monitor progress on implementing the education agreement. Although Rehn's visit was largely symbolic (because the agreement itself was largely symbolic) she expressed concern at the increased repression of Kosovar Albanians especially highlighting attacks upon schoolteachers at a press conference held at the Grand Hotel in Pristina. Amazingly, she responded favourably to Rugova's proposal that Kosovo be placed under international administration. This provoked Milošević to sever his cooperation with the UN.[96] The Yugoslav government refused to grant permission for an office in Pristina although it did allow the UN's Commission on Human Rights to establish offices throughout the rest of the country.[97] For its part, the WEU expressed concern with the situation and proposed that pressure be brought to bear on Milošević to persuade him to accept an EU monitoring mission in Kosovo.[98]

Although there was a slight increase in the level international engagement, manifested by the education agreement and opening of the US Information Centre these were more symbolic than substantive. Ibrahim Rugova became increasingly marginalised in the face of the rapidly emerging UÇK thanks to the lack of international support for his non-violent strategy. International society remained reluctant to intervene to prevent violence because it feared losing Serbian cooperation in Bosnia. However, events in Albania in 1997 provided the means for the UÇK to transform itself from a small clandestine terrorist group into a mass armed uprising bringing the long-standing threat of violent conflict to fruition.

1997 began much as 1996 had ended, with increasing Serb repression, sporadic UÇK terrorist attacks, and limited international interest. Having called for an international protectorate to be established, a suggestion that was not even recorded by her political masters in Geneva and New York, Rehn began the new year by condemning what she described as terrorist attacks by the UÇK.[99]

At the beginning of 1997, the prevalent perception that the Kosovo conflict should be regarded as an internal Yugoslav problem became official EU policy. Although Hans van den Broeck, the EU's external affairs commissioner, seemed to imply that the long-awaited internationalisation of the conflict had arrived when he commented that 'the normalisation of relations between the [European] Union and Belgrade cannot be dissociated from the Kosovo issue', he went on to clarify the point by arguing that 'this initiative should not be interpreted as a wish on the part of the EU that Kosovo should become completely independent...the Union believes that the province should regain a certain amount of autonomy, comparable to the situation prior to 1989'.[100] This new found EU interest in Kosovo spurned some new initiatives, such as the linking of inclusion in the PHARE programme and the granting of autonomous trade preferences with the existence of 'real dialogue' on Kosovo and the creation of a Conflict Prevention Network tasked with gradually increasing the involvement, presence, and visibility of the EU in the province.[101]

The US remained more sceptical about progress in Bosnia and the human rights situation in Kosovo and did not share the EU's optimism. In an atmosphere of increasing repression and the radicalisation of growing sections of the Kosovar Albanian population these initiatives were too little, too late. Indeed, they created as many problems as solutions for Rugova precisely because the assumptions that underpinned them required a renunciation of his long-standing claim for independence without establishing a noticeable international presence on the ground. A few weeks later, the EU decided that Serbia had indeed done enough and decided to grant it trade preferences, effectively lifting the last vestiges of the EU's sanctions regime against it though the US maintained its 'outer-wall' of sanctions.[102]

The trigger for the granting of trade preferences was Yugoslav engagement in 'meaningful dialogue' by sending a delegation to meet with Kosovar Albanian representatives at a roundtable in New York. The roundtable was hosted by the Carnegie Corporation and other NGOs on 7–9 April 1997. According to one of its organisers, Alan Cassof, the most important aspect of the meeting was that although the sides were represented at a fairly low level there had been general consensus that resolution could only be found through dialogue and consent. Moreover, both parties agreed to host a series of such roundtables in Belgrade and Pristina. However, it is important not to overestimate their importance. Milošević's Socialist Party was not represented and although the parties recognised the need for continuing dialogue, no timetable was set. As with the implementation of the education agreement, this allowed for considerable slippage and the roundtable never met again. Nevertheless, Yugoslavia was allowed to retain its autonomous trade preferences.[103]

In 1997, Albania descended into anarchy fundamentally changing the political landscape in Kosovo. Throughout post-communist Albania, so-called pyramid banking schemes were created as a way of creating wealth rapidly.[104] The schemes relied on the inflow of new deposits to fund payment of extraordinarily high rates of interest on old accounts. In a society with high unemployment, low wages, and a low standard of living, such schemes though clearly unworkable proved very attractive. In the autumn of 1996 the World Bank and IMF warned of the economic dangers presented by the schemes but neither anticipated the sudden collapse of many such enterprises over the winter. After these first collapses, investors rushed to withdraw their deposits bringing other larger schemes into doubt. In March 1997, anxious Albanians converged on one of the largest pyramid scheme providers, Sudja Holdings. When it became clear that no payments would be forthcoming angry crowds took to the streets, destroying property, looting shops and fighting with the police.

Two months of anarchy followed. As the scale of the looting increased, weapons stolen from abandoned military barracks began to spread amongst the protestors. Enver Hoxha's communist Albania, more concerned with internal opposition than external aggression, had based its defence policy around pillboxes and small arms. As a result, it was estimated that Albania had 200,000 pillboxes and over two million small arms. These fell into the hands of informal local militia who demanded Berisha's resignation. In the midst of all this an election was held that Berisha failed to win, causing him to step down eventually. The flood of Albanian refugees landing on the Italian coast prompted Italy to lead a UN authorised operation (Operation Alba) into Albania to help restore order. The operation was successful but the cost of anarchy was around 2,000 deaths and the release of a vast quantity of weapons into Albanian society. It was reported that at the beginning of 1998 an AK-47 could be purchased for less than US$40. Many of these arms began to find their way into the hands of the UÇK, changing the organisation from a closely knit radical group employing low level 'terrorist' tactics into a broader guerrilla army capable, by March and April 1998, of seizing and holding around one-quarter of the territory of Kosovo, albeit briefly.

Anarchy in Albania and the increase of UÇK activity in Kosovo prompted states to pay more attention to the region in the latter half of 1997. The Contact Group first became interested in Kosovo in September. Responding to the Albanian catastrophe, the growing presence of the UÇK, and the increasing radicalisation of the Kosovar Albanian community that manifested itself in mass demonstrations in Pristina, the Contact Group announced its 'concern' with the situation and despatched Klaus Kinkel (the German Foreign Minister) and Robert Gelbard (Bill Clinton's special representative to the Balkans) to Pristina for talks with Rugova and the Serbs. Kosovo was not yet top of the group's agenda as its rather feeble expression of concern suggests and the trip was ultimately cancelled because of Serb objections.[105] Two months later, NATO's governing body, the North Atlantic Council expressed its first interest with the situation in Kosovo, though NATO ambassadors were not as yet prepared to do anything other than 'express concern'.[106]

Two further initiatives at the end of 1997 suggested that Western states were becoming more interested in Kosovo as a result of the crisis in Albania (which showed that conflict in the region would create massive flows of refugees clambering to get into Western Europe) and the escalation of violence in Kosovo. At an EU–US summit held in Washington, in December, Western states for the first time condemned Serb activities in Kosovo and resolved to mount a coordinated effort to promote human rights there.[107] Klaus Kinkel (German Foreign Minister) and Hubert Védrine (French Foreign Minister) travelled to Belgrade to persuade Milošević to accept third party mediation in Kosovo. Belgrade's response was wholly negative. Not only did Milošević refuse to meet the foreign ministers, the Serbian Prime Minister, Milan Milutinović (a close Milošević ally) also bluntly informed them that Kosovo was an internal affair and therefore 'nobody else's business'.[108]

Summary

The period of *limited engagement* came to an end when Milošević instructed the CSCE Mission of Long Duration to leave Yugoslavia and Owen removed Kosovo from the ICFY minorities working group mandate. Because there was no violent conflict in Kosovo its future was viewed as a price worth paying for peace in the western Balkans. This was based on two flawed assumptions that Milošević was pivotal to peace and, secondly, that his cooperation would be jeopardised if resolving the Kosovo conflict was included in a long-term regional strategy for peace. The period of limited engagement was brought about by the rise of Milan Panić. The Panić interlude should therefore be viewed as an opportunity missed for conflict prevention. The assumption that Milošević would jeopardise peace in Bosnia if the Kosovo issue had been introduced to international negotiations was not seriously tested, by either Lord Carrington, Lord Owen or Richard Holbrooke.

Between the summer of 1993 and the start of violent conflict in 1998 international society's engagement with Kosovo can be described as *malign non-engagement*. The non-engagement was malign because it resulted from a dominant view that it was necessary to sacrifice Kosovo's future to 'save' Bosnia. The strategy is criticised here not because of the failure of prevention nor indeed because of the calculation that stopping the Bosnian war was more important than resolving the human rights situation in Kosovo. It is criticised because of the absence of prevention, the failure to even try to place Kosovo on the agenda.

This *malign non-engagement* was one of the main causes of the subsequent war. By denying the possibility of internationalisation, refusing to incorporate Rugova into the peace process, and accepting Serbia's claim to Kosovo, international society directly contributed to Rugova's marginalisation and the rise of the UÇK. The violence of 1998 was therefore not in spite of international efforts in Kosovo but because of them.

3
Towards Intervention

In March 1998 a nine-month long international conversation began about the nature of the Kosovo conflict and the scope of appropriate responses. At various times during this period the launch of NATO air strikes against Yugoslavia looked like a real possibility. At other times, support within the Alliance for armed intervention wavered. The new British government was instrumental in persuading doubting partners – which at times included the US – about the efficacy of threatening the use of force. Concurrently, the UN, Contact Group, EU, and the Russian and American governments pursued diplomatic initiatives to quell the escalating violence. These initiatives were not always complimentary and were occasionally deliberately designed to scupper the plans of other states and organisations. The Yeltsin–Milošević agreement in June 1998 tried to draw the wind from the sails of hawks in the West (such as Tony Blair) who called for armed intervention against Yugoslavia.

While there was certainly a distinct shift from the *malign non-engagement* of the previous five years it is very difficult to characterise international engagement between March and October 1998. This was a period of *debating intervention* in which states and organisations considered many policy options. There were, however, three important characteristics that set this period apart from everything that had gone before. First, and for the first time, international society decided to directly address the causes of the conflict. There was a direct correlation between the amount of violence in Kosovo, the interest that international society showed in the conflict and the amount of resources it committed to resolving it. Sceptics have argued that the UÇK had a conscious policy of drawing the West into its conflict by provoking Serb reprisals against the civilian population in Kosovo.[1] The BBC, for example, transmitted interviews in which several leading members of the

UÇK stated that they believed that the Serbs would respond to guerrilla attacks by killing civilians. However, it is important to distinguish between the belief that the Serbs would kill civilians from evidence suggesting that there was a deliberate policy to attract such reprisals. In the time I spent with UÇK leaders such as Selimi, Remy, and Lerak, I found no evidence that there had been such a policy and much evidence to suggest that they continued think that the West would not help them. This belief persisted until the first NATO bombs began to fall on Pristina.

Prior to 1998, Kosovo was seen as a price worth paying for an end to violence elsewhere in the former Yugoslavia, primarily because there was no large-scale violence there. In March 1998, changing perceptions of political necessity dictated to some that something should be done to resolve the Kosovo conflict. This became imperative in its own right rather than an addendum to more serious matters elsewhere. There was a discernable shift from emphasising the self-determination aspects of the conflict, which delegitimised the plight of the Kosovar Albanians in the eyes of many states because of the secessionist overtones, to an emphasis on massive human rights abuse. Policy-makers began to see the relationship between the issue of self-determination and the abuse of human rights. The precise reason for, and nature of, this conversion is the source of much of the discussion in this and subsequent chapters.[2]

The third characteristic was a decisive shift in the apportionment of blame for the Kosovo tragedy by international society. This is most clearly demonstrated by comparing UN Security Council Resolutions 1160 (31 March 1998) and 1199 (23 September 1998). Resolution 1160 called for an immediate cessation of violence but in invoking Chapter VII of the UN Charter failed to precisely identify where the source of the 'threat to international peace and security' lay. By the time of Resolution 1199, however, that threat was clearly identified as emanating from Serb MUP and VJ action against the civilian population of Kosovo. This alone created the possibility for alternative and more aggressive courses of action by the West.

This growing interest was directly related to the increase of violence in Kosovo.[3] Whatever one thinks of the merits or otherwise of the UÇK it is fair to say that without it, and without its resilience in the face of a Serb onslaught, Kosovo would never have attracted the heightened level of international engagement that it did in 1998.[4] The increase in violence posed three particular problems for world leaders, especially those in Western Europe and North America. They were:

- The Bosnia syndrome. A fear that Kosovo could witness a repeat of the bloodshed in Bosnia, which many of the leaders had criticised their predecessors for not responding more decisively to.[5]
- The refugees syndrome. In 1998 it came to be believed that violent conflict in Kosovo would cause massive refugee flows and that steps were therefore needed to prevent and escalation of violence.
- The Balkan Wars syndrome. A pervasive (though misguided) perception during the Bosnian war was that conflict in the southern Balkans would spread uncontrollably, drawing in Macedonia, Albania, Bulgaria, Greece, Turkey, and probably Russia as well.[6]

The period of *debating intervention* in 1998 was crucial to what happened in 1999. It was in 1998 that NATO members discussed the appropriateness of using military force. It was also in 1998 that the question of the role of the UN and Russia was discussed. When Richard Holbrooke and Slobodan Milošević reached an agreement on 16 October 1998 that allowed the deployment of the OSCE's Kosovo Verification Mission, the debate within NATO had been largely resolved, though significant doubts and differences of interpretation still remained. The military planning for Operation Allied Force was conducted under an Activation Warning issued by NATO's governing body, the North Atlantic Council, on 24 September 1998, yet very few accounts of the war consider international diplomacy in 1998 in any detail.[7]

The Donji Prekaz massacre and the new Kosovo agenda

In March 1998 everything changed about international society's engagement with the Kosovo conflict. Only twice in the entire period covered by this book did something that actually happened in Kosovo shape international responses. The first was the massacre of the Jeshari family in the village of Donji Prekaz on 5 March 1998; the second was the massacre of 45 people in the village of Racak, ten months later.[8] At the beginning of 1998, Milošević continued to be viewed as a peacemaker and as the most important guarantor of the Dayton settlement.[9] This provided the Yugoslav president with room for manoeuvre in his attempts to quash the emergent UÇK. The Contact Group described the UÇK as the 'so-called Kosovo Liberation Army', and awarded it equal responsibility for the escalating violence alongside the Serbian forces.[10]

Foreign diplomats in Belgrade played down the UÇK's significance with some choosing to portray it (not wholly inaccurately at this juncture) as a fragmented and disorganised group. Such a portrayal overlooked the fact that the rebel army was spreading its operations throughout Kosovo and had even begun holding territory in the Drenica valley.[11]

The travels and statements of American special envoy, Richard Gelbard, between 23 February and 1 March give a good indication of international policy at this time, which continued to be based on the assumptions that informed the period of *malign non-engagement*. Gelbard, a senior envoy despatched by President Clinton, first visited Milošević and held private discussions with the Serbian leader. Gelbard reportedly told Milošević that he faced a choice: Continue to be an instrument of peace in the region by facilitating a political agreement in Kosovo as he had done in Bosnia three years earlier and be rewarded with a relaxation of the 'outer wall' of American sanctions against Yugoslavia that had survived Dayton, or face increasing isolation 'into a downward spiral of darkness' if the violence in Kosovo increased.[12] As the albeit watered down 'Christmas ultimatum' of 1992 remained in force should the Serbs have chosen to solve the Kosovo question by use of force the threat of 'increasing isolation' must have sounded reassuringly undemanding. It may also have persuaded Milošević that the ultimatum had been superseded by a more flexible American policy.

Concurrent with Gelbard's visit to Belgrade, the US announced that it would ease the sanctions regime and allow the Yugoslavs to establish a consulate in New York. However, the denial of access to international financial institutions that was a prominent element of the 'outer wall' of sanctions was not rescinded. The lifting of these sanctions had been explicitly linked to conditions in Kosovo and the US administration reiterated the point that any further relaxation of sanctions would be dependent on progress towards peace in the province.[13] The decision to relax the sanctions regime was imprudent to say the least. Tension and violence in Kosovo was higher than at any time before or after Dayton and the human rights situation was actually deteriorating, yet the sanctions regime was relaxed.

After his meeting with Milošević, Gelbard then travelled to Pristina. In a statement directed at both the Serb and Albanian communities, the envoy warned that 'the violence we have seen growing is incredibly dangerous'. While criticising the spiralling violence, which he said had been 'promulgated' by Serbian forces, the main thrust of his condemnation fell onto the UÇK. Gelbard remarked that 'the UÇK is without any question a terrorist organisation', commenting that he had seen many such organisations throughout his career in the State Department. He went on to condemn the UÇK's terrorist activities, a condemnation that was reiterated by the State Department on 2 March.[14] Taken together, Gelbard's meetings in Belgrade and Pristina appeared to give Milošević a tacit green light to use military force against the UÇK. Although Gelbard has been heavily criticised for his comments about the UÇK, particularly in view of the fact that a brutal Serbian crackdown began almost immediately after his visit, he was not alone in holding this view. British diplomats in Belgrade shared the opinion that it would have been desirable for the Serbs to eradicate the UÇK, which they believed threatened regional stability.[15] However, both the Americans and British hoped that such a counter-insurgency operation would be conducted swiftly and without harm to the civilian population. Given that neither the VJ nor MUP had any tradition of conducting limited counter-insurgency operations and a well-established recent record of ethnic cleansing and brutality against civilians the Anglo-American preference seems distinctly misguided.

The diplomatic picture changed almost overnight on 5 March. Only a fortnight after it had relaxed the sanctions regime against Yugoslavia and denounced the UÇK as terrorists, the administration in Washington was being asked about the possibility of using air power against Serbia.[16] Even before the assault on the Jeshari family compound at Donji Prekaz, there was evidence to suggest that far from being discriminate in their targeting of the UÇK, VJ and MUP forces were escalating the conflict and targeting civilians. On 2 March, a Kosovar Albanian demonstration in Pristina was forcibly broken up by Serb riot police, killing one, leaving two in comas, and injuring 150.[17]

The Yugoslav government also began preparing the way for a wider offensive. On the same day as the demonstration in Pristina, a high level delegation from Belgrade's Ministry of Justice arrived in the Macedonian capital of Skopje for meetings with President Gligorov. According to James Pettifer, it is believed that the purpose of the visit was to persuade Gligorov to grant the Serbs a right of 'hot pursuit' of UÇK fighters across the Macedonian border and to establish a subsequent arrest and extradition agreement.[18] Gligorov rejected these proposals because he was keen to insulate Macedonia, which has a sizable and restive Albanian minority of its own, from the conflict in Kosovo.[19] The Serb plan was also a non-starter because of the presence of Western troops along the Macedonia-Kosovo border as part of the UNPREDEP mission in Macedonia, which was withdrawn later in 1998 at China's behest after Macedonia signed a mutual recognition and trade agreement with Taiwan.[20]

The much-predicted Serb onslaught began on 5 March. 58 people were killed in the attack on the Jeshari family at Donji Prekaz, including ten children and 18 women.[21] This was not the first such attack. A few days earlier, the Ahmeti family – who unlike the Jeshari's did not have known UÇK connections – was given similar treatment. The scale of the Donji Prekaz attack and the close proximity of the bodies allowed organisations like Amnesty International, Human Rights Watch and Physicians for Human Rights to conduct detailed analyses of the bodies and interview witnesses. The reports they produced were widely disseminated throughout Europe and North Europe.[22]

The international response to the 5 March massacre was immediate though not as decisive as some had hoped. The British Foreign Secretary, Robin Cook, was in a unique position to react to the massacre. Whilst Donji Prekaz burned on 5 March, Cook was in Belgrade threatening Milošević with isolation from the EU. At the time, it was reported that Milošević was unwell with a cold and did not want to see the British minister, though we can speculate as to alternative motives for his unusual shyness. When he did see Milošević, Cook informed the Yugoslav president that the normalisation of relations between Yugoslavia and the EU depended on Belgrade adhering to the standards of a modern European state, indicating that 'Kosovo is a major test for that'.[23] He went on to demand that Milošević implement the education agreement so that the schools and university in Kosovo could be reopened to Kosovar Albanians. Given what was going on in Donji Prekaz at precisely the same time as Cook was sitting on Milošević's couch, his choice of words on this occasion was unfortunate to say the least. The British Foreign Secretary informed the Yugoslav president that 'so long as they [the schools] are closed, there is a breeding ground for terrorism'.[24] Milošević steadfastly rejected the claim that his forces were acting unreasonably.

The Donji Prekaz massacre brought a rapid about-turn in US policy towards Yugoslavia. The limited economic concessions that had been made on 23 February were immediately rescinded. Yugoslav Airlines (JAT) had its landing rights removed, the consulate in New York was put on hold, and the Yugoslav mission to the UN was limited in size.[25] In the immediate aftermath of the massacre, US Secretary of State Madeleine Albright visited Italy and Germany to discuss options for action before arriving in London for a meeting of the Contact Group.

Madeleine Albright's personal preference for a decisive response to the Serbs is well documented. As a child, Albright had only narrowly escaped the Nazis and in 1995 she was horrified by what see saw of the massacre in Srebrenica.[26] Along with Blair and Cook, Albright consistently voiced the opinion that military pressure should be brought to bear on the Serbs. Unlike Blair and Cook, though, Albright did not have the decisive vote on the direction of US foreign and defence policy and was but one (albeit influential) voice amongst many in foreign policy making circles. If Albright's visit to Italy was intended to garner support for decisive action against the Serbs she was to be disappointed. Whilst the Foreign Minister, Lamberto Dini – a member of the Italian Communist Party – shared Albright's concern about the increase of violence in Kosovo, he did not share her belief that a military response was necessary. After the meeting, Dini told the press that 'we must make every effort to redirect the situation *within the limits of diplomacy*'.[27] This argument was somewhat different from Albright's position. Asked whether the prospect of armed intervention was discussed, Albright replied that it had not been but went on to comment that 'we have a broad range of options available to us and *we do not rule anything out*'.[28] On one hand, therefore, Dini was quite clearly drawing limits to what an acceptable response should be while Albright continued to insist that all options – including armed intervention – remained on the agenda.

The following day, Albright flew to Bonn to meet the German Foreign Minister, Klaus Kinkel. Throughout 1998, Kinkel insisted that any action against Yugoslavia should be authorised by the UN Secretary Council. From the outset, the US believed that this would not be forthcoming because of the threat of Russian and Chinese vetoes. At his 8 March meeting with Albright, Kinkel proposed a three-track response to the violence, which fell well short of the decisive response sought by the Secretary of State. The first track was consultation with the Security Council and a consideration of strengthening UNPREDEP in Macedonia. The second track was an expansion of the WEU military presence in Albania. The third track was involvement of the OSCE and the despatch of an EU negotiating mission fronted by Felipe Gonzalez, the former Spanish premier.[29]

If Albright was hoping for a concerted action from the Contact Group she was to be very disappointed. The Group's statement issued after it met on 9 March condemned the Serbs and UÇK in equal measure. The Contact Group did agree a package of policies aimed at halting the violence and facilitating a political settlement. These included a recommendation that the UN Security Council impose an arms embargo on Yugoslavia (which would also cover the supply of arms to the UÇK, mirroring the controversial UN Security Council Resolution 713), and further sanctions including visa restrictions for Yugoslav government officials and a moratorium on government financed export credit for trade and investment, including assistance with privatisation in Serbia.[30] The Russians refused to implement these last two provisions but did agree to enforce them should Yugoslavia fail to comply with the Contact Group's demands. The Contact Group demanded the withdrawal of special police units (MUP) from Kosovo and the cessation of violence, the granting of access to the International Committee of the Red Cross (ICRC) and other humanitarian organisations, and a commitment to political dialogue with the Kosovar Albanian leadership. Should Milošević fail to comply, the Contact Group threatened further punitive economic measures including the freezing of Serbian funds held abroad.

The Contact Group's demands were far weaker than Albright had hoped. Robin Cook, embarrassed by Milošević four days earlier, again referred to the UÇK as terrorists, telling Milošević that, 'if you want to beat terrorism, you have to isolate the terrorists'.[31] That said, a debate on intervention had begun indicating the beginning of a new phase in international engagement with Kosovo. The Western media began to ask its political leaders whether armed intervention was being considered and whilst most NATO allies insisted that such an option was not being discussed, Madeleine Albright had confessed that she had not ruled out this alternative.

After the Contact Group meeting, the American foreign policy making establishment began its own debate about the future direction of its policy towards the region, severely restricting the State Department's leadership for an eight-week period. This internal debate revealed the extent to which Albright's ability to formulate American policy was constrained. Richard Gelbard, Albright's nominee as Clinton's special envoy to the Balkans, became increasingly unpopular within policy-making circles. Although his very public comments about the nature of the UÇK echoed the thoughts of most diplomats, many linked them directly with the upsurge in violence in Kosovo. They viewed Gelbard's comments in a similar way to the perceived green light for the invasion of Kuwait that the American Ambassador to Baghdad gave to Saddam Hussein in 1990.[32] Gelbard attempted to make amends for his apparent weakness during his next visit to Belgrade. In talks with Milošević, the American envoy condemned the escalation of violence in Kosovo, placed the blame fully at the feet of the Serbs and denounced the 'heavy handed and disproportionate' police action, insisting that 'this [Serbian] government has trampled on the rule of law'.[33] This about-turn had the opposite effect to that which was desired by Gelbard. Rather than seeing him as a tough diplomat like Holbrooke, Gelbard's condemnation angered Milošević and made himself appear weak. After all, Holbrooke had never changed his mind so blatantly. Milošević refused to see the envoy thereafter. Albright's deputy, Strobe Talbott and the President's National Security Advisor, Sandy Berger, advised that Richard Holbrooke be brought back from his job at the Crédit Suisse First Boston Bank to retake his position as special envoy to the Balkans. Albright opposed the move, fearing that Holbrooke's return would diminish her already weak control of American policy to the region. The case for sending Holbrooke was boosted in mid-March when the diplomat-turned-banker received a fax from Ibrahim Rugova inviting him to mediate direct talks between the Kosovar Albanian leader and Slobodan Milošević. Talbott and Berger's case was further strengthened by Milošević's refusal to see Felipe Gonzalez who was acting as the EU and OSCE's special envoy. As a source told Tim Judah:

> There was an eight week period of no contacts and the situation was deteriorating. Madeleine was issuing statements with the 'Euros' saying something had to be done – and nothing was being done. Milošević would not see Gonzalez for the OSCE, nor Gelbard and his forces were taking ugly actions. So, Madeleine reluctantly agreed that Holbrooke should take a trip.[34]

Holbrooke made his first Kosovo-related visit to Milošević in early May after several weeks of policy paralysis during which time the situation on the ground in Kosovo had changed dramatically.

As Milošević was refusing to see the EU and OSCE envoy, Felipe Gonzalez, Klaus Kinkel and Hubert Védrine (French Foreign Minister) decided to take their arguments directly to the Yugoslav president once again. Milošević agreed to make progress towards political settlement with the Kosovar Albanians though on the ground the violence contin-ued to spread to cities such as Pec. Two days after his meeting with the foreign ministers, on 22 March, Milošević and the newly re-elected unofficial president of Kosovo, Ibrahim Rugova, concluded (another) education agreement. The agreement (which was never put into prac-tice) accepted Robin Cook's earlier demand that the schools and univer-sity in Kosovo be opened to Kosovar Albanians by allowing Albanians to use school buildings in the afternoons. Milošević persuaded the Contact Group to conclude that 'there has been progress in some areas of concern, notably some movement in Belgrade's position on dialogue on a range of issues including the autonomy of Kosovo and the … imple-mentation of the education accord'.[35]

March ended with the adoption of UN Security Council Resolution 1160. This resolution reflected the uncertainties about what an appropriate response to the escalating violence should be. The Chinese Ambassador insisted in the Council that the Kosovo problem was an internal matter for the Yugoslavs and only two weeks before he allowed the Resolution to pass by abstaining had suggested that he would oppose any international involvement.[36] With one eye on the troublesome Chechens, the Russians insisted on measures to cut off international support for the UÇK and resolutely opposed any tightening of the sanctions, which the Foreign Ministry in Moscow claimed would have 'dire implications for the entire Balkan region'.[37] To satisfy the Russians and Chinese, the Resolution condemned the Serbs and UÇK with equal vigour and reaffirmed Yugoslav sovereignty and territorial integrity. Furthermore, although the resolution was adopted under Chapter VII of the Charter it used the words 'calls upon' to recommend action by the parties rather than demanding action or threatening enforcement. Thus it 'called upon' Yugoslavia to begin work with the Contact Group towards a political settlement, 'called upon' the Kosovar Albanian leadership to condemn terrorist action, and 'called upon' both parties to begin urgent direct negotiations. Finally, the Resolution reaffirmed a four-week deadline for the withdrawal of special MUP forces from Kosovo, the granting of access to humanitarian organisations, and acceptance of an OSCE mission to the province.[38]

Resolution 1160 appeared to favour the Serb position because it contained no enforcement mechanism and legitimised Serbia's two key claims, that Kosovo was part of Serbia and that the UÇK were terrorists. However, the Yugoslav government responded by criticising the Council's decision. It contended that Resolution 1160 represented a dangerous precedent because 'an internal question of a Member State of the United Nations has been considered without its consent'.[39] This was mistaken because by invoking Chapter VII the Council found that Kosovo presented a threat to *international* peace and security. Unwittingly, the Belgrade government put its finger on the most significant aspect of the resolution. For the first time, Kosovo was not considered to be a purely internal matter for Serbia. It now posed a threat to international peace and security. Therefore it was permissible for the UN to consider a whole new range of policy options that had been excluded for the previous decade because Kosovo had been seen as a wholly internal matter. After all, dealing with an international threat does not require the consent of the host government before action can be taken.

Although at face value Resolution 1160 appears to be a pointless exercise in diplomatic obfuscation it reflected an important shift in the international engagement with the Kosovo. Key assumptions remained, about the nature of the UÇK and the illegitimacy of Kosovar Albanian claims to independence. However, the most fundamental assumption that dated back to the 1991 ECCY Conference at The Hague, namely that Kosovo's destiny should be intimately linked to Serbia's was broken. The escalation of violence and mounting evidence of atrocities committed by the VJ and MUP made Kosovo an international problem in its own right for the first time.

A new decisiveness

In the face of continuing violence in Kosovo and growing evidence of an impending refugee crisis caused by MUP and VJ attacks on the civilian population the international response remained stultified after the passage of Resolution 1160. This was partly caused by the lack of American leadership owing to the struggle over Holbrooke's future role. The Russian government seized the opportunity to contribute to the international effort by laying the groundwork for the Yeltsin-Milošević agreement of 16 June that took the wind out of the sails of hawks in the American and British governments who had begun to talk about the possibility of punitive air strikes against Yugoslavia. Bolstered by its belief that Resolution 1160 scored a decisive blow against the UÇK, the Russian Federation began to work on a framework for the re-integration of Yugoslavia into international society. Milošević's assurances that special MUP forces had been withdrawn from Kosovo were enough to persuade the Russians that he was complying with the Security Council's wishes. Russia opposed the idea of enforced international mediation because the conflict was essentially a domestic one that they believed should be dealt with by the Yugoslav government.[40]

Regardless of Russia's opinions on the matter, the Yugoslav government did not comply with the Security Council's calls for an end to the violence. The OSCE noted that while the situation in Kosovo itself remained relatively calm there was no progress on beginning political dialogue largely because the Serbian government had not put a framework for negotiations in place despite Rugova's LDK having brought a negotiating team together.[41] The EU agreed with the OSCE's assessment but also pointed out that contrary to his assurance to the Russians, Milošević had not reduced the number of special MUP units in Kosovo and although their operations had been scaled down they continued to restrict Kosovar Albanians' freedom of movement.[42] Both the OSCE and EU also noted that Milošević was still preventing Felipe Gonzalez from carrying out his mediation role.

In an attempt to increase his legitimacy, Milošević called a referendum on international mediation for Kosovo, on 23 April, the eve of the end of the four week period for compliance stipulated by the Contact Group and Resolution 1160. The question, crudely put together on badly printed unnumbered ballot forms, asked Yugoslav citizens, 'do you accept foreign representatives taking part in resolving the problems of Kosovo and Metohija?'.[43] The Kosovar Albanians did not participate in the vote and neither did large numbers of Montenegrins who supported the reformist President Milo Djukanović, who was attempting to frame an independent Montenegrin policy separate from Serbia's. Not surprisingly, therefore, the referendum returned a 94.73 per cent result against international mediation from a total vote of 73 per cent.[44]

Tim Judah argues that Milošević's subsequent decision to negotiate with Richard Holbrooke days after the referendum was symptomatic of his inconsistent behaviour. Milošević's decision to negotiate also reflected his belief that Holbrooke saw him as a crucial guarantor of Balkan stability, as opposed to Gonzalez who, the Yugoslav President feared, would seek to remove him from power.[45] While Judah is correct to point out that domestic Serbian politics had a greater influence on Milošević's policy towards Kosovo than has been hitherto acknowledged, the referendum was more significant than Judah suggests.[46] Milošević feared a repeat of Dayton and was therefore keen to prevent international mediation in talks between himself and Rugova. As Yugoslav President he was happy to talk about Kosovo with Richard Holbrooke but as Rugova was not President of a recognised state (as Tuđman and Izetbegović were at Dayton) Milošević believed that he should not be allowed access to the negotiations. Such access would, Milošević feared, legitimise Rugova's claims. The referendum gave Milošević the veneer of democratic legitimacy and influenced the shape of the negotiations for the following ten months. Not until Rambouillet did the Kosovar Albanians actually participate in substantive talks with either the Serbian authorities or the Contact Group. Milošević did meet Rugova to discuss the education agreement but this further marginalised the embattled Kosovar Albanian moderate in the eyes of his constituents. What the Holbrooke–Milošević meeting in April 1998 achieved, however, was the beginning of what appeared to be political dialogue based upon a series of plans produced by the American Ambassador to Macedonia, Christopher Hill. Hill had been a senior member of Holbrooke's negotiating team at Dayton.

The situation in Kosovo took a turn for the worse towards the end of April. The Albanian Foreign Ministry claimed that Yugoslav fighter aircraft repeatedly infringed its airspace[47] and there were reports that MUP and VJ, forces were being massively reinforced in preparation for a major offensive in the west of the province. UN Secretary-General, Kofi Annan, told the Security Council that he was 'concerned about the deteriorating situation in Kosovo and the absence of progress in the negotiations'.[48] Nevertheless, the Russian and French governments indicated that they would not be prepared to consider imposing comprehensive sanctions against Yugoslavia as the US proposed. For its part, the US was becoming more proactive leading to a hardening of different opinions within the Contact Group. This was indicated by the fact that a Contact Group gathering held at the end of April was a meeting of officials rather than ministers.[49]

Holbrooke's arrival in the region created a new decisiveness and reinvigorated Madeleine Albright's view that only diplomacy backed by the threat of punitive measures would persuade Milošević to change his course of action. Holbrooke began his new job by doing what he had done two and a half years earlier. He created a procedural framework for the negotiations. Next, he instigated a symbolic meeting between Milošević and Rugova. Milošević clearly had nothing to lose. Rugova had much to lose but the American diplomat was able to persuade him to attend by promising an audience with President Clinton the following month.[50]

Richard Holbrooke's early meetings with Slobodan Milošević led to two significant developments. Firstly, the Yugoslav President accepted American assistance in facilitating genuine dialogue between Belgrade and the Kosovar Albanians with a view to reaching a political settlement. The dialogue would take the form of a weekly meeting between Milošević and Rugova. Christopher Hill was invited to work on putting together a comprehensive settlement, beginning the so-called 'Hill process' that began in earnest in July. Secondly, noting that the UN Sectretary-General, the OSCE and the Contact Group had all complained about their lack of access into Kosovo to monitor events, Holbrooke persuaded Milošević to accept a Kosovo Diplomatic Observer Mission (KDOM) whereby foreign diplomats already based in Belgrade would 'double-hat' as human rights monitors in Kosovo.[51] The KDOM was despatched in July and soon received a derisory and predictable nickname.

On 9 May the Contact Group backed up Holbrooke's tough words by strengthening the sanctions against Yugoslavia and banning all foreign investment. Worryingly for Milošević, President Clinton began to publicly support Albright's hawkish stance. In answer to a media question about the possibility of 'sending troops' to Kosovo, Clinton made it clear that 'no option should be ruled out'. Tellingly, in giving his answer he twice made reference to the 'lessons of Bosnia', indicating that the administration would act decisively, including using military force if necessary, rather than risk a repeat of the Bosnian impasse.[52]

The summer and autumn of 1998 saw heightened international involvement in the Kosovo crisis along three tracks: The Hill process, observation and monitoring, and the debate about the use of force. The debates and activities that began in March 1998 came to an end with the so-called 'October agreement' concluded by Slobodan Milošević and Richard Holbrooke on 16 October. By that time, international society had a clearer picture of what a political settlement for Kosovo could look like and what sorts of tools (NATO air power and a peacekeeping force) would be necessary to coerce acceptance of and compliance with the settlement. The period between March and May 1998 was one of transition from *malign non-engagement* to *debating intervention*. During this period there were several important shifts in international perceptions about the importance of the Kosovo conflict:

- The massacre at Donji Prekaz and subsequent increase in violence forced the UN Security Council to recognise that Kosovo was an *international* problem.
- The despatch of Richard Holbrooke gave a sense of direction to US policy, particularly with the deployment of KDOM and commencement of the Hill process.
- Whilst doubts remained about what constituted appropriate action, the increase in violence forced states to consider options that had hitherto been unacceptable. On 9 May, Clinton had not ruled out the use of force and unlike Lamberto Dini two months earlier, the Italian Prime Minister (Romano Prodi) reiterated the need to keep all options open.

For the first time since 1992, states and organisations that were engaged with the Kosovo conflict began to reassess some of their core assumptions. There was a growing sentiment that Kosovo posed a distinct set of problems and that it was no longer acceptable to consider the issue as inherently linked to the broader question of what to do with Serbia. In 1992, one of the three reasons for the marginalisation of Kosovo from the negotiations about how to manage the dissolution of socialist Yugoslavia had been that the Kosovar Albanians did not control any of the province's territory. By the middle of 1998, however, the UÇK had seized control of about 40 per cent of the entire province and the threat of a major conflict on the scale of the Bosnian war seemed to be a real possibility. Another of the considerations back then had been the absence of large-scale violence but by 1998 that reality had changed as well. It was no longer so 'politically necessary' to appease the Serbs. Perceptions of political necessity now dictated that something be done about Kosovo. This perception came eight years too late and there was still no agreement about precisely *what* should be done.

The Hill process

Although Madeleine Albright agreed to send Richard Holbrooke to Belgrade she insisted on keeping her man, Robert Gelbard, as special envoy with responsibility for the Balkans. The Secretary of State wanted to keep Holbrooke under control but the diplomat had other ideas. Holbrooke wanted his own team around him, including Christopher Hill and General Wesley Clark, who had both been involved in the Dayton process. His first priority, therefore, was to rid himself of Gelbard. Albright, though, was equally keen that he should be present in the negotiations. This presented the Secretary of State with a dilemma. On one hand, she knew that Holbrooke was better placed than anyone to persuade Milošević to halt the violence and conclude some kind of political settlement. On the other, she also knew that once he got started he would take over and shape American policy in the region and that she could not be sure that the diplomat would be as forceful as she wanted. As it happened, this latter fear was well founded. The Holbrooke–Milošević deal in October 1998 made several concessions to the Yugoslav president and came just as key NATO allies such as France and Germany had come around to the view that punitive air strikes were warranted. Portents of this were given when Holbrooke succeeded in removing Gelbard with Milošević's unwitting help. Milošević agreed to meet Holbrooke but steadfastly refused to accommodate Gelbard. With the new diplomatic offensive in danger of being stillborn, Milošević asked for clarification about who headed the US initiative. Under pressure from Talbott and Berger, Albright faxed Belgrade to instruct the Serbs that Holbrooke was head of the mission. Thus, that first meeting took place with Hill, not Gelbard, at Holbrooke's right hand. Soon afterwards, Christopher Hill was officially named as special envoy to Kosovo and Gelbard was permanently sidelined.[53]

Efforts to construct a political settlement began to take shape once Richard Holbrooke took over the US effort and gave the task of drawing up a settlement to Christopher Hill.[54] The first problem for Hill was the issue of Kosovo's final status. There were three possible alternatives; autonomy within Serbia, independence, or partition. Each of these was unacceptable to one or both of the parties. Moreover, Russia believed that any solution should only come about with Milošević's freely given consent.[55] Christopher Hill and Jim O'Brian (who had worked with Hill and Holbrooke at Dayton) were thus charged with charting a path though these competing interests – the first time that international society had attempted to address these issues.

Although Hill was given a degree of flexibility about what he could put in his plan, there were several working assumptions that needed to be taken on board. First, the plan was to be based on the principle of autonomy and therefore had to reaffirm Yugoslavia's sovereignty and territorial integrity. Secondly, although any plan would clearly alter the constitutional makeup of Yugoslavia it was not to do this explicitly. There could be autonomy for Kosovo but that did not necessarily mean republic status because such status would then imply a right of secession. Thirdly, there must be protection for all the national communities in Kosovo. Any plan had to include safeguards and legislative vetoes for national groups to prevent them suffering under the tyranny of the majority. A final assumption was that a post-agreement Kosovo would be a properly functioning democracy. Some argued that this was a worrying thought for Milošević because the sudden addition of two million or so Kosovar Albanian voters would have seriously threatened his parliamentary majority.[56]

Between May and November, Hill shuttled between Belgrade and Pristina refining specific points of his plan and mediating between the parties.[57] This task was made much harder on 29 May when the Kosovar Albanian negotiating team led by Ibrahim Rugova refused to continue with the agreed weekly meetings with Milošević. This impasse was provoked by a renewed bout of MUP and VJ activity in the Decani region, in which many Kosovar Albanians were killed and thousands forced from their homes. The decision to end face-to-face meetings certainly hampered Hill's operations but did not stop them. Instead he adopted a form of extended 'proximity negotiations' of the type later employed at Rambouillet, whereby the mediators passed messages between the protagonists. In some respects this style of diplomacy suited Hill because it allowed him to develop a comprehensive settlement and present it to the parties without their interference and obstruction at the drafting stage. An important breakthrough was made on 2 September, when Hill persuaded the Kosovar Albanian negotiators to defer a decision on

Kosovo's final status indefinitely, a concession that Rugova's rivals (in particular, Adem Demaçi, Hashim Thaçi, and Rexhep Qosja) vehemently opposed.

Christopher Hill completed a draft agreement in July. At a meeting in Bonn on 8 July, the Contact Group called on the negotiating team to formulate a plan to resolve the conflict, noting that both the status quo and the independence option were unacceptable.[58] Given that the Contact Group, backed by the UN Security Council, had already obtained an agreement for dialogue and that the basic principles adhered closely to Serbia's negotiating position, Hill sought out the UÇK for discussion on the proposals. On 29 July, Hill travelled with Veton Surroi and Blerim Shala to the rebel stronghold of Likovac in the Drenica valley and handed them a copy of his draft agreement.[59] The UÇK was not, however, given a formal opportunity to respond. If they had, the regional commanders would have rejected the plan outright for three principal reasons. First, there was no mechanism by which independence could be achieved and the achievement of independence was the one point that united all political factions in the Kosovar Albanian community from Rugova to Hashim Thaçi. Secondly, the UÇK commanders argued that any agreement that allowed the MUP and VJ to remain inside Kosovo, in any capacity, was unacceptable. Finally, knowing the quality of an agreement signed by Milošević first hand, the UÇK commanders insisted that any deal must include the deployment of an armed international force to implement it, preferably led by NATO.[60]

Hill refused to incorporate these ideas into his plan because he believed it to be more important to win Milošević's agreement and international acceptance than it was to appease the UÇK. The first draft, which Hill presented on 1 October, contained many of the elements of the interim settlement later proposed at Rambouillet.[61] As with the Rambouillet proposal, there would be four levels of governance: The commune, the national community, provincial and federal. The bulk of the powers devolved from Belgrade would go to the local communes, which would provide local policing, health and education provision, housing and planning regulation, and emergency services.[62] Above the communes, each national community (left undefined by Hill) would elect a 'national council' that would have executive functions and would administer the affairs of that community. The 'national council' would ensure that legislation passed by the Kosovo Assembly did not infringe on the rights of its citizens and symbolise the principle that all national communities were equal.[63] This idea was further distilled by the time of the Rambouillet summit. In the interim settlement proposed there, the national communities held a power of veto over any legislation passed by the Kosovo Assembly that was deemed to discriminate against the national community.[64]

There were several important omissions from the first Hill plan, reflecting areas where finding compromise was problematic. The paragraphs on policing were annotated 'to be developed further'. The principle of commune primacy (akin to the cantonment of Bosnia proposed in the Vance-Owen plan) suggested to Hill that policing should be organised by the communes. However, the relationship of these local police units to federal and provincial police forces, which were controlled by the MUP, provided a stumbling block in his talks with the Yugoslav Interior Ministry. There was a separate annex containing a draft law on enforcement and security but it did not contain details about the exact nature of these problematic relationships. The first Hill draft also contained no details on what VJ and MUP special police forces would be allowed to remain in Kosovo and where they should be deployed. The plan was envisaged as a final rather than interim settlement, though by way of a compromise with Kosovar Albanian demands it did include a mechanism for the assessment of progress and suggestions for improvement after a three-year period. There being no indication as to how the plan would be implemented the problem of who would decide whether the plan would be revised was bypassed. Finally, although Hill repeatedly stressed the importance of an international presence in Kosovo in the form of an OSCE monitoring mission, Serb intransigence on the matter – bolstered by the result of the referendum on international mediation – resulted in this being omitted from the first draft.[65]

Before the Kosovo delegation had an opportunity to respond to the plan, Milošević and Holbrooke came to an agreement to end the escalating violence and deploy an OSCE verification mission, radically altering the conditions in which the negotiations continued. What the Hill process had done, however, was lay the basic framework for the political settlement called for by the UN Security Council and get the Serbs and Kosovar Albanians thinking about the possibility of negotiated compromise in an institutional setting, something that had not been possible before because of the limited nature of the international engagement.

Observation and reporting: KDOM and the OSCE

Between the end of June and the end of July the number refugees and internally displaced people climbed dramatically from approximately 100,000 to around 300,000.[66] After the agreement to create the KDOM,

150 diplomats were despatched to the province on 6 July. According to Holbrooke, the KDOM's major advantage was that it facilitated Russian participation without permitting it to have a major input into the diplomatic initiatives being pursued by the Americans.[67] The KDOM was formally launched by Richard Miles, the US Chargé D'Affaires in Belgrade and his Russian counterpart. The mission's mandate was to observe and report on the general freedom of movement and security situation in Kosovo. It was expected to specifically report on the actions of the various 'security' organisations (VJ, MUP, UÇK) and on the condition, whereabouts, and number of internally displaced persons. Its main contribution would be confidence building.[68] In the event, the KDOM's size and makeup prohibited it from having any practical impact on the fighting in Kosovo.

Kofi Annan reported evidence of the mounting humanitarian tragedy unfolding in Kosovo to the UN Security Council. Using information gathered by the OSCE, Annan noted that the intensification of violence had caused a large increase of civilian casualties.[69] This prompted the Contact Group to tighten the sanctions regime against Yugoslavia when it met in Birmingham on 16 May, sanctions implemented by President Clinton on 9 June despite continuing opposition from the Russian government.[70]

The weight of effective reporting and attempts to make immediate improvements to the quality of life in Kosovo fell onto the shoulders of the OSCE, which had still not re-established a permanent mission in Yugoslavia. Based on information gathered by third parties on the ground, the OSCE was able to assess the continuing increase in violence and escalation of the UÇK's efforts to control territory. However, it ruefully noted that there was no evidence that Milošević was altering his stance towards the EU/OSCE mission headed by Felipe Gonzalez and little prospect of him accepting the deployment of an OSCE mission in Kosovo.[71]

The reason for Milošević's intransigence in these matters became apparent in late summer. The VJ and MUP launched a major offensive on UÇK strongholds in the Drenica region. One by one these villages fell displacing tens of thousands of civilians and prompting the UÇK to flee into the mountains. Milošević did not want international observers hindering and delaying the advance of his forces. He also wanted the operation to be concluded swiftly because the West had begun talking about using military force to bring the conflict to an end.

Debating intervention

During spring and summer of 1998 international society debated whether to use force to coerce the Serbs into ceasing their repression and accepting a political settlement. The debate was concluded in a side room at Heathrow Airport on 6 October when it was implicitly agreed that NATO could, in principle, use air power against Yugoslavia without the explicit authorisation of the UN Security Council. Importantly the Russian Foreign Minister, Igor Ivanov, was present at that very meeting and played a key role. How, though, did the Western allies reach this decision and why did Milošević's closest ally abandon him to his fate?

The use of force against Yugoslavia became a real possibility in June 1998, but Russian President Boris Yeltsin scuppered the plans when he brokered an agreement with Milošević on 16 June. The first leader to move beyond saying that 'all options were being considered' was the British Prime Minister, Tony Blair. In a June speech in the House of Commons, Blair warned Milošević that NATO would not tolerate an intensification of the conflict in Kosovo. Blair stated that, 'I don't believe we could afford to have a situation of disorder spreading in that part of the world and I think this is a clear enough message to Mr. Milošević.' Holbrooke supported this view, insisting that decisive action was necessary to prevent a wider regional conflict. Referring to Operation Deliberate Force in 1995, when NATO had bombed the Bosnian Serbs, Blair argued that, 'we must make sure that we do the same again'.[72] Reacting to these demands for firm action, the North Atlantic Council, NATO's governing body, decided (at the request of Albania) to deploy a preventive force along the Albania–Kosovo border.[73]

Several NATO members were sceptical about the advantages of using force. Some, such as Greece, Italy and Spain were doubtful for political reasons. Greece has close cultural and religious ties with Serbia and the overwhelming majority of Greeks opposed any form of armed intervention against Yugoslavia.[74] The Italian government feared that NATO involvement would inflame an already volatile situation creating a fresh influx of Albanian refugees. With one eye on the Basque separatists, Spain was also reluctant to allow NATO to become a supporter of a secessionist movement and take military against the host state.[75] Turkey also confronted this dilemma in relation to its troublesome Kurdish community, but concluded that the need to display Islamic solidarity with the predominantly Muslim Kosovar Albanians should took precedence over these concerns.[76] Other states, most notably Belgium, France and Germany, were concerned about the legality of using force against Yugoslavia. German Foreign Minister Klaus Kinkel believed that NATO could only act if it had the explicit authorisation of the UN Security Council, particularly as the allies agreed that Kosovo was rightfully part of Serbia. The French Foreign Minister, Hubert Védrine, supported Kinkel's view. Such an approach would be 'logical and legitimate', Védrine argued. However, given that such a Resolution would have to be allowed to pass by both Russia and China it was generally accepted that one would not be forthcoming. In response to these German concerns, Madeleine Albright and Richard Holbrooke repeatedly insisted that the UN should not hold a veto on NATO action.

In order to secure agreement among the NATO allies on the use of force, the American and British governments conducted a sustained and multi-faceted diplomatic offensive throughout the summer and early autumn of 1998. Shortly before an EU summit in Cardiff at the beginning of June, Blair visited Italian premier, Romano Prodi, and persuaded him of the importance of maintaining a strong NATO position. They agreed on a set of words that warned Milošević that 'every option remained open'.[77] This, and a similar joint statement made with President Clinton clearly revealed a change in Italy's position since Foreign Minister Dini's insistence that any engagement be limited to the diplomatic level.

Before embarking on his trip to persuade sceptical allies of the need to use force, Blair consulted with his own government. According to sources within Downing Street, while the official line was one of 'ruling nothing out', Blair made it clear to the cabinet that 'the only question that matters is whether you are prepared to use force. And we have to be. Reports indicate a level of butchery that risks escalating into another Bosnia'.[78] What is clear is that Tony Blair, who as leader of the opposition had strongly criticised John Major's handling of the Bosnian war, was determined not to make the same mistakes as his predecessors. The strength of his conviction was revealed by the fact that while the British government insisted that any action be taken on a multilateral basis, Downing Street asked the Ministry of Defence to investigate options for acting unilaterally. At this point (early June) some leading figures within the British government not only advocated the use of air strikes but also believed that a forcible ground intervention would be necessary. One British official stated that, 'the only thing that would change Milošević's actions would be [military] action in and over Kosovo itself'.[79] Robin Cook reinforced the UK's tough stance when he stated that Milošević had 'crossed the threshold. The use of tanks and artillery...against civilian centres is wholly unacceptable'.[80] However, there was little international support for the UK's position. There was no support whatsoever for a land intervention and while there was more support for the employment of air strikes, several allies were concerned about the threat to air crew that would be posed by Serbia's sophisticated air defence system, the legality of the operation, and the danger that the Alliance would not achieve its goals.[81]

To support its efforts, the Blair government drafted a Security Council resolution authorising NATO air strikes against Yugoslavia as a way of deterring the Serbs from further ethnic cleansing. The text, co-written by the British and American delegations, invoked Chapter VII of the Charter and authorised the use of 'all necessary means' to halt the violence in Kosovo.[82] The draft resolution set a deadline for Slobodan Milošević to halt attacks in Kosovo and in a reference to the Hill process demanded that he 'take necessary further steps' to reach a political settlement. The EU supported this move at its conference in Cardiff and resolved to encourage international efforts in Kosovo, 'including those which would require an authorisation by the United Nations Security Council'.[83] However, the Greek foreign minister argued that the EU should adopt a more conservative stance to enable Milošević to participate in peace talks with Rugova.[84] In the end, the draft resolution was never presented to the Security Council because the Russians made it clear that they would veto any resolution that authorised the use of force against Yugoslavia and the British and American governments calculated that it would be better to not present a resolution to the Council than to lose a vote.

There was some progress in the Security Council with the passage of Resolution 1199 on 23 September, which was used by the British Foreign Office to justify Operation Allied Force at the outset. Russia voted in favour of this resolution and China abstained. Resolution 1199 had a much stronger tone than Resolution 1160 and was more forthright in placing the blame for the violence and refugee crisis at the feet of the Serbs. The source of the threat to international peace and security posed by Kosovo was identified as 'the recent intense fighting in Kosovo and in particular the excessive and indiscriminate use of force by Serbian security forces and the Yugoslav Army, which have resulted in numerous civilian casualties'.[85] Whereas Resolution 1160 merely 'called upon' the parties to take certain actions, Resolution 1199 made several 'demands'. The demands included an instant ceasefire and immediate efforts on the part of the Yugoslav government and Kosovar Albanian leadership to alleviate the humanitarian catastrophe. Four key demands, which had been previously agreed by the Contact Group on 12 June, were aimed directly at Milošević:

- The cessation of all security forces activity affecting the civilian population.
- The enabling of 'effective and continuous' international monitoring in Kosovo.

- The facilitation, in agreement with the ICRC and UNHCR, of the safe return of refugees and internally displaced persons.
- Rapid progress to a clear timetable towards political settlement with the Kosovar Albanians.

Interpretations of Resolution 1199 varied considerably. Madeleine Albright emphasised that it was a Chapter VII resolution, and for her it sent a clear message: 'The international community says with one voice, that, if Belgrade does not now choose to end offensive operations in Kosovo, it must be compelled to do so'.[86] Albright and Secretary of Defence, William Cohen, clarified their interpretation a week or so later. The Secretary of State referred to the 'combination of the threat of the use of force and diplomacy' and Cohen backed this up by stating that 'the purpose of having a credible military threat is to indicate that in the absence of meeting those demands he faces such a threat'.[87]

The Russian government interpreted the resolution rather differently. Ambassador Lavrov emphasised the fact that the resolution condemned UÇK terrorism and called upon the Kosovar Albanian leadership to do likewise. More importantly, Lavrov noted that the resolution stated that the Security Council would consider further action if Yugoslavia did not comply. He pointed out that 'no use of force has been authorised by the Council at the present stage. No sanctions against Belgrade have been imposed'.[88] The latter point held particular significance for Moscow because Yugoslavia owed it over US$200 million in unpaid oil revenue that Russia could ill-afford to write-off.[89]

By October 1998 most NATO allies had become generally, if uneasily, supportive of the idea of air strikes, though this was at the expense of ruling out a land invasion. The US came on board to the idea of using military force in mid-June, with Clinton echoing Tony Blair's fear that Kosovo could become 'another Bosnia' if decisive action was not taken.[90] The key reason for this change of policy lay in Richard Holbrooke's view that diplomacy with Milošević had to be backed by a credible threat of force in order to be successful.[91] Holbrooke's preference for diplomacy backed by force brought him closer to Albright's position and hence introduced an element of coherence that had previously been lacking in American policy. Bob Dole supported Clinton's robust stance. Dole publicly urged the President to take tough measures against Yugoslavia, including the imposition of a no-fly zone and threat of air strikes.[92] The fact that the US advocated the use of force immediately helped to persuade those allies that were concerned about the threat of military losses because the US would shoulder the bulk of the burden particularly if that burden was primarily in the form of air and missile strikes.

The root of the Russian decision to offer a tacit nod of approval to NATO at the Heathrow Airport gathering lay in an agreement struck by Milošević and Yeltsin on 16 June, only a day after the Alliance had carried out a large combined air exercise – Determined Falcon – over northern Albania. In the days before the 16 June agreement, NATO was building a head of steam that made it appear as though air strikes were imminent, though in actuality there remained considerable disagreement about the appropriateness of using force and the Activation Warning to initiate military planning was not issued by the North Atlantic Council until 24 September. The purpose of Determined Falcon was, as one NATO official put it, 'to create as much noise as possible' and demonstrate the Alliance's ability to initiate air attacks on Yugoslavia at a moments notice.[93] A day later, British Defence Secretary George Robertson insisted that 'NATO wanted Mr. Milošević to understand that diplomacy to end the Kosovo violence was being backed by the threat of force'.[94] This followed an earlier assertion by Robertson that:

> The full power of NATO is considering all options, including the most radical…military options that could, and might have to be made available. President Milosevic should be under no illusion about this.[95]

In the same week, NATO members of the Contact Group along with Canada and Japan publicly announced their intention to obtain a UN Security Council Resolution authorising the use of 'all necessary means' to resolve the Kosovo conflict.[96] These threats were given more credence by Kofi Annan's decision to welcome NATO's initiative, implying that the UN supported the threat of force.[97]

These threats (which lacked substance because there was no agreement in the North Atlantic Council about actually using force) greatly alarmed Russia. It is important at this juncture to avoid the crude but popular view that Serbia and Russia are traditional allies joined together by a sense of pan-Slavic unity. This simply did not influence Russian foreign policy though in its domestic rhetoric the government had to appear decidedly anti-NATO. This, however, had more to do with Russian self-esteem than with pan-Slavic unity.[98] Yeltsin feared that if NATO acted unilaterally, Russia would be sidelined and allowed to have no input into provisions for the final settlement. In a meeting with Klaus Kinkel, the Russian Foreign Minister Yevgeny Primakov rejected the idea of sanctions and flatly ruled out accepting Western military intervention.[99]

Russia's response to the growing calls for armed intervention was somewhat incoherent. We noted earlier that it had a vested interest in protecting the Serbian economy as Russia was in no position to write off a US$200 million debt. To this end, Primakov made it clear to the Contact Group that Russia opposed both the use of force and application of sanctions against Yugoslavia. However, in a two-day visit to Brussels in which he spent much time at NATO's headquarters, the Russian Defence Minister, Igor Sergeyev, sent out mixed signals. His negotiating style was surprisingly co-operative given the divergence of policy between NATO and Russia. One report recorded that he 'pleaded' with NATO not to use force.[100] Moreover, Sergeyev put his name to a joint statement with NATO that condemned Serbia's 'massive and disproportionate use of force'.[101]

This conciliatory stance derived from Russia's belief that it had outmanoeuvred the West. On 16 June, Milošević travelled to Moscow for talks with President Boris Yeltsin and concluded a rapid agreement that covered three of the four Contact Group (and UN Security Council) demands. Yeltsin persuaded Milošević to promise that 'talks on the whole package of Kosovo problems, including forms of autonomy, will progress without a break in accordance with international standards and in line with a timetable agreed by both sides'.[102] The Yugoslav President also agreed to accept Resolution 1160 and refrain from further violence against the civilian population. Furthermore, he gave a commitment to grant unimpeded access to humanitarian organisations such as the ICRC and UNHCR.

Missing from the agreement was a commitment to withdraw VJ and MUP forces as demanded by the Contact Group and Resolution 1160. The Yeltsin–Milošević agreement stated that Belgrade would work towards a withdrawal once the UÇK's 'terrorist activity' had ceased.[103] Nonetheless, the agreement was nothing short of a diplomatic triumph for Russia. Yevgeny Primakov told the West that the concessions extracted from Milošević were the 'maximum possible' and created the possibility for a political settlement, placing the onus on the Kosovar Albanians to respond positively.[104] Although the West remained cautious, reminding Milošević of his responsibility to withdraw his forces, the argument for air strikes was now dead in the water.

Russia's triumph was short lived. Having given Yeltsin a rare foreign policy success by promising to restrain his forces in Kosovo, Milošević then allowed the VJ to begin reinforcing its positions in Kosovo the very next day and by the end of the month VJ tanks were being employed against villages on the outskirts of Pristina.[105] Yeltsin was stunned and angered at this humiliation. Milošević's promises to his Russian 'ally' had meant as much as his many earlier promises to NATO, the UN and OSCE. As a result, Russian policy perceptibly changed in the summer of 1998, demonstrated by the stronger tone of Resolution 1199.

A day before that resolution, the North Atlantic Council, met in Portugal and decided by 15–1 to approve a phased bombing campaign against Yugoslavia. Greece, whose vote was pivotal because North Atlantic Council decisions require the consent of all members, demanded that the decision be deferred until after the passage of the Security Council Resolution that was being debated concurrently in New York. This gives Russia's decision to vote in favour of the Resolution even greater significance. Had it used its veto and voted against the draft Resolution, Greece would have prevented the issuing of NATO's Activation Warning that ultimately paved the way for Operation Allied Force. Given that the North Atlantic Council vote was widely reported in the media and the fact that Russia has a permanent diplomatic presence at NATO headquarters, we must assume that Sergei Lavrov, the Russian Ambassador at the UN, was aware of the ramifications even though he stated afterwards that Resolution 1199 did not authorise the use of force and that Russia would have vetoed it if it had.[106] Many commentators argued after NATO's intervention that had Russia known that the allies would use an expansive interpretation of Resolution 1199 to justify air strikes it would not have allowed it to pass. They also insisted that NATO's actions weakened the Security Council and lessened the chance of similar resolutions being passed in the future.[107] However, what we can deduce from the inter-relationship of decisions made by the Security Council and North Atlantic Council is that not only was Russia aware of the implications of the strong language and Chapter VII nature of Resolution 1199, it was also aware that its passage would directly facilitate NATO's Activation Warning. By reneging on his agreement with Yeltsin, Milošević had lost his last ally and created a basic level of implied consensus between NATO and Russia on the principle of air strikes.[108]

Russia's new ambivalence to the question of air strikes was revealed more explicitly at the now infamous meeting at Heathrow Airport that took place on 8 October. Prior to the meeting, key NATO allies were continuing to insist that the Alliance should obtain a new Security Council Resolution that expressly authorised the use of force. Two days before the meeting, Jacques Chirac argued that the use of force 'must be requested and decided by the Security Council'.[109] However, Tim Judah points out that Chirac went on to clarify the point, saying, 'the humanitarian situation constitutes a ground that can justify an exception to the rule'.[110]

Partly by chance and partly by volition, 8 October saw Robin Cook, Hubert Védrine, Klaus Kinkel, Igor Ivanov (Russian Foreign Minister), Madeleine Albright and Richard Holbrooke come together at London's Heathrow Airport. The discussion turned to the need for a Security Council resolution authorising the use of force against Yugoslavia. Holbrooke has gone on record with his account of proceedings:

> Ivanov said: 'If you take it to the UN, we'll veto it. If you don't we'll just denounce you. Kinkel says he wants to take it to the Security Council as do the British and French. Madeleine and I say: 'That's insane!' So, Kinkel says: 'Let's have another stab at it'. But Ivanov says: 'Fine, we'll veto it'. And Kinkel asks again and Ivanov says: 'I just told you Klaus, we'll veto it ... '. He says: 'If you don't we'll just make a lot of noise.[111]

Not only did Russia indirectly facilitate the passage of NATO's Activation Warning by not opposing Resolution 1199 when in all probability Ambassador Lavrov at the UN knew that the North Atlantic Council would not agree the Activation Warning if the Resolution did not pass, but the Foreign Minister now told key NATO allies in no uncertain terms that Russia would not act to physically hinder the Alliance should it choose to use force against Yugoslavia. Because of domestic concerns, Russia could not be seen to be supporting NATO but Yeltsin was deeply upset by Milošević's refusal to adhere to their agreement. An important issue to arise from all this, though, is the question of what the Russians were telling Milošević. One of the reasons for the Yugoslav President's intransigence at Rambouillet and prior to Allied Force was his belief that he would receive material assistance from Russia.

Summary

The period of March–October 1998 saw a critical debate on intervention that was partially resolved in early October in a collective NATO decision about the legitimacy of using air strikes in principle. Intervention was placed on the agenda for three main reasons, all of which related closely to the fact of an armed conflict (the one element that had been missing from Kosovo for the previous eight years). These were the Bosnia syndrome, Balkan Wars syndrome and refugees syndrome. The spread of violence in Kosovo changed international perceptions of political necessity and provoked a reassessment of important assumptions. Specifically, the assumption that Kosovo was an internal matter for Serbia was revisited. On 31 March, the Security Council decided that the conflict constituted a threat to international peace and security. This important decision gave international society new types of policies that it had not previously made available to itself, such as the credible threat of military force. The Security Council decision thus began an important debate within NATO and between NATO and Russia about the use of force. The key aspects of this debate were:

- Can the Security Council be persuaded to authorise the use of force against Yugoslavia?
- If not, would it be permissible for NATO to use force?
- How would international society (most notably Russia) respond to this unauthorised use of force?
- What sort of armed force should be used?

In the course of six months of debate each of these issues was resolved to the satisfaction of the North Atlantic Council, though questions of law, precedence and prudence remained. Once it became clear that Security Council authorisation would not be forthcoming because of public opposition from Russia and China, the German, British and French governments were persuaded that explicit Security Council authorisation was not necessary. The Greek government was confident that Resolution 1199 provided enough legitimation for the Alliance's Activation Warning. This was largely because Russia gave clear indication that it would at least tolerate NATO's use of force and turned down an opportunity, which it was presented with as a result of Greece's decision to delay the decision until after the passage of Resolution 1199, to prevent the Activation Warning. On the question of what sort of force should be employed, Tony Blair's early preference for all military options to be considered – including the possibility of a ground invasion – received no support from allies and so was quickly dropped, only to be resurrected during Allied Force.

4
The Kosovo Verification Mission

The transition from *debating intervention* to *unarmed intervention* was orchestrated by Richard Holbrooke. The American diplomat persuaded Slobodan Milošević to comply with the demands made by Security Council Resolution 1199. Provided with ammunition by NATO's Activation Warning, which was issued immediately after Resolution 1199 was passed, Holbrooke embarked on what he believed was a final diplomatic mission to Belgrade. Using diplomacy backed with force, he persuaded Milošević to accept a series of demands including the reduction of troop levels in Kosovo to that before the outbreak of violence in 1998, the imposition of a general ceasefire, an international mission to verify compliance, and a deadline for the beginning of meaningful political dialogue based on a revised version of the Hill plan. The despatch of the OSCE KVM to verify the agreement marked the start of a more intrusive international engagement. However, the KVM never deployed its full complement of 2,000 and by the beginning of January 1999 it was quite obvious that the Holbrooke–Milošević agreement was unravelling in the face of renewed violence.

The defining characteristics of this period derive from the nature of the KVM, which was widely perceived in the West as Milošević's last chance to avoid war with NATO:

- The KVM was a traditional peacekeeping mission in the narrowest sense. It was there with Yugoslav consent and it was widely understood that it could not operate without that consent.
- NATO's co-operation with OSCE verification in the form of the aerial reconnaissance mission, 'Operation Eagle Eye', and the stationing of a European-led NATO 'extraction force' in Macedonia to provide a rapid withdrawal capability for the KVM suggested a growing militarisation of international policy.

- The continuation of negotiations and subsequent revisions of the Hill plan suggested that there was hope of finding an interim political settlement though the portents for failure were also present as deadlines passed without progress.
- The KVM was based on an agreement between the West and Slobodan Milošević. The Kosovar Albanians were neither included nor consulted during the negotiations. As a result, the agreement was generally viewed in a negative light by the Kosovar Albanian community and elements of the UÇK believed themselves to be not bound by the accord though its leadership did conclude a separate ceasefire agreement with Holbrooke.

The Milošević–Holbrooke agreement

The Milošević–Holbrooke agreement, which was finalised between 13 and 15 October 1998, was facilitated by the increased likelihood of NATO air strikes against Yugoslavia. With key alliance members such as the UK and US suggesting publicly that Resolution 1199 provided enough authorisation for air strikes the Alliance moved to link the decision on whether to use military force directly to the fate of Holbrooke's diplomatic mission in Belgrade.[1] The decision to link force and diplomacy was based on the belief that it was this that ultimately brought the parties to Dayton in 1995. In fact, no such link had existed. Back then, although Milošević believed that Holbrooke had the power to call in air strikes, the use of air strikes during the negotiations was not at Holbrooke's behest, though the American diplomat noted that they greatly enhanced his negotiating position.[2]

The move to turn NATO's Activation Warning, which called upon member states to contribute forces and commence planning, into an Activation Order that gave the Supreme Allied Commander Europe (SACEUR) control of the air assets and authority to actually begin attacks commenced in early October 1998, in tandem with Holbrooke's diplomatic mission. On 9 October, the North Atlantic Council approved the operations plan for a phased air campaign and for the first time began to examine the possibility of a limited deployment of ground troops. This would be 'after a ceasefire or in order to monitor a ceasefire'. The Council stressed however that no decision had been made on this latter possibility and no Activation Warning had been issued.[3] The move to back diplomacy with a credible threat – and possible use – of force was emphatically endorsed by the European Parliament. Hans van den Broek, a European Commissioner, echoed the parliament when he noted that, 'Russia must not have the right of a veto when it is a question of putting an end to crimes against humanity'.[4] That threat became more credible on 8 October when the Pentagon revealed that it had assigned 260 strike aircraft to the mission should the diplomatic effort fail and the British and American embassies in Belgrade withdrew their non-essential staff.[5]

American diplomats have been remarkably candid about the actual progress of the negotiations. What is interesting from these decidedly one-sided but not necessarily erroneous accounts is the role that the credible threat of force played. The threat, which was constantly repeated, allowed Holbrooke and General Mike Short to take a bullish approach to their talks with Milošević, even though as we will see later, the actual substance of the agreement they secured was not overly onerous for the Yugoslav president. This prompted some commentators to criticise Holbrooke for not using his strong position to extract more concessions from Milošević.[6]

In order to reinforce the message that the West was planning to use force if the Serbs did not fall into line, Holbrooke insisted that General Michael Short, who would be commanding Operational Plan 10601 – Allied Force, accompany him to Belgrade. Holbrooke recalled that Short's presence in Belgrade had an immediate effect on Milošević. The Yugoslav president turned to Short and said, 'so, you're the one who will bomb us'. Holbrooke explained that during the flight to Belgrade he and Short had already decided on a form of words that Short would use to explain his position. The General responded to Milošević by telling him: 'I've B52s in one hand and U2s [high altitude surveillance aircraft] in the other. It's up to you which I'm going to use'.[7] Holbrooke told the BBC that he was in no doubt that General Short's presence had a profound impact on the Yugoslav president: 'Milošević knew he was telling the truth. Now that threat was completely real and it resulted in the ceasefire agreements'.[8]

Despite the threats, Milošević continued to negotiate strongly and obfuscate in the face of NATO's demands. To allow aerial verification of the ceasefire and reduction of Yugoslav force levels to those of the beginning of 1998, Holbrooke demanded the withdrawal of Serbian anti-aircraft missiles from Kosovo. When Milošević explained that this was impossible because the missiles were immobile, Short interjected pointing out that the US Air Force and spy satellites had been observing the missiles and that the Serbs had been moving them every day. Presented with this evidence, Milošević backed down and promised to withdraw them.[9]

As the talks continued, without agreement on key aspects such as the need for an international monitoring mission, NATO issued its Activation Order (ACTORD). On 13 October, NATO Secretary-General Javier Solana declared that Richard Holbrooke had briefed the North Atlantic Council. The American envoy told them that progress was being made and that this was largely due to the Alliance's credible threat of force. As a result, the Council issued a delayed Activation Order for both limited air strikes and a phased air campaign in Yugoslavia, which would commence within 96 hours of the announcement.[10] It was widely believed that the attack would be spearheaded by Tomahawk cruise missiles fired at Yugoslav air defences by American and British ships and submarines stationed in the Adriatic Sea. After the initial attack there would be an operational pause to allow Milošević time to agree to Holbrooke's terms. If he failed to do so, the phased air campaign planned by the September Activation Warning would commence.[11]

Holbrooke's generally positive assessment of the situation persuaded some wavering alliance members to agree to the ACTORD because the likelihood of it being acted on was low, though Holbrooke himself rejects this interpretation of events. Instead, he argues that on the night that the phased and delayed campaign was ordered there were only two options on the table in the North Atlantic Council: Order an immediate attack or order an attack after 96 hours. Member states had already agreed to the plan and the idea of bombing in principle (shown by the agreement to issue the Activation Warning) but were concerned that it should be synchronised with the diplomatic activity in Belgrade.[12] Subsequent press reports that 'NATO had pulled back from the brink' when confronted with the possibility of actually using force were therefore misleading, he argued.[13]

Within hours of Solana's statement, Milošević announced that 'accord has been reached that problems in Kosovo and Metohija and in connection with Kosovo and Metohija be resolved by peaceful means, by political means'.[14] Holbrooke flew back to Brussels from Belgrade to brief NATO that the Yugoslav president had indeed verbally agreed to a peace deal. The task over the following two days was to commit this verbal agreement to paper and translate it into practice.

On 23 October, Zivojin Jovanović, Yugoslavia's permanent ambassador to the UN, gave the agreement some substance by writing to the Security Council's president outlining its key principles. He informed the Council that the Yugoslav government had agreed to accept a 'full-scale' international monitoring mission led by the OSCE.[15] The other principles included a commitment to begin work towards a political settlement by 2 November, a renunciation of violence, the principle of autonomy, and the principle of democratic governance.[16] To this latter principle was added a pledge to hold elections in Kosovo within nine months of the agreement.[17] These principles underpinned the oral agreement with Holbrooke. Fundamental to their acceptance by the Serbs was the fact that they reaffirmed Yugoslav sovereignty over Kosovo. Milošević and the Serbian government noted that the agreement 'fully preserves the territorial integrity and sovereignty of Serbia' and 'avoids conflict and creates conditions for a political dialogue ... within the framework of the legal systems of the Republic of Serbia and the FRY'.[18]

Two further written agreements were reached to put the accord into practice. One was between Yugoslavia and NATO and the other between Yugoslavia and the OSCE. On 15 October, General Wesley Clark and Memeilo Feridle, the VJ's Chief of Staff, reached agreement on the military aspects of implementation. According to Javier Solana, the agreement had three primary purposes: Securing the immediate withdrawal of the special MUP forces responsible for much of the violence, establishing an air verification component that would allow unarmed NATO aircraft to operate over Kosovo, and maintaining the Alliance's willingness and capability to act should the Yugoslavs not be in compliance.[19] In the event, the bulk of the agreement dealt with detailed provisions to ensure the protection of the air verification mission.[20]

Throughout the protracted negotiations the main point of disagreement had been the need for an international presence in Kosovo. The Serbs had continuously insisted that there should be no such presence because the problem was an internal Yugoslav one. Western states believed that an agreement would not be worth the paper it was written on unless there was an international presence to ensure compliance. Two factors combined in the middle of October to bring these two positions together. First, Milošević's military intelligence made him believe that the UÇK was a vanquished force. As a result, he reckoned that allowing an international presence in Kosovo would not lead to a resurgence of terrorism. Furthermore, his own forces would be able to comply with the West's demands because to all intents and purposes the enemy had been defeated. Secondly, Milošević preferred the idea of OSCE involvement to a potential NATO or UN deployment. There were several reasons for this: OSCE verifiers would be unarmed, OSCE missions tend to be much smaller than UN or NATO missions, the organisation's decision making process requires consent from all 55 members meaning that the mission's mandate would reflect the lowest common denominator, and Milošević already had experience of working with the OSCE's predecessor, the CSCE.

The day after the NATO–Yugoslavia accord was concluded, the OSCE's Chairman-in-Office, Polish Foreign Minister Bronislaw Geremek, flew to Belgrade to reach an agreement with Yugoslav Foreign Minister Jovanović. This agreement provided the basis for the OSCE's Kosovo Verification Mission. The mission was to have five principal roles:

- Verify compliance with the military aspects of the Holbrooke–Milošević agreement.
- Establish a permanent presence throughout Kosovo.
- Maintain a close liaison with the VJ, political parties and other appropriate authorities within the province.
- Supervise elections.
- Report and make recommendations to the OSCE Permanent Council and the UN Security Council.[21]

In order to carry out this mission, Foreign Minister Jovanović agreed to accept, '2,000 unarmed verifiers from OSCE member states'. The media tended to claim that the verifiers were civilians. In fact, most verifiers were serving or retired military personnel and the OSCE–Yugoslavia agreement stated only that they be 'unarmed' not that they be civilian. Although the agreement states that the KVM would have 2,000 verifiers it went on to say that this figure also included headquarters and support staff. As a result, the actual number of people that could be physically deployed as verifiers was substantially fewer than the 2,000 frequently referred to though this was a much-debated point.

The Holbrooke–Milošević and subsequent NATO and OSCE agreements created a new phase of *unarmed intervention*. For the first time since 1993, international society established a permanent presence in Kosovo. There was also a clear timetable for progress towards political settlement (2 November) and an authorised regime of punitive measures should Yugoslavia not comply. There were, however, serious problems. The US decision to reach a unilateral agreement with Milošević created a number of rifts within the Alliance. The British government, for example, was concerned that having spent so much energy building an international consensus on the use of force that harmony would now be destroyed. Working on the assumption that the Serbs would not comply, several British officials privately expressed the view that the agreement marked a significant backward step as building consensus on using force would now be much harder given Milošević's apparent cooperation.[22]

Not many commentators at the time noted that the agreement was fatally flawed by the fact that the Kosovar Albanians were not involved.

The three agreements made no demands of the UÇK and its political leadership openly stated that it felt itself to be outside the agreement, though it did later conclude a ceasefire agreement with the KVM. The other problem caused by Kosovar Albanian non-participation was that the political terms of the settlement were wholly unacceptable to them because there was no provision for independence or even a mechanism for investigating its possibility. It was widely perceived in Kosovar Albanian society that the agreement preserved the status quo and offered it international legitimacy. The agreement was rejected by virtually every Kosovar Albanian leader, though once deployed the OSCE found widespread support for its activities.

Unarmed intervention

The OSCE was only informed of its new role in the Balkans when Holbrooke announced his agreement with Milošević to the world. Branislaw Geremek immediately travelled to Belgrade to secure the agreement outlined above before returning to Vienna as the OSCE Permanent Council adopted the appropriate mandate authorising the mission. Geremek told observers that implementing the KVM provided both 'a tremendous challenge and a tremendous opportunity' to the organisation.[23] The Chairman-in-Office was not overstating the problem. If the KVM had reached its 2,000 target for personnel it would have become the OSCE's largest mission, ten times the size of the second largest in Bosnia. Furthermore, it would have been four times larger than all the other OSCE missions put together.[24]

The KVM drew broader international legitimacy from Security Council Resolution 1203. The Resolution passed on 24 October 1998 under Chapter VII of the Charter demanded full compliance with Yugoslavia's agreements with NATO and the OSCE.[25] Importantly, however, some elements of the undertaking were more robustly demanded than others and this reflected the KVM's priorities. Most robust was its demand for full compliance with Resolutions 1160 and 1199 and their military aspects in particular. The Council was less demanding on the question of progress towards a political settlement. The resolution merely, 'stresses the urgent need to the authorities of the Federal Republic of Yugoslavia and the Kosovo Albanian leadership to enter immediately into a meaningful dialogue'.[26] Nevertheless, the resolution did give the KVM a high degree of international legitimacy.

Holbooke made four key claims about the veracity of the agreements. Firstly, he emphasised the fact that they made provision for 'verifiers' rather than observers or monitors. Milošević, he claimed, had insisted on observers and monitors a demand Holbrooke rejected as, 'bureaucratic babble words'.[27] Instead, Holbrooke insisted that the mission would be proactive, reflected in the use of words such as 'verify' and 'compliance'. Secondly, Holbrooke interpreted the 2,000 figure as a minimum rather than maximum aspiration. According to the agreement, he argued, 'it is 2,000 or more'. He continued, 'Ambassador Walker [Head of the KVM] has the right to bring in any additional people at any time'.[28] This view was at considerable variance with Walker's understanding. Walker suggested that the 2,000 figure had been reached without an assessment of what the KVM would be doing and that it was a ceiling. In January 1999 Walker told a press conference that 'the number 2,000 was always a fairly arbitrary one'. He continued, 'if the Chairman-in-Office is correct in his estimate that we need 1,500...we will stop there'.[29] Holbrooke's third point was that the ground verification system would also fulfil other important roles. Chief amongst those, he insisted, was election supervision within nine months and training and advising an indigenous Kosovar Albanian police force. The final aspect of the agreement that Holbrooke focused on was both parties' recognition of Christopher Hill's role as mediator in the search for a political settlement.

The OSCE Permanent Council's decision to appoint William Walker as Head of Mission was not without controversy. The decision was influenced by the desire to continue with the American diplomatic leadership that had won the Holbrooke–Milošević agreement in the first place. The American administration's choice of a representative as senior as Walker indicated that it intended to remain deeply involved in the peace process. To ensure a sense of Euro-Atlantic balance though, Walker's deputy was Gabriel Keller, a former French chargé d'affaires in Belgrade. Walker and Keller did not get on at all and the European proved to be a constant thorn in Walker's side. William Walker was selected because he was the most senior available American diplomat with recent practical experience in the region. His previous job had been as the UN's Special Representative to the Secretary General in the United Nations Transitional Authority in Eastern Slavonia (UNTAES). That had been a very successful mission, which had handed over authority of Eastern Slavonia to the Croatian government in 1997 having fulfilled its mandate.

Walker's appointment created suspicion among conspiracy theorists. According to Diana Johnstone, the KVM's objective was to establish the primacy of NATO in Europe by revealing the impotence of the OSCE.

She insists that:

> The mission's fate was sealed in favour of the second alternative when the European majority in the OSCE was somehow persuaded to accept US diplomat William Walker to head the KVM. Walker was a veteran of Central American 'banana republic' management, who had collaborated with Oliver North in illegally arming the 'Contras' and had covered up murderous state security operations in El Salvador as US ambassador there during the Reagan administration.[30]

It is not at all surprising that Johnstone is unable to furnish evidence for this claim. The OSCE was selected because it was the only organisation that Milošević would accept. To argue that the KVM was designed to fail in order to allow NATO to establish its authority is simply absurd. The American administration invested much political capital in winning the agreement and Walker's appointment should be seen as indicating determination to ensure that the KVM provide robust verification. Others have argued that the 'deliberate' torpedoing of the KVM was planned to lend legitimacy to air strikes. This too is absurd given that in October 1998 Alliance members believed that they had enough legitimacy to issue the Activation Order. With the Activation Order issued the authority to order strikes was delegated to the SACEUR, Wesley Clark. As we saw in the previous chapter, by the time of the Holbrooke–Milošević agreement, the Alliance did not believe that it needed more legitimacy than it already had.

The task of establishing the mission proved to be problematic and by the time of its withdrawal in March 1999, only 1,300 of the projected 2,000 verifiers had been deployed. Based on his meetings with the Permanent Council and the American diplomatic team led by Richard Holbrooke, Walker concluded that his mission would have two primary roles: Averting the impending humanitarian emergency that threatened Kosovo's sizable internally displaced population and creating a stable environment in which negotiations towards a political settlement could continue.[31] Although the OSCE's members agreed to send the mission and approved Walker as its head, its Permanent Council had considerable difficulty defining its precise role. At a meeting in Warsaw, Walker was advised that the mission should be robust from the outset and should contain several human rights experts. The Russian, Ukrainian and Belarussian representatives rejected this interpretation of the mandate and insisted that human rights verification did not form part of the OSCE–Yugoslav agreement.[32] Nevertheless, the majority view in the organisation, a view taken on by Walker, was that as the so-called 'human dimension' formed a crucial part of the Helsinki Final Acts (1973), which set out the principles on which the CSCE/OSCE would be based, every OSCE mission must have a human rights element at its core.

Even before deployment, therefore, the KVM confronted three challenges:

1. *Scale.* The KVM was substantially larger and had a much higher profile than any previous mission undertaken by the OSCE.
2. *Mandate.* The mission was based on overlapping mandates from the UN, its own Permanent Council, the Holbrooke–Milošević settlement, the NATO–Yugoslav accord, and the OSCE–Yugoslav agreement. To make matters worse, there were different interpretations of what that mandate was.
3. *Precedent.* Such an operation had not been envisaged by the OSCE when it took on a traditional peacekeeping role. As a result it did not have the necessary logistical or organisational structures in place. These had to be created in October and November 1998.

Recruitment was a problem that dogged the KVM throughout its deployment. Because the mission's primary task was the verification of compliance with the military aspects of the Holbrooke–Milošević agreement and subsequent OSCE–Yugoslavia and OSCE–UÇK accords most contributing member states provided personnel and material through their Ministry's of Defence. This created two sets of problems. Many of the Defence Ministry's had not worked with the OSCE on such an operation before so there was some confusion about appropriate operating procedures. Moreover, most of the personnel seconded from member states were either currently serving or retired military officers. This was partly due to the military nature of the task and partly because of the perceived risks to the verifiers.[33] While on one hand this bias was partly needed because only verifiers with military experience would be able to ensure compliance with the military aspects of the agreements (complete withdrawal of special MUP forces and the return of VJ force levels to its January 1998 strength) on the other hand it meant that other aspects of the mission's work – for example in the human rights field – took longer to develop. Walker himself observed that by the end of the KVM's presence in the province, in March 1999, only 80 of the 1,350 international staff had been processed and assigned to full-time human rights tasks.[34] To overcome this problem and increase the mission's field knowledge several Western states agreed to incorporate the KDOM into

KVM. This happened in the cases of the UKDOM (UK) and EUKDOM (EU), but American diplomatic observers retained their separate identity. This prompted some observers to conclude that USKDOM was providing field intelligence for Washington and conducting covert operations alongside the UÇK.

The problem of guaranteeing the physical security of KVM personnel troubled policy-makers throughout Europe. Under the OSCE–Yugoslavia agreement, the Yugoslavs guaranteed the security of KVM personnel. Resolution 1203 authorised NATO to deploy an 'extraction force' in neighbouring Macedonia that could be used if a forcible withdrawal of the KVM became necessary. These provisions did not mitigate the fact that tactical level security was based upon the consent of the belligerents. KVM verifiers would be defenceless against attack. Being unarmed also meant that they could only be proactive in limited ways. In the British House of Commons, for example, John Wilkinson – the Conservative MP for Ruislip–Northwood – commented:

> May I express the gravest reservations about the insertion of unarmed British personnel, especially British service personnel, in a region of such brigandry and banditry as Kosovo?[35]

Although the protection of the KVM was an important issue and became more so as violence began to increase at the beginning of 1999 and OSCE staff became a target for intimidation, the fact that the verifiers were unarmed had some advantages. Being unarmed was crucial in winning Milošević's acceptance of the mission. On the ground, neither side could perceive the KVM as a threat because it had no weapons. This encouraged the local perception that the mission was an impartial verifier allowing it to accomplish tasks that it would not have otherwise been able to do.

Ceasefire and withdrawal

The KVM's first task was to verify Yugoslav compliance with the military aspects of the agreements within the 96-hour period agreed by Milošević and Holbrooke. On 16 October, NATO decided to extend that deadline although it was clear that the Serbs were far from compliance. The Kosovar Albanian leadership reacted by arguing that this decision proved that Milošević had successfully seen off the threat of air strikes.[36] The perception that NATO had blinked when confronted by a clear failure to comply with a deadline increased the difficulty the Alliance would later face in persuading both delegations at Rambouillet about the credibility of the threat of force. The decision to extend the deadline and call off air strikes, which were due to be launched at 5 a.m. was taken after extensive debate amongst the permanent representatives at NATO headquarters in Brussels. Once again a briefing to the Council by Holbrooke proved to be crucial in making the decision. Holbrooke told the Council that although many VJ and MUP units remained deployed throughout Kosovo the Serbs had indicated an intention to withdraw them and thus the deadline should be extended. He argued that extending the deadline would also allow the OSCE to deploy some of its verifiers in order to build up an accurate picture of what was happening on the ground.

As with other deadlines set in the Balkans over the previous decade, there was very little movement towards compliance with NATO's demands until two days before its expiry. On 25 October, Milošević agreed a further deal with SACEUR Wesley Clark and the chairman of the Alliance's Military Committee, General Klaus Naumann. Although Robin Cook reiterated the threat to Yugoslavia, telling Milošević that he must comply immediately or face the consequences,[37] it was clear that the consensus in the North Atlantic Council on using force was diminishing as the Serbs made incremental moves towards compliance. The British Ministry of Defence estimated that by 26 October VJ troop levels in Kosovo had been reduced to around 12,000, lower than the 12,950 troops stationed in the province before the armed conflict began in January 1998. Compliance with regards to MUP forces was less forthcoming though. The Ministry estimated that whereas the pre-conflict levels were around 6,030 the number that were still deployed on 26 October remained as high as 9,500–10,000.[38] This variance in compliance reflected Milošević's preference for using MUP forces rather than the less trustworthy VJ for internal 'policing' operations. Nevertheless, the headline figure of 7,500 troops withdrawn appeared enough to satisfy the Alliance. Many subsequent writers argued that Milošević did indeed comply at the outset with the military terms of the agreement. This is not the case. At no time did overall force levels come down to those agreed with Holbrooke.

There was a great deal of scepticism among Kosovar Albanians because they had not been involved in the negotiating process prior to the Holbrooke–Milošević agreement and were not consulted about the terms of the OSCE deployment. For many, it appeared that Milošević had done just enough to stall NATO air strikes without actually changing the situation on the ground. The UÇK was particularly sceptical. Commander Shaban Shala, a member of the UÇK's inner circle, commented that, 'it looks like Milošević has drawn them [Holbrooke and the other US diplomats] into his game', noting that while there had been a limited withdrawal the Serbs had deployed an entire tank battalion and anti-aircraft weapons close to UÇK strongholds and refugee camps in central Kosovo.[39] However, under pressure from US diplomats the Kosovar Albanian fighters declared a unilateral ceasefire but tempered it with the qualification that it would only hold if Resolution 1199 was implemented.[40]

It was widely predicted that because the UÇK was not party to the agreement it would move its forces into areas being vacated by Serb forces. For the Serbs, this provided a rationale for not withdrawing whilst for moderate Kosovar Albanians such as Veton Surroi, editor of *Koha Ditore*, this was merely a symptom of the failure to engage the Albanian community in the peace process.[41] It was soon apparent after the 26 October deadline that the UÇK was indeed moving into areas formerly policed by the Serbs. In the Drenica valley, which the rebels had held prior to the Serbian summer offensive, the UÇK literally moved into gun placements built and manned by the VJ and MUP before their withdrawal and uniformed guerrillas set up checkpoints throughout the province.[42] A day later, the UÇK was persuaded to make a formal declaration in which they promised to adhere to the ceasefire, not set up checkpoints and not begin any new offensives as long as the Serbs did not move into areas in which UÇK fighters were deployed.[43] It was not clear whether they would observe these pledges or indeed whether the commanders were capable of controlling all their forces. The VJ and MUP maintained a public presence along the eastern side of the Djakovica–Klina road and the MUP established new positions in the Malisevo area, in a clear violation of its international obligations.[44] In response, the UÇK attacked the MUP headquarters in Malisevo on 9 November. MUP forces retaliated by attacking Kosovar Albanians in Stimlje.[45]

KVM practicalities

The KVM did not begin to get fully organised until mid November. Prior to that, it only had a small physical presence on the ground and could do little to promote inter-communal confidence or ameliorate the security situation. The mission was separated into five regional centres commanded by a headquarters in Pristina. Whilst at the outset, the mission's goal was to verify Yugoslav compliance with the military aspects of the agreement it soon took on a broader role. According to Brigadier-General Maisonneuve, who served with the Canadian OSCE contingent in Prizren, the mission's primary function was to preserve the ceasefire.

As a result, it found itself reacting to breaches of the ceasefire rather than doing the intrusive verification envisaged by Walker and verifying compliance with the 'human dimension' elements of the directive from the OSCE's Permanent Council in Vienna.[46]

Verifiers enjoyed near complete freedom of movement and access to barracks and other security forces locations occupied by both belligerents. They also performed independent investigations, accompanied the authorities when they conducted criminal investigations, verified compliance with the human dimension requirements, provided assistance to humanitarian organisations working to return the 600,000 or so internally displaced persons to their homes, aided reconstruction planning, and began preparing for an election by conducting electoral registrations.[47] Walker decided that the mission should be as visible as possible throughout the province to help promote confidence in both communities. Thus, the KVM adopted a decentralised structure based on small field offices. While this certainly succeeded in raising the mission's profile, the lack of leadership and guidance from the top created disparity between the priorities and operating procedures of different field offices.

Political progress

The litmus test for the Holbrooke–Milošević agreement was progress towards a political settlement. Milošević agreed that progress would be made by 2 November. A day before this deadline Christopher Hill presented the Serbs with a revised version of the plan he had tabled at the beginning of October. Hill had strengthened key parts in order to make the settlement more appealing to both sides. The new plan contained much more detail than the original, particularly on the subject of law and policing. To win Kosovar Albanian acquiescence the new proposals fortified Kosovo's legal status within the federation, making it an entity in its own right.[48] Moreover, the province would now have a president, giving it a very public external personality. Finally, to persuade the Serbs the revised plan gave greater and better-defined powers to the local communes and provisions for the autonomy of national communities were reinforced.[49]

It was not until some eight days after the expiry of NATO's deadline that Yugoslavia responded to the revised Hill plan though there was little suggestion in the meantime that the Alliance should take action against the Yugoslavs. Indeed, in its 10 November statement, the Yugoslav Ministry of Foreign Affairs denied having seen the new plan. With the KVM on the ground, a ceasefire more-or-less holding, and a president being ostensibly cooperative there was little will in the West for a resumption of hostilities. The Serbs created a facade of dialogue because the 2 November deadline for progress on political dialogue had been a key part of the Holbrooke–Milošević agreement. On 18 November they organised their own conference in Pristina in which a new plan was presented. According to Marc Weller, 'it [the Serb conference and plan] was seen by Kosovo as a cynical attempt to undermine the internationalised Hill process'.[50] The Serb plan was supported at the conference by the Yugoslav, Kosovo Serb, Gorani, Romani, Egyptian, Turk, and Muslim 'national communities', though the delegates had all been hand-picked by Belgrade. Although ostensibly modelled on the Hill plan there were several crucial changes in the Serb proposals. As with the proposal subsequently produced after Rambouillet, this scheme gave all the 'national communities' a veto, increased the power of Serbia *vis-à-vis* the province, and refused to recognise the Kosovar Albanian political leadership.[51]

Explaining the Serb position and his problems with Christopher Hill's proposals, Milošević told Western journalists that, 'its [the Hill plan] shortcoming is that the plan is favouring Albanians. Our approach is different. We think that no national community in Kosmet should be favoured. Each national community in Kosmet has to be equal with other national communities'.[52] What he meant by this was that each national community should have a national veto, effectively giving the Serbs a veto over any decision reached by a future Kosovo Assembly. The president outlined his position more bluntly later in the interview, 'police in Kosovo is from Kosovo', he claimed, 'and Kosovo is Serbia'.[53]

The publication of the revised Hill proposal on 1 November achieved two things. It exposed the lack of progress being made on political dialogue and the Serbs failure to comply with the Holbrooke–Milošević agreement. It also set in motion political dialogue between the West and the Kosovar Albanians. Indeed, a characteristic of all negotiations towards a political settlement that were conducted between the deployment of the KVM and Allied Force was that the Kosovar Albanians engaged in detailed and constructive dialogue whilst the Serbs did not.

Fehmi Agani, a senior member of Rugova's LDK, was given the job of negotiating with Hill. A major step was the agreement of Rexhep Qosja's opposition party to accept the principle of an interim settlement. This meant delaying the aspiration of independence for three years whilst increasing Kosovo's wider international legitimacy. Some in the LDK also saw the principle of the interim settlement as important because it meant that for the first time international society was not ruling out the possibility of independence at some point in the future. Nevertheless, after consultation with Hill on this second draft, Agani concluded that he had 'serious objections' to the plan, though he was sure that improvements could be made.[54]

Despite this willingness to engage in dialogue, the third published revision of the Hill plan gave further concessions to the Serbs principally increasing the power of Serbia over the province and further bolstering the role of the national communities. Given the erosion of alliance consensus on using force following Milošević's apparent decision to cooperate in October, winning Serb agreement was given primary importance. This was a mistake that was also made at Rambouillet. Persuading the Kosovar Albanians to defer their independence claim once again had been difficult enough. By altering the proposed settlement in Serbia's favour, Hill forwent the opportunity to reach an accord with at least one of the belligerents. Agani's optimism that an agreement could be reached was soon dissipated. Adem Demaçi, the UÇK's political spokesman denounced the third draft Hill proposal, which was unveiled on 2 December. He described the revised settlement as, 'utterly unacceptable', lamenting that, 'Mr. Hill is either unfamiliar with the Albanian question or else is taking sides with the Serbs'.[55] Noting that the third draft proposal offered worse terms than the second draft had done, Demaçi called for the US State Department to reconsider Hill's position. Although more constructive in his comments, Agani said that he believed the new plan to be 'a return to the old and unacceptable proposals'.[56] Furthermore, a commission of Kosovo Assembly members noted that the new plan severely curtailed the assembly's legislative jurisdiction.[57]

The publication of the third draft of the Hill plan sounded the death knell for the process, which had begun in the summer of 1998. The Serbs continued to refuse to engage in constructive dialogue and failed to meet their obligations under the Holbrooke–Milošević agreement. Nevertheless, the chimera of cooperation and the dramatic reduction of violence that accompanied the KVM's deployment meant that the consensus on using force that had produced the Activation Order in October disappeared. Early optimism amongst Kosovar Albanian political leaders that an equitable interim political settlement could be won at the expense of accepting a three-year moratorium on independence was dashed as Hill appeared to give more weight to Serb demands than he did to Kosovar Albanian demands.

The unravelling peace

The lack of progress towards a political settlement persuaded several UÇK members to take up arms again. In November 1998 there was a noticeable increase in the number of attacks against Serb civilians and security forces and Kosovar Albanian opponents. In Bukos, a 25-year-old Kosovar Albanian was shot in the head in an incident widely thought to have been related to organised crime. The UÇK also attempted to prevent KDOM and KVM personnel from moving freely in their attempts to investigate the incident.[58] The UÇK were not the only ones responsible for inhibiting the work of the KVM or intimidating its verifiers. In the first half of November, VJ forces opened fire over clearly marked orange KVM vehicles, prompting Javier Solana to issue a stern warning.[59]

Whilst William Walker continued to insist that the KVM would be 'forward leaning, proactive, assertive and intrusive'[60] both sides breached the ceasefire arrangements with increasing regularity. Over the weekend of 7 November, MUP forces ambushed and killed five members of the UÇK. In retaliation, the Kosovar Albanian guerrillas kidnapped and killed two Serbian policemen.[61] Despite this, the overall security situation in November was relatively benign and the scale of violence remained considerably lower than it had been prior to the KVM's deployment. A KVM report to the UN recorded that whilst there had been 'sporadic ceasefire violations' there had been no significant combat between the belligerent armed forces.[62] Furthermore, the report stated that the KVM had successfully created a more secure environment that had facilitated the return of 75,000 internally displaced persons though another 175,000 remained displaced. The majority of these found shelter with family members elsewhere in the province but a good many continued to live outdoors, providing a major cause of concern as winter approached. There were also problems housing the returnees. Because of the destruction to housing caused by the Serb offensives in the summer many refugees, the report concluded 'are forced to stay in the houses of their more fortunate neighbours and thus are still displaced, albeit within their own villages'.[63]

Steady progress towards a more secure environment was made throughout November and early December despite the sporadic violence. On several occasions the presence of verifiers defused potentially serious situations. For example, on 10 December 1,000 Serb civilians marched into territory held by the UÇK to protest at the disappearance of 50 Serbs over the previous few months. The protestors set out from Orahovac, having assured the KVM verifiers that accompanied them that they would not enter UÇK held territory. However, they decided to march towards the UÇK stronghold at Dragobilje. As they did so, they were joined by Serb police and MUP forces increasing the likelihood of an armed confrontation. This was averted when OSCE verifiers arranged a meeting between the Serb leaders and local Kosovar Albanians in which the Serbs presented their grievances and came to a vague agreement to begin cooperation on finding the whereabouts of all missing persons in the province.[64]

On 14 and 15 December, two incidents indicated a further deterioration in the security situation and a return to larger scale violence. On 14 December, MUP forces ambushed UÇK units that were trying to enter Kosovo from Albania near Prizren. The media and KVM reported that at least 31 people from a group of around 140 were killed in the ambush. Although the vast majority were indeed UÇK members the attack did constitute a violation of the Holbrooke–Milošević agreement. In what appeared to be a reprisal, though the UÇK never accepted responsibility, two masked gunmen burst into a Serb student café, 'Panda', in Pec and shot dead six young Serb civilians.[65]

The killings in Pec provoked a strong reaction from the Serb community. Serb demonstrators condemned the KVM for failing to protect them and for favouring the Kosovar Albanians. Serb youths pelted verifiers with stones, forcing them to withdraw from the town. The emerging popular view that the KVM was not impartial was deeply damaging to the mission because of its dependence on consent to be able to go about its business. The removal of consent by one of the belligerents reduced the mission's ability to create a more secure environment. The situation was believed by the West to be so serious that Richard Holbrooke returned to the region for the first time since his agreement with Milošević. Holbrooke's visit to Belgrade and Pristina in the immediate aftermath of the killings had two purposes. First, it was hoped that he would add new impetus to Christopher Hill and Wolfgang Petritsch's efforts to make progress towards a political settlement. Progress was not forthcoming, however, because both sides appeared implacably opposed to the underlying principles of the proposals. The second purpose of the visit was to warn the belligerents that the consequences of violence would be catastrophic for both. Although NATO's Activation Order remained in place, Holbrooke chose not to refer to the potential for military action by the Alliance presumably because of the diminished consensus on the issue.

Holbrooke's efforts were in vain and the ceasefire collapsed on Christmas Eve. The Serbs launched a major offensive against UÇK positions in villages around Podujevo. KVM verifiers reported that the Serbs used tanks and artillery in their attacks and that there was 'sporadic shelling' in the area.[66] According to the Kosova Information Centre, a service provided by the parallel government, MUP forces launched a major offensive and surrounded the villages of Glamnik, Obranca, Burince, and Lapastica, all known to be UÇK strongholds. The report said that the Serbs had encountered strong resistance from the UÇK.[67]

The increased violence around Christmas raised fears about the security of KVM personnel. The US responded by sub-contracting its verification contribution to a private security firm.[68] This increased suspicion that the American's main effort remained focused on its KDOM contingent, which had not folded into the KVM. Despite the dangers, many verifiers remained optimistic about their role in the province. One verifier, UK Brigadier Ian Mcleod (retired) commented that, 'being unarmed is better, you're not a threat to them. Both sides offer their protection. We're here by consent like any policeman in the UK'.[69] Moreover, commenting on the view that the mission was not actually achieving anything, given the failure of political dialogue and increasingly numerous ceasefire breaches, another verifier claimed that 'our presence means the local Albanian population is no longer scared of the Serb police to come and pray after nightfall'.[70] Tellingly, the verifier chose not to comment on the mission's contribution to Kosovo Serb security concerns.

The wider international perception of events in Kosovo was not as optimistic as these opinions expressed by KVM verifiers. Responding to the Serbs Christmas Eve offensive, the SACEUR General Wesley Clark, told reporters that 'the Serbs are violating their commitments to NATO'.[71] Although William Walker, Richard Holbrooke and others were later to admit that the Serbs never reached full compliance with either the political or military aspects of the Holbrooke–Milošević agreement, this was the first time that a prominent player had openly drawn attention to the fact without first stating that progress towards compliance was moving apace. Adjoining General Clark's statement was a NATO intelligence assessment which revealed that MUP force levels were being increased again, that the VJ forces which remained in the province had not returned to barracks in accordance with the agreement, and that both forces were maintaining road-side check points.[72] It was becoming clear to Western states that the agreement reached in October was unravelling and that an unarmed verification mission could do little when confronted with diminishing levels of consent caused by a widespread perception in both communities that political dialogue was not proceeding as hoped. As an unnamed NATO official put it at the time, 'we are not seeing the sort of wholesale attacks on civilians, the shelling of villages, that we saw last summer. The Serbs are pushing it, but they are keeping below a threshold level at which NATO would have to get involved'.[73]

The Racak massacre[74]

On 15 January 1999 there was a major exchange of fire between MUP forces and the UÇK around the village of Racak. The precise reason for the MUP's decision to attack the village on this particular day remains obscure because the Kosovar Albanian rebels had held it since October. At around 8 a.m. MUP forces entered Racak accompanied by a camera crew from Associated Press. This in itself was unusual. Given that even attacks directed against the UÇK contravened the Holbrooke–Milošević agreement and Yugoslavia's subsequent agreements with the OSCE and NATO it appears strange that the Serbs would have wanted international media coverage. Moreover, never before had the Serbs actively encouraged a foreign media presence to witness an attack on a village. Associated Press had been invited to film the fighting between the MUP and UÇK and thus to direct attention away from the main business of the day in Racak: A reprisal against Kosovar Albanian civilians for the killing of three Serb policemen in Dulje on 8 January. The KVM was also invited to observe the exchange and verifiers stationed themselves on a hill overlooking the fighting, but with only a partial view of Racak.

Witnesses reported that the Serb operation began at 6.30 a.m. At this point it is widely believed that the population of Racak numbered around 3–400. T-55 tanks belonging to the VJ and MUP armoured vehicles were deployed around the perimeter of the village. Seeing these deployments, the first families began to flee to Petrovo and UÇK members also withdrew from the village to positions in the hills around it. A female eyewitness told Human Rights Watch that around 40 MUP officers opened fire on the village from the hillside. The fire was aimed at the people fleeing below. Bullets hit the witness's husband and son. A 74-year-old man in the same group said he saw his grandson, granddaughter, and daughter injured at this time. Many villagers sought refuge from the fire in Sadik Osmani's house. At around 11 a.m. MUP officers took 30 men from the house. They were forced to lie on the ground in the courtyard. Two hours later, 23 of these men were led away by the officers. The people left in the house suspected that they were being taken into police custody in Stimlje. However, at 3 p.m. villagers heard shots coming from the direction where the bodies were later found.

Although KVM verifiers were able to see some of the events from their hillside location their view was only partial. Contradicting their apparent openness with regards to Associated Press the Serbs explicitly told the verifiers not to enter Racak. The verifiers first entered the village in the late afternoon and immediately heard unconfirmed reports that men and women had been separated and the men taken away by blue-uniformed MUP officers. They withdrew from the village as darkness fell in accordance with the KVM's standard operating procedures. At about 4 a.m. villagers discovered the bodies of 45 people scattered on a hillside, 25 together in a small gorge. They also discovered the bodies of nine uniformed UÇK fighters. The verifiers returned early on the morning of 16 January accompanied by foreign journalists. The government had reported that 15 'terrorists' had been killed in the fighting but informal briefings given by verifiers to the press in Pristina on the night of the 15 January aroused a great deal of interest about what had happened in Racak. The KVM's spokesman, Berend Borchardt was amongst this first inspection team. He told the press that he believed the dead to be 'ordinary farming people' most of them wearing Wellington boots and none of them wearing the sort of footwear appropriate for military activity. Two British journalists who were also present at the scene were given access to the bodies and confirmed the verifiers reports that most of the victims had been shot at close range and that many had also suffered serious knife wounds.

William Walker arrived at Racak at around midday. He was first briefed by the verification team on the ground and then visited the site where the bodies were. He later recalled:

> The dead were mostly elderly men, all in peasant work clothes, and had died where they were discovered. The evidence of deliberate execution was overwhelming. I so described the incident in a press conference that afternoon, blamed the security forces and asked the government to permit the entry of investigators from the ICTY.[75]

Walker was immediately declared a *persona non grata* by the Serbian authorities and ordered to leave Yugoslavia.

On the day of the initial attack on 15 January the Serbian Deputy Prime Minister, Nikola Sainović spoke on the telephone with the Interior Minister General Sretan Lukić. Unbeknown to them, the conversation was being tapped by the CIA and the subsequent tapes found their way to the *Washington Post* newspaper. Speaking from Belgrade Sainović opened the conversation by enquiring about on-going operations around Racak. The Deputy Prime Minister was clearly concerned about international news reports of a massacre there and the two engaged in lengthy and detailed discussions about what to do. Sainović recommended two courses of action. First, the border with Macedonia should be sealed to prevent Louise Arbour, the chief prosecutor for the International Criminal Tribunal for Former Yugoslavia (ICTY), who was on her way to the region from entering Yugoslavia. Secondly, Lukić was instructed to order his forces to retake and hold Racak, which had fallen back into UÇK hands on the night of the 15 January after the MUP had withdrawn.[76]

On 17 January the Serb security forces launched a renewed attack on Racak. Around 100 people were in the village at the time (including verifiers and journalists) and were forced to flee in the face of the attack. This meant that the bodies, now laid out in the village mosque, were left unattended. On 19 January, Louise Arbour was prevented from entering Kosovo.

Having retaken Racak, MUP officers took the victims bodies from the mosque to the Serbian Forensic Medicine Institute in Pristina. Two days later a combined Serb and Belarussian team of pathologists began an autopsy on many of the bodies. Two days after that, on 21 January, a Finnish team of pathologists headed by Helena Ranta arrived having been instructed by the EU to investigate and report on the causes of the deaths. According to the Serb and Belarussian pathologists the bodies showed no signs of execution and all had gunpowder traces on their hands indicating that they were indeed UÇK guerrillas as Belgrade had claimed. Helena Ranta disputed these findings. Two months later in a detailed report Ranta pointed out that the Serbs reached these conclusions by using a paraffin test method. She argued that this method had been recognised as unreliable as long ago as 1968 and that using modern methods revealed there to be no evidence that any of victims had fired weapons prior to death.[77]

Ranta released her final report on 17 March. She concluded that there was no evidence that the victims were anything other than unarmed civilians and that many of them had been shot a close range, execution-style. Ranta went on to conclude that what happened at Racak on 15 January was in her mind without doubt 'a crime against humanity'. Seven key points emerged from this and other reports.

1. The dead were unarmed civilians who had not fired weapons.
2. The bodies had been moved before inspection but there were many reasons why this would have happened and nothing suggests that they had been moved by the UÇK in order to create the appearance of a massacre.
3. KVM verifiers were correct to identity that many of the dead had been shot at very close range.

4. The Serbian pathologists concluded that there had been fabrication of evidence before they had conducted autopsies.
5. The fact that the bodies were left unsupervised between 17 and 21 January increases the possibility that they had been moved and tampered with by the Serbs.
6. The Serb and Belarussioan pathologists used outdated methods and reached unsupported conclusions.[78]
7. The Serbs had actively obstructed the ICTY investigation.[79]

By piecing together reports by different organisations, many of which were frequently critical of NATO, it is possible to build a detailed picture of events in Racak. Nevertheless many commentators in the West continue to argue that the massacre was 'staged' by the UÇK in an attempt to persuade NATO to intervene against the Serbs. Their key arguments are that, first, the Serb attackers were accompanied by the cameras of Associated Press and verifiers of the KVM, neither of which reported a massacre. Secondly, the television pictures show the village to be deserted, so any Kosovar Albanian casualties must have been UÇK fighters. Thirdly, the verifiers were not shown the bodies until the next morning, giving the UÇK time to gather the bodies of its fighters and arrange them to give the appearance of a massacre. Fourthly, the Finnish pathologists generally agreed with their Serb counterparts and Ranta steadfastly refused to describe what happened at Racak as a massacre. Finally, William Walker deliberately overreacted and refused to investigate the events properly because his remit was to find grounds to legitimise an armed NATO intervention.[80]

These arguments are wildly inaccurate. The Associated Press cameraman's pictures actually show very little. Indeed, witness reports suggest that the killings probably took place after he had left Racak. The fact that there were no villagers caught on camera was because those who remained were hiding in Sadik Osmani's house at the time. The claim that the Serb forces were accompanied by KVM verifiers is simply erroneous. Verifiers were expressly told not to enter the village and were only given a partial view by their vantage point. If most of the killings were committed in the general area where the bodies were discovered the KVM verifiers could have neither seen them or observe people being led out of the village in that direction. The verifiers did not see the bodies until next morning because they had not been discovered until the early hours of that morning. Most villagers believed that the victims had been taken to a police station but some did tell verifiers on the night of the 15 January that they heard gunshots from the direction of where the bodies were subsequently found. Much was made of the fact that Ranta did not describe what happened in Racak as a massacre. The Finnish report is a highly detailed and technical piece of work. The word 'massacre' is not a precise legal term, so Ranta instead referred to what happened as a 'crime against humanity', which is a crime that falls under the jurisdiction of the ICTY. The Finnish report departed substantially from the Serb and Belarussian pathology report. The final point concerning NATO's desire for a war ignores the fact that international consensus on using force had waned considerably since October.

Given the weight of evidence it is strange that the conspiracy theory has taken such a hold among Western commentators. The reason for this can be traced back to the discord between Walker and his deputy, Gabriel Keller. It was the French newspaper, *Le Monde*, which first exposed the so-called conspiracy. A day after the massacre, Keller briefed French journalists that 'there was something wrong' with the apparent massacre. This prompted journalists and academics to piece together the story of a staged massacre, a story that continues to hold credence in the West today. That story hinges on there being significant lapses of time during which the UÇK would have been able to move bodies in order to stage a massacre and a belief that some NATO states were intent on unleashing air strikes. Thanks to numerous detailed reports we now know that no such time lapses occurred. Subsequent debates within the Alliance about how to respond to the massacre suggest that there was no consensus on using force.

Summary

Although the KVM remained in place until the eve of Operation Allied Force, the Racak massacre effectively sounded the death knell for the period of *unarmed intervention*. Because it was unarmed, the KVM relied on high levels of consent from both parties and progress towards a political settlement. Ultimately, the Hill plan failed to satisfy either side and there was very little international interest in using sticks and carrots to coerce acceptance.

Herein lay the major problem. Milošević had only agreed to accept the KVM when threatened with NATO air strikes. Although the Activation Order that was issued in October remained in place it was clear that consensus within the Alliance on using force had diminished. There were two major reasons for this. Firstly, there was a dramatic reduction of violence. Both sides acknowledged that they were constrained by the presence of verifiers. This was greatly aided by the fact that the Serbs believed the UÇK to be a vanquished force and because the mission was deployed in winter, the harshness of which precluded significant military operations. There was widespread evidence that both sides were preparing for further clashes in the spring. Nevertheless, the absence of burning villages made it very difficult to sustain the consensus on using force.

The second reason for the loss of consensus was the facade of progress on political dialogue. Maintaining political dialogue based on the Hill proposals remained the preferred policy in the West despite the 2 November deadline having passed almost unnoticed. What Western states shared with the Yugoslav president was a belief that Kosovo should remain part of Yugoslavia and that a political settlement be based on the creation of democratic local political institutions to manage conflict. There was therefore little desire to increase tensions by threatening to use force in a situation where violence initiated by the MUP and VJ had decreased substantially.

With Racak, however, the period of *unarmed intervention* came to an end. Its exposure in the media galvanised the Contact Group into action. After a two-week period of consultation, the Group adopted a new strategy based on *coercive diplomacy* and grand summitry.

5
From Rambouillet to Paris

The peace conference that began in the French chateaux at Rambouillet on 6 February has been described as the greatest 'what if' of international society's engagement with the Kosovo conflict.[1] While this is something of an overstatement given the missed opportunities of the early 1990s that were discussed earlier, there is little doubt that in February 1999 the interim settlement proposed at Rambouillet represented the best last chance for peace. The amount of consensus in the West on whether to use force increased in the immediate aftermath of the Racak massacre, so that although the KVM remained in place, international involvement reluctantly shifted from *unarmed intervention* to *coercive diplomacy*. This transition occurred in the final two weeks of January with debate in the West about whether to act on NATO's Activation Order. This involved discussion about whether to issue an ultimatum to the belligerents and the likelihood of achieving an international consensus on using force to impose an interim political settlement. While these debates proved inconclusive, the Russian government was persuaded of the need for an international summit aimed at securing acceptance of a peace plan based on arrangements being worked on by Christopher Hill even though that process was underpinned by an explicit threat of force by NATO.

Responding to Racak: debating force

NATO's response to the Racak massacre was almost immediate. On the day that the Yugoslav government ordered KVM chief William Walker to leave the country, General Wesley Clark (SACEUR) and General Klaus Naumann (Chairman of the NATO Military Committee) were despatched to Belgrade to reaffirm NATO's military resolve.[2] They carried with them a message from the Alliance's Secretary-General, Javier Solana. Solana condemned the massacre as 'a flagrant violation of international humanitarian law' and demanded that Milošević co-operate with the ICTY in its search for the perpetrators. Solana's statement reminded the Serb president that NATO's Activation Order remained in place but stopped short of making a renewed threat of force – this was a debate that the Alliance and other states were about to have.[3] A few days earlier, though, Solana had told journalists that, 'it is difficult to see what more we can do without using force',[4] a conclusion that many people were beginning to reach. William Walker decided to support the diplomatic initiative by flying to Belgrade to respond in person to Milošević's decision to expel him from Yugoslavia. The KVM chief's planned trip was put on hold though when advisors warned that taking to the air would provide the Serbs with an opportunity to divert Walker out of the country. Heeding this advice, Walker opted to remain in Pristina.[5]

The North Atlantic Council sent Clark and Naumann because they believed that sending military men to Belgrade would persuade the Yugoslav president that the Alliance was serious and its threats credible. This was a tactic that Richard Holbrooke had used several times before and Clark had played an active role in Holbrooke's negotiations with Milošević prior to both the Holbrooke–Milošević agreement of October 1998 and the Dayton agreement in 1995. Naumann, though, was more sceptical about the chances of success. He told the British parliamentary committee on defence that:

> We had been sent against our advice to Belgrade. We had asked not to be sent since we knew that the task we had been given was not a military task. I should say the instruments that the [North Atlantic] Council had kindly provided us with to persuade Mr. Milošević were not really a stick but what I would call a rubber baton.[6]

These reservations were confirmed by Milošević's reaction to the renewed threat. Naumann's account of his discussions with Milošević reveal that rather than changing his course of action, the Yugoslav president was not at all worried about the threat of NATO air strikes:

> He [Milošević] said to us 'I will solve the Kosovo problem once and for all in spring 1999'...We asked him, 'how will you do it Mr President?'. 'We will do to them what we did to the Albanians in Drenica in 1945'. So we said to him, 'Mr. President, we do not know what you did to the Albanians in 1945. Would you be so kind as to

elaborate. It is quite simple [he said]. We got them together and we shot them'. That was his answer.[7]

The Alliance's new coercive diplomacy was not resonating in Belgrade. Indeed, this very point was made on the same day by the American Ambassador to NATO, Sandy Vershbow. Vershbow told the BBC that should Milošević refuse to succumb to the Alliance's threats, an air campaign could be launched within days. However, he correctly gauged the nature of the on-going discussions in Belgrade when he observed that Milošević 'doesn't seem to understand how serious the situation is... I don't think our patience will last very long'.[8]

It is not difficult to see why Milošević was unperturbed by the renewed threats. He had heard much the same before. Moreover, the Russian government was swift to react to NATO's threats by repeating its opposition to the use force and Robert Gelbard (famous for labelling the UÇK as terrorists only days before the first Serb onslaught in March 1998) insisted that the Kosovar Albanian fighters shared the blame for the increase of violence.[9] Although lacking resonance, the threats were backed up with action. The North Atlantic Council decided to increase the readiness of its assigned forces so that air operations over Yugoslavia could take place only 48-hours after a political decision to act.

These mixed messages were caused by a lack of consensus within the Alliance and even within particular Alliance members about how to proceed. In the US, the Pentagon and White House opposed the use of force. William Cohen and Sandy Berger were both sceptical about the utility of force particularly because the strategy did not have a clear military or political end state.[10] These two departments agreed that the best response to the unravelling of the peace process would be to 'beef up' the KVM by deploying more verifiers and equipping them with helicopters, whilst trying to reinvigorate the Hill process.[11] The problem with the 'October-plus' (as it became known) plan was that it contained no means by which to achieve the latter objective. It was the lack of progress towards a political settlement rather than inadequacies on the part of the KVM that had led to the unravelling of the Holbrooke–Milošević agreement. Without anything new to offer it was unclear how 'October-plus' would get off the ground without being seen as yet another fudge designed to evade acting on the threat of force that had been made some months earlier.

The Racak massacre turned this debate in favour of the hawks in the State Department. Madeleine Albright, the Secretary of State, was very disappointed with the 'October-plus' formulation and warned that the

KVM would be unable to halt the excessive use of force by the Serbs because it lacked enforcement capabilities. Racak graphically demonstrated this point. In the immediate aftermath of the massacre the State Department argued vociferously for an immediate limited cruise missile attack against Yugoslavia, similar to the attacks planned by NATO in October 1998. The Pentagon remained reticent, arguing that any use of force be linked to a political end state, something that remained elusive. To overcome this concern, Albright set to work linking the threat of force with a political goal. The result was put to the other departments on 19 January, only four days after Racak. It was based on an idea that Sandy Vershbow had aired sometime earlier. Vershbow had argued that Kosovo should be turned into a UN protectorate through the use of force if necessary.[12] Albright's plan involved using a credible threat of force to coerce the parties into accepting a comprehensive peace plan. This would be based on the Hill plan but with one important addition: There would be a robust NATO-led peacekeeping force to enforce compliance. The Bosnian and KVM experiences persuaded Albright that the imposition of a NATO led force was absolutely essential if any credible and long-lasting peace was to be achieved. Furthermore, it was clear that neither the US nor its European allies (with the possible exception of the UK) would countenance deploying ground forces in anything less than a 'permissive' environment as it came to be known. Put another way, Albright had to find a way to persuade the Serbs and Kosovar Albanians to accept such a KFOR force, as Holbrooke had done when he persuaded the Serbs, Croats and Bosnians to accept the deployment of IFOR in 1995.

It was not only in the US that such debates were taking place. In France, a sceptical media had been briefed by Gabriel Keller to doubt the validity of the Racak massacre. This prompted Gaullists to question the American diplomatic strategy, arguing that it provided evidence of US dominance over Europe.[13] The battle lines in Paris were not drawn along the right-left axis but along perceptions of the role of the US in Europe.[14] Similarly, Gerhard Schröder's centre-left coalition in Germany was unsure of how to respond to Racak. The previous October, the Budestag had voted by a massive majority of 500 to allow its armed forces to participate in a NATO intervention in Kosovo.[15] There was a huge difference, though, between participating in a post-agreement peacekeeping force and actually attacking a sovereign state. In particular, there was a danger that the smaller party in the government coalition, a red-green coalition (Bündnis 90/Die Grünen) that included several pacifists, would reject ultimatum diplomacy and the use of force putting the government's majority in jeopardy. As these debates raged around Europe and North America, it is hardly surprising that Milošević was receiving mixed messages giving him reason enough to doubt NATO's credibility.

This lack of credibility was reinforced by a shortage of forces available to the Alliance in the immediate vicinity of Kosovo. As we noted in Chapter 4, NATO had established a small French led force inside Macedonia. This force was there to extract the KVM should its position have become untenable. However, sources within defence policy circles point out that this deployment was something of a hollow gesture. Numbering less than 4,000 the extraction force lacked firepower and mobility.[16] Indeed, the British parliamentary defence committee concluded that if it had been called upon to conduct its extraction mission in the face of opposition from Serb forces it would probably have been unsuccessful. As the committee put it, 'had Milošević sought to put the extraction force to the test, even only in its limited role as a rescue mission, its limitations and NATO's credibility might have been rudely exposed'.[17] To redress this credibility problem, the Pentagon deployed the aircraft carrier, *USS Enterprise*, and two support ships both capable of firing Tomahawk cruise missiles into the Adriatic. The British government also increased the number of aircraft it had based in Italy at the Gioia del Colle airbase and the French did likewise, announcing the deployment of a carrier into the region.

Having won inter-departmental consensus (albeit lukewarm in some quarters) for her plan for an ultimatum linking the threat of force to acceptance of a political settlement, Albright now set about persuading allies, some of whom were keener than others. On 21 January, Bill Clinton and Tony Blair spoke on the telephone and agreed that force should be used if the diplomatic initiative that they were about to promote through the Contact Group failed to impress Milošević. A day later, Albright travelled to London to present the plan to the Contact Group. She argued that the only way forward was to set down an ultimatum demanding agreement within a specific timeframe and threatening that force would be used if compliance was not forthcoming. The Secretary of State later elaborated on her proposed strategy:

> If President Milošević refuses to accept the Contact Group proposals, or has allowed repression in Kosovo to continue, he can expect NATO air strikes. If the Kosovo Albanians obstruct progress ... they cannot expect NATO and the international community to bail them

out. ... If the two sides do reach agreement, we will need to concentrate our efforts on making sure that it is successfully implemented.[18]

Albright's attempts to persuade her European allies initially floundered. The main problem that the allies had with the American plan was the time period that she proposed. The Secretary of State insisted that the ultimatum should be issued immediately and a 96-hour deadline set for compliance to be completed. Several NATO members were also uneasy with the demands being made of the Serbs, which as well as including unlimited access for the ICTY also insisted that they allow the KVM to set up a radio station.

Albright's initial proposals to the Contact Group fell somewhere between the original 'October-plus' plan, based on maintaining and bolstering the KVM and her subsequent post-Racak plan. State Department officials believed that the Contact Group would baulk at the prospect of demanding a political settlement and imposing a NATO-led peacekeeping force, so Albright was advised to tone down her demands to make them more immediately realisable.[19] In fact, this compromise had the opposite effect. Many allies believed that using force in response to non-compliance on these limited demands on marginal issues was disproportionate. As one source at NATO headquarters in Brussels put it, 'that would mean that if Milošević failed to comply with all the demands, NATO would be obliged to launch air strikes, and I don't think anyone in the Alliance would want to bomb if Milošević refused to set up a radio station for the verification team'.[20] Several allies, particularly France and Italy, were also concerned that threatening or actually using force against Yugoslavia would encourage the UÇK to continue or widen its campaign and they were keen not to be seen to be supporting armed separatists.

The Americans agreed to rethink the ultimatum and relate it directly to a political settlement based on the Hill plan – which had been Albright's preferred approach in the first place. Even the Russian representative concurred. The Contact Group agreed to meet again in London a week later on 29 January to continue work on the basis of the American plan. In between the two meetings, Albright flew to Moscow for informal talks with the Russian Foreign Minister, Igor Ivanov, the man who had given NATO a tacit nod of approval at the Heathrow airport meeting. Although Ivanov continued to insist that using force against Yugoslavia would be unacceptable to Russia, he did concur that the *threat* of force could be used to persuade the Serbs to attend a peace conference aimed at reaching a political settlement.[21] As well as Yeltsin's lasting irritation with Milošević, Ivanov's position was shaped by two considerations. Firstly, he was keen to ensure that the Contact Group, which Russia was a member of, held primacy over NATO in the diplomatic process. Indeed throughout the subsequent negotiations, both Ivanov and Hubert Védrine, the French Foreign Minister, argued that NATO should only use force if invited to do so by the Contact Group. This was not something the French government had insisted on in 1998 when it authorised the passage of the Activation Order. It was a position they developed in response to their growing belief that the US was dominating the diplomatic effort in a way that it had not done before.[22] Secondly, Ivanov concurred with Albright's assessment that threatening force was likely to be the only means of persuading Milošević to negotiate sincerely and the Russian Foreign Minister was primarily driven by a desire for a political solution that included Russia as a key player.[23]

The Contact Group reconvened at Lancaster House in London on 29 January to revisit the ultimatum plan. Russian acceptance of the plan persuaded reluctant allies such as Germany to concur and thus agreement was reached reasonably swiftly. The Contact Group summoned the Yugoslavs and Kosovar Albanians to send delegations to the Rambouillet château near Paris and instructed them that should they fail to reach an agreement within 21 days international diplomacy would be replaced by NATO military force. The proposed settlement would include provision for its enforcement by a NATO-led armed force. The negotiations would be mediated by three diplomats: Christopher Hill, whose plan would underpin the talks, Wolfgang Petritsch the EU's regional envoy, and a Russian negotiator later confirmed as Boris Mayorski. They also made several immediate demands. These included compliance with Security Council Resolution 1203 and cooperation with the ICTY in its investigation of the Racak massacre. Lest there be any doubt about the Group speaking with one mind, the final paragraph of its statement spelled the situation out clearly:

> The future of the people of Kosovo is in the hands of leaders in Belgrade and Kosovo. They must commit themselves now to complete the negotiations on a political settlement within 21 days to bring peace to Kosovo. *The Contact Group will hold both sides accountable if they fail to take the opportunity* now offered to them, just as the group stands ready to work with both sides to realise the benefits for them of a peaceful solution.[24]

The Contact Group's adoption of Albright's ultimatum plan was swiftly endorsed by Kofi Annan, the UN Secretary-General and the Security Council, and was supported by the North Atlantic Council. Kofi Annan joined Igor Ivanov in supporting the threat of force to achieve a political solution. Recalling what he described as the 'lessons of Bosnia', he observed that, 'the bloody wars of the last decade have left us with no illusions about the difficulty of halting internal conflict by reason or by force – particularly against the wishes of the government of a sovereign state', adding 'but nor have they left us with any illusions about the need to use force when all other means have failed'[25] before going on to indicate that the situation in Kosovo may have reached such a stage. The Security Council also demonstrated that Russia was taking a full part in the coercive diplomacy by issuing a presidential statement endorsing the Contact Group's decision within hours of that decision being taken.[26]

A day after the Contact Group decision, the North Atlantic Council debated the measures that the Alliance should take to add credibility to the threat of force. The Council gave Javier Solana the authority to instruct SHAPE (Supreme Headquarters Allied Powers Europe, NATO's European Headquarters) when to commence the air attack. Sir John Goulden, the British representative on the Council at the time insisted that this decision made NATO's threat more credible but drew attention to an important caveat. Whilst delegating the authority to Solana, the Council insisted that the decision to act should only be taken after intensive consultation with the allies' political leaders.[27] Goulden identified two problems that undermined this decision's efficacy. First, he argued that the Council's decision may have been premature because the tripwires for using force (the fate of the forthcoming Rambouillet conference) had not yet been triggered and the decision as to when they had been triggered lay in the hands of the political leaders, reducing Solana's effective authority to launch the military campaign. Secondly, he noted that although the modified Hill plan included provision for a substantial NATO-led peacekeeping force, the Alliance had not begun planning such an implementation mission let alone making the necessary preparatory deployments. NATO could have been expected to begin deployment as early as 21 days after the Contact Group statement but the North Atlantic Council had not even called for troop contributions.[28] The Activation Order for the implementation force (KFOR) was not issued for another three weeks, largely because the American administration was divided on the issue of whether it should contribute ground troops. Although the Contact Group was adopting an essentially

American plan, the President's National Security Adviser told journalists not to count on them sending troops to enforce the settlement.[29]

The Contact Group gave Robin Cook the task of delivering the ultimatum to Milošević. Once again, there was little to suggest that Milošević took either the threat, or Cook's presentation of it, at all seriously. Emerging from the meeting, the British Foreign Secretary revealed that Milošević had agreed to study the international peace plan and respond within a few days and that he had pressed the Yugoslav leader to call an immediate halt to the violence. There was little evidence of this on the ground, however. On the same day that the Contact Group met in London, Serb forces killed 24 men in the village of Rogovo. Although the UÇK later admitted that 17 of them were in fact UÇK fighters, the Rogovo killings exposed the fact that Racak was not an isolated incident and that the ceasefire agreed in October was now a dead letter. After Cook had left Belgrade for Pristina to present the ultimatum to Kosovar Albanian leaders, Milošević swiftly unveiled his reply. He insisted that although talks were a possibility, there could be no immediate ceasefire, no prospect of independence, and as Kosovo was part of Serbia the conflict should be resolved without outside interference.[30] Foreign Minister Jovanović went one step further, denouncing NATO's ultimatum as 'an open and clear threat of aggression against the FRY'.[31] Jovanović overlooked the fact the ultimatum was issued not by NATO but by the Contact Group, which included Russia.

Cook's mission fared little better when he met leading Kosovar Albanians. UÇK leaders, Hasim Thaçi and Jakup Krasniqi replied only that they too would respond in a few days and not before the organisation had done some serious soul-searching. Some, such as Adem Demaçi, argued that it should not be involved in the negotiations at all because the proposed settlement did not offer a path to independence. Others heeded Albright's threats and argued that the UÇK should be involved in the talks but should not sign an agreement that did not provide a clear mechanism for independence. Regional commanders such as Remy and Selimi remained deeply sceptical, particularly about promises of an armed implementation mission led by NATO. They were also concerned that their political leadership would be coerced into signing an agreement that did not meet their demands if they went to Rambouillet. Of all the Kosovar Albanians Cook met, only Ibrahim Rugova promised to attend and it became clear that putting together a coherent, representative, and authoritative Kosovar Albanian delegation would be a difficult task.

As the Serbs and Albanians debated amongst themselves, NATO continued apace with its military preparations for both potential air strikes and the deployment of an implementation force. In Brussels, NATO's military planning staff began drawing up plans for the rapid deployment of five brigades, three of them armoured, with reserves based in Macedonia. Sources at NATO headquarters in Brussels indicated that Javier Solana was prepared to use his authority to authorise air strikes within 96 hours should there be a repeat of the Racak massacre whilst negotiations were on-going,[32] a position at considerable variance with the caveats outlined above by Britain's representative to the North Atlantic Council.

Cook indicated that there would be no action against Milošević for not sending a team to Rambouillet if the Kosovar Albanians failed to send a properly representative delegation. This slightly changed the rules of the game. Now, the Kosovar Albanians simply had to attend. If they did not the Serbs would not have to attend either. If they did, the Serbs would be bombed by NATO if they did not also attend. It is not surprising, therefore, that both sides agreed to attend within a day of each other. The Contact Group constructed its threats in such a way that both sides realised that either they should both go or neither go. As the UÇK recognised that it could not win a war against the Yugoslavs, particularly if international society cut the flow of money from émigré's in Switzerland, Germany, and the US, non-attendance was not really an option and Adem Demaçi was swiftly marginalised by the liberation army's political leadership. After a meeting of the general staff, on 2 February, Jakup Krasniqi announced that the UÇK would indeed send representatives to Rambouillet with the proviso that they lead the Kosovar Albanian delegation.[33]

Milošević decided that he would send a delegation as soon as he heard that the Kosovar Albanians would be attending. The decision came at the end of a masquerade aimed at reinforcing domestic support for the Yugoslav delegation's tough negotiating stance. After denouncing the Contact Group ultimatum and airing unacceptable proposals, the government – in the shape of Deputy Prime Minister and idiosyncratic former opposition leader, Vuk Drasković – announced that the decision whether to attend would be made by parliament, which was in fact little more than a rubber stamp for Milošević. On 4 February, the parliament duly voted by 227–3 in favour of sending a delegation. However, it explicitly instructed the delegation to block any attempt to part Kosovo from Serbia or impose an international presence that was greater than the KVM presence already in place.[34] The radical nationalist,

Vojislav Šešelj, whose party supported the government in this, told parliament that NATO, 'would be prevented with all available means' and declared, 'a national allergy to the mere name of France'.[35] Nevertheless, the Contact Group secured the agreement of both parties to attend the conference.

As was noted earlier, the plan that was to be presented at Rambouillet was heavily based on the ill-fated Hill plan. Certainly, the basic list of principles were similar to those in the Hill plan, though there were three notable additions. The settlement offered at Rambouillet was an interim arrangement with a process of international arbitration about the province's final status after a three-year period. There was more in the way of international implementation and oversight. Although KFOR's so-called military annex attracted a lot of attention, the OSCE was envisaged as the lead agency in the international implementation effort. Also, the so-called military annex, which was not shown to the Kosovar Albanian delegation until two days before the second deadline contained a bombshell for them: Not only would the UÇK have to adhere to a ceasefire it would also have to disband and hand over its weapons to the NATO-led peacekeepers.

It was therefore after a considerable amount of doubt and international debate that the strategy of *unarmed intervention* was abandoned in favour of *coercive diplomacy*. Consensus had to be built within individual states, among NATO members, and between NATO and Russia. The problem with coercive diplomacy is that the threat must be credible and the on-going public international debate detracted from that credibility, ultimately leading to its failure. There was very little that was new in the initial interim settlement that was proposed at Rambouillet but there were three changes which if anything made the proposals *more* unpalatable to both sides.

Rambouillet – the greatest what if?

The parties gathered at Rambouillet on 6 February. Getting them there proved to be more problematic than the organisers had first anticipated. The Yugoslav authorities attempted to prevent the three UÇK representatives from leaving Pristina airport, arguing that they were terrorists who did not have proper documentation. The rest of the Kosovar Albanian delegation insisted that they would not leave Pristina without their colleagues. In Paris, Ratko Marković insisted that there could be no negotiations with 'killers and kidnappers' while Wolfgang Petritsch insisted that the UÇK had to be involved if the talks and subsequent settlement were to have any credibility.[36] Cook and Védrine intervened once it became apparent that the Kosovar Albanian delegation would not be arriving. The foreign ministers instructed Belgrade that the talks would not go ahead without the full compliment of Kosovar Albanian delegates and that the Yugoslav government would be held responsible for the failure, with all the consequences that entailed. Under pressure, the Serbs relented and allowed the delegates to depart.[37]

Rambouillet is a 30-roomed, three-floored, French châteaux, about 30 kilometres from Paris. This layout was well suited to proximity-style negotiations. The two parties had their own floors with separate facilities and the mediators who spent two weeks shuttling between them had theirs. The international presence within the châteaux was immense. Each of the six Contact Group members maintained their own diplomatic staff, occasionally increased with foreign ministers and their entourages. In an effort to recreate the seclusion that was achieved at Dayton, the delegates were forbidden from leaving the conference compound. This isolation was never achieved because of Rambouillet's geographical position, the proliferation of mobile phones, and the fact that Milošević remained in Belgrade, ostensibly fearing that he would be apprehended by the ICTY should he step foot in Western Europe but also assuming that his absence would reduce the likelihood of meaningful progress.

The negotiations were based on discussion of an interim settlement and the adjoining implementation annexes that were presented by the Contact Group. The delegations were to work separately and submit written revisions or points of clarification. If the revisions were acceptable to both sides they would be adopted by the Contact Group plan. If they were not accepted, the original plan would remain unchanged. The mediators laid down ten non-negotiable principles and insisted that any proposed changes be consistent with them.[38] These principles were:

- An immediate end to the violence.
- Peaceful settlement of the conflict through dialogue.
- The agreement would be an interim one for the period of three years.
- There could be no unilateral change to this interim status.
- The territorial integrity of Yugoslavia and its neighbours must be respected.
- The rights of members of all national communities must be respected.
- There would be free and fair elections in Kosovo, supervised by the OSCE.

- Neither party should prosecute anyone for crimes related to the Kosovo conflict (with the exception of the ICTY).
- There would be an amnesty and release of political prisoners.
- There would be international involvement and full co-operation by the parties on implementation.

A minor diplomatic crisis was caused when the Serbian delegation began the conference by insisting that the Kosovar Albanians sign a declaration endorsing these principles. This they could not do because accepting the principle of maintaining Yugoslavia's territorial integrity meant giving up the one aspiration that united the delegation. The Serbs refused to continue with the negotiations until their adversaries had accepted the basic principles in writing. The Contact Group responded with carrots and sticks. The French delegation insisted that adherence to the principles was a precondition for participation, so although the Kosovar Albanians would not sign a declaration they had inferred their acceptance of the principles by appearing at Rambouillet.[39] The two delegations interpreted the principles differently and were encouraged to do so by the mediators who controlled the flow of information between the parties. While the Serb delegates saw the territorial guarantee as set in stone, the Kosovar Albanians were advised that as the settlement was an interim one accepting Yugoslavia's territorial integrity during the interim would not prejudice their chances of full independence when the province's final status was decided. Meanwhile, the British and American delegations wielded sticks in order to put an end to Yugoslav intransigence. Madeleine Albright announced her intention to visit the talks and Robin Cook publicly identified the Serb delegation as being responsible for obstructing progress.[40] Ultimately, the sticks and carrots persuaded the Yugoslavs to drop their demand and allow the negotiations to continue.

Both delegations contained an eclectic mix of people, which made the mediators' task harder than it already was. The Serb delegation was made up of low-level officials. Although the Serb President, Milan Milutinović, a close Milošević ally of long standing, attended towards the end of the negotiations the delegation was initially fronted by Ratko Marković, Serbia's Deputy Prime Minister. This emphasised Milošević's belief that the Kosovo problem was an internal Serb republic matter, and not a matter either for international society or even the Yugoslav federation.[41] The Serb delegation also consisted of representatives of Kosovo's numerous ethnic groups including Roma, Gorani, and Turks, and even a loyal Kosovar Albanian delegate who was head of an unheard of political party. Marc Weller, who was present at Rambouillet in his capacity as legal adviser to the Kosovar Albanians, noted that the constitution of the Serb delegation reflected the fact that they were not there to play a major role in the forthcoming diplomatic struggle and that when the delegation began to indulge in serious negotiation it was considerably strengthened by the addition of Milutinović and professional negotiators and constitutional experts.[42]

The Kosovar Albanian delegation included virtually every prominent member of the community's political elite, with the lone exception of Adem Demaçi who did more damage to his own political standing than he did to the negotiations by staying away. At the insistence of the UÇK, Hashim Thaçi was elected as head of the delegation. The LDK was represented by Rugova (who still considered himself to be the President of Kosovo) and Fehmi Agani. The second largest political party, the United Democratic Movement (LBD), which had broken away from Rugova after the Dayton failure was represented by its leader Rexhep Qosja and former political prisoner, Hydajet Hyseni. Veton Surroi, editor of the independent newspaper *Koha Ditore* proffered the necessary compromises between these disparate factions. It was Surroi who was responsible for keeping the negotiations on track when there appeared to be little consensus on whether to accept the interim settlement or not.

Negotiations – week 1

The conference was opened by the co-chairs, Robin Cook and Hubert Védrine on 6 February amidst a general mood of pessimism. It was clear from the outset that there were major problems. Not only were the two sides poles apart in their aspirations; they were negotiating a settlement that closely resembled one that they had both previously rejected. The mediators were also divided. There was particular resentment among NATO allies who were not part of the Contact Group and were therefore being expected to endorse a threat of force to support a diplomatic initiative that they were not involved with. This predicament particularly exercised the Greek government, whose public was overwhelmingly opposed to the Alliance's position.[43] Moreover, there was concern in some quarters that NATO was not itself represented in the châteaux. General Naumann told the British parliamentary defence committee that:

> We saw one weakening of NATO's involvement and that was the phase of the Rambouillet and Paris talks where NATO was not admitted to be present. We were not allowed to offer any advice at all. That

led to some problems of cohesion within the [North Atlantic] Council since they all knew that five of the council members [the Contact Group members] had some national information but, as always in international negotiations, the degree of sharing was never 100 percent.[44]

The work began with the presentation of a proposed political settlement contained in a framework agreement and three implementation annexes: One on a proposed constitution for Kosovo, one on provisions for elections, and one on an implementation ombudsman.[45] Although the Kosovar Albanian delegation began detailed scrutiny of the proposals the debate in the first few days focused on their demand for an immediate cessation of hostilities. Not surprisingly, the Serbs rejected this idea. Progress was made when the two sides issued a joint statement condemning a bomb attack that killed three Kosovar Albanians in the centre of Pristina on 6 February. On other fronts, however, the omens were more troubling. The Serbs leaked a story claiming that the Kosovar Albanians had signed the ten core principles mentioned earlier. This immediately increased the amount of pressure that Thaçi and Krasniqi were put under by both Demaçi and the regional UÇK commanders who had direct mobile telephone links with their representatives in the châteaux. The claim was fatuous and was denounced as such by the Contact Group.[46]

While the Serb delegation did very little that was constructive in the first week, the Kosovar Albanian delegation set to work putting together written and oral submissions on the proposed settlement. In retrospect, some participants have come to believe that this cooperation may have had the opposite effect to the one that was intended. It persuaded the Contact Group that they could probably count on Kosovar Albanian agreement rather than highlighting areas for revision. On 8 February, Blerim Shala delivered an oral submission to the Contact Group that welcomed the proposals but insisted that the final document include a clause on a referendum on independence and a future role for the UÇK.[47] On the same day, the delegation created a working group under Fehmi Agani, tasked with producing a written response to the proposals. When the delegation submitted written comments they noted that while the underlying principles were acceptable, revisions would have to be made. In particular, in addition to the two points mentioned above, they insisted that the powers allotted to 'national communities' be reconsidered because as they stood they would give the Serbs an effective veto over all Kosovo legislation.

In contrast to the frenetic activity in the Kosovar Albanian delegation, the Serb delegates failed to respond to the proposals. Robin Cook returned to the châteaux on 9 February, insisting that the talks were 'three-quarters of the way there'.[48] Precisely what grounds the British Foreign Secretary was basing this assessment on is unknown. His very presence at the talks suggested to many observers that they were in danger of collapse. Moreover, splits were beginning to open up between the mediators. The Russian representative, Boris Mayorski, openly denounced the Kosovar Albanian insistence that there should be military intervention in Kosovo (which the other five members of the Contact Group believed to be part of the plan) and repudiated suggestions that there should be any compromise to Yugoslavia's territorial integrity.[49] This came at the very time that a NATO representative was admitted to the châteaux and Madeleine Albright was telling television viewers on *France Channel 3* that a decision had been taken to bomb Serb targets if the talks failed due to Serbian recalcitrance.[50]

With the talks seemingly on the brink of collapse before the end of the first week owing to the lack of Serb participation, the mediators welcomed the arrival of Serbian Prime Minister, Milan Milutinović. The Serb delegation immediately issued a statement that reiterated the ten core principles – hardly evidence of five days of productive negotiation.[51] However, Milutinović was joined by several constitutional experts, which prompted the delegation to become a little more proactive. The Serb president identified what he described as:

> An intrinsic contradiction between a verbal commitment to sovereignty and territorial integrity of Serbia ... while at the same time is it sought to offer and prepare proposals related to constitutional solutions for a sovereign country or even the solutions with a conferral character, actually intending to limit its sovereignty and integrity.[52]

He continued by calling for face-to-face negotiations with the Kosovar Albanians and repeating the demand that they sign the Contact Group's ten principles. In less formal comments, Milutinović offered the first indication that Yugoslavia would attempt to take NATO on, calculating that the Alliance lacked the political will and cohesion to see its threats through. He insisted that, 'this is our land and we shall fight to defend it, even if NATO is stronger'.[53]

As the first deadline approached, NATO members attempted to increase the pressure on the Serbs. The US finally agreed that it would contribute to the planned NATO-led peacekeeping force. Moreover, Albright suggested that a deal could be reached with the Kosovar

Albanians, throwing down a challenge to the Serbs. This brought members of both delegations together for the first time. To support this intensification of the diplomatic pressure, the EU promised a £350 million package of aid to Yugoslavia in the event of an agreement and not for the first or last time Boris Mayorski contradicted his earlier comments by suggesting that Russia would contribute troops to a future peacekeeping operation provided that Milošević agreed to it.[54]

Not surprisingly, the Contact Group concluded that enough progress had been made to allow the talks to be extended by a further week. This, despite the facts that the Serb delegation had not formally responded to the original plan, that the detailed concerns of the Kosovar Albanian delegation had not been addressed, and that the sensitive issues of final status, international implementation, and the dismemberment of the UÇK had not yet been raised.

Negotiations – week 2

The second week began with more evidence of splits amongst the NATO allies in the Contact Group. Madeleine Albright was criticised by EU officials for her likening of Hashim Thaçi to Gerry Adams. One official observed that, 'quite honestly, she's been unimpressive on the details' and 'it's clear that she hasn't grasped the full deal under discussion'.[55] Eager to prevent the US dominating proceedings and shaping the military responses, the French government insisted that any decision to use force by NATO be subordinate to a prior Contact Group decision. It also argued that force only be used with Security Council authorisation and that the OSCE take the role of lead agency in Kosovo.[56] The French received support from Germany, Italy and Russia, though the American and British governments rejected their proposals.

Evidence of splits among the mediators increased the recalcitrance of the parties because the divisions undermined the credibility of NATO's threats. The UÇK representatives refused to consider disbanding their army. Pleurat Sejdiu, one of their political representatives, argued that 'the UÇK is considered like an army by the Kosovan people and it will stay like that', while on the ground in Kosovo one of their regional commanders, Remy, insisted that, 'we'll put our weapons in warehouses only when we have liberated Kosovo'.[57] The mood music coming from the Serb delegation was equally unpromising. Milan Milutinović chose the beginning of the second week to reiterate his opposition to the proposed KFOR implementation force and the idea of an international armed presence in Kosovo per se.

With the talks floundering, the US broke with its Contact Group partners and launched a unilateral diplomatic initiative by despatching
Christopher Hill along with the chief Serbian negotiator Nikola Sainović
and British and French representatives to Belgrade for direct negotiations with Milošević. Although the Yugoslav president was not present
in Rambouillet, it was obvious to the mediators that he was keeping
in close touch with the Serb delegation and that if there was to be deal,
a hope that was looking increasingly forlorn, it was Milošević's agreement that would have to be obtained. Though an understandable
response to the obstacles being faced in Rambouillet, the American decision to take the case directly to Belgrade further splintered the Contact
Group. The German and French representatives feared that the US was
trying to strengthen the case for punitive strikes by stealth. More troubling, though, was the message that the Hill visit sent to the Kosovar
Albanian negotiators inside the châteaux. Wolfgang Petritsch was
reportedly so distressed at the decision to break the conference's fundamental rules that he chased Hill's car to the airport in an attempt to prevent him leaving Paris. Not only did the visit suggest that Rambouillet
was no longer the centre of the negotiations, the Kosovar Albanians
feared that key parts of the agreement were being unilaterally altered in
Belgrade. Moreover, the visit further alienated Russian mediator, Boris
Mayorski, who made formal protests to the American, British and
French governments and threatened to leave the conference. This
response underlined the fact that the Russian position was not driven
by a desire to protect their Slavic brethren as has so often been argued,
but rather by a keenness to be at the heart of the diplomatic process.
The mission to Belgrade could only have been beneficial to the Serbs,
yet Mayorski denounced it nevertheless.

Kosovar Albanian fears were realised almost immediately when, only
hours after the visit, the Serb delegation produced a written response
(their first) to the proposed interim settlement. According to Marc
Weller, this response 'was incompatible with the non-negotiable principles and the overall structure for a draft to the settlement'.[58] The Serbs
indicated their general acceptance of the political aspects of the agreement but insisted that they could not accept the forced withdrawal of
MUP units from the province let alone a NATO military presence there.

Things continued to get worse for the Kosovar Albanians when, a day
after the Serb proposals, the Contact Group delivered a substantially
revised version of the interim settlement. The Kosovar Albanian delegation was instructed that the Serbs had agreed to many of the proposals
and that the negotiations would now focus on the key aspects that

concerned them, leaving the majority of written points submitted by the Kosovar Albanian delegation unanswered.[59] The new draft strengthened the powers vested in the national communities giving them a veto over Kosovo legislation and attempted to resolve the thorny issue of Kosovo's constitutional status by placing it firmly under Belgrade's suzerainty.[60] There was worse to come with the presentation of the much-criticised 'military annex', which demanded the disbanding of the UÇK.

The military annex has been widely blamed for the failure of the talks and held by some as evidence that NATO members deliberately sabotaged the talks as a pretext for using force.[61] It was not for its provisions on the UÇK that it received this reputation, rather it was for its clauses on NATO's right of access throughout the whole of Yugoslavia. To many, the annex appeared to give NATO a right to station troops throughout Yugoslavia. It is not difficult to see where this view came from. Paragraph 8 of the annex gave KFOR 'free and unrestricted passage and unimpeded access throughout the FRY'. However, it is important to note that KFOR's rights outside of Kosovo were transitory and were aimed at securing the most efficient logistical routes to the province. Because the wording of the whole agreement tried to emphasise Yugoslavia's territorial integrity it was more difficult to limit the geographic scope of the annex. There is no doubt that the annex was unfortunately worded. It was hastily written and applied templates already in use for Croatia and Bosnia, both of which have very similarly worded Status of Forces agreements with NATO.

Although NATO has been blamed for this clumsiness, it is important to bear in mind that the Alliance was not itself formally represented at Rambouillet and therefore did not have officials on hand to explain the annex. It is also interesting to note Boris Mayorski's position on the implementation annexes. Whilst not wanting to be party to them he neither attempted to revise them nor block their delivery to the parties. Moreover, Milan Milutinović and the delegation in Rambouillet did not rule the annex out of hand. We will see in the next chapter that it was only once Milošević had decided that he could either rely on the Kosovar Albanians not signing or on NATO not gathering enough consensus for a protracted air campaign that he pointed to the military annex as reason enough for not signing the agreement. Once he had made this decision, Milošević also refused Christopher Hill's offer of the opportunity to rewrite the annex.

The portents were not looking good for the Kosovar Albanians. Only two days before the original deadline set by the Contact Group they had been offered an agreement that was substantially worse for them than the original, a settlement that included the complete dismemberment of the UÇK. Simultaneously, any consensus that had existed within the Contact Group on using force was rapidly eroding with Yeltsin warning Clinton in the strongest possible terms not to use force, though the White House later claimed that it never received such a message.[62] Sensing that the new draft had gone a long way to winning Milošević over, the chairmen – Robin Cook and Hubert Védrine – attempted a final push to persuade the Serb people to put pressure on their president to sign the agreement. Importantly, erroneously, and disastrously for the Kosovar Albanians, Cook and Védrine told the Serb media that 'the Kosovo Albanians will have to give up their demand for independence'.[63] Christopher Hill supported this renewed initiative to win Serb agreement by returning to Belgrade. On this occasion, however, Milošević refused to even see the American ambassador. This diplomatic initiative only compounded Kosovar Albanian disquiet with the way that the negotiations were progressing and reduced the likelihood of reaching agreement still further. What is more, they disaffected the Kosovar Albanians without persuading the Serbs to move any closer to signing an agreement. With each concession the Serbs secured the less likely it became that the Kosovar Albanians would sign. It was this refusal to sign that Milošević was banking on.

On 20 February, the day of the original deadline, it was clear that the two sides were little closer to reaching an agreement than they had been two weeks earlier. The Serbs had still not agreed to important parts of the settlement, were implacably opposed to the very idea of international implementation, and had yet to even offer a detailed response to key sections. The Kosovar Albanians, meanwhile, had responded in detail but had seen the proposed settlement altered in the Serbs favour and had been presented with a demand to disband the UÇK. Nevertheless, under pressure from Madeleine Albright who had returned to Rambouillet, the co-chairs extended this second deadline by 48 hours. This came after a day in which helicopters came to pick up the delegates and then departed with no one inside. It is difficult to see precisely why the deadline was extended given that so many issues remained unresolved. However, Albright's return to the fray rapidly changed the focus of the mediation effort. Whereas the main effort of the second week had been directed towards persuading the Serbs to accept the agreement by making changes to the draft settlement, Albright's intervention shifted the focus onto the Kosovar Albanians. It may have been that the mediators had expected the Kosovar Albanians to sign any agreement they were presented with. Whatever the reasons there had been very little effort to take their concerns on board until the decision was taken to extend the final deadline.

The decision to switch the main effort towards persuading the Kosovar Albanian delegation to accept the interim settlement was partially prompted by the changing conditions on the ground in the province. On 20 February, reports of Serb troop movements and reinforcement accompanied reports of increased violence around Pristina, suggesting that Milošević had decided to achieve his aims through military force rather than negotiation. Over the next two days Albright took command of the negotiations, focusing on direct talks with Milutinović and Thaçi. Meanwhile, the delegations at last began swapping detailed views on the substance of the proposals.

Milutinović continued to argue that Serbia accepted the political aspects of the agreement but could not accept an armed international implementation force. Thaçi was in an equally difficult position. He was telephoned by Adem Demaçi and informed that he was no longer the political head of the UÇK, a claim that he later found to be baseless. On 22 February Sulejman Selimi was named overall UÇK commander. Selimi telephoned Thaçi and instructed him on pain of death not to sign the agreement unless it guaranteed NATO intervention and independence.[64] The pressure on Thaçi was intensified by a reputed death threat from a member of the Serb delegation and a demand from Milan Milutinović that Interpol apprehend the UÇK leader on charges of terrorism. Tim Judah records that this pressure made Thaçi so paranoid that he refused the offer of a glass of wine from one of the mediators and drank half a bottle of his own whisky instead and on occasions came close to tears.[65]

In the early hours of 22 February after much intensive debate with the Kosovar Albanian delegation, Albright's team presented them with a revised draft of Chapter 8, Article 1(3), which detailed what would happen at the end of the three-year interim period. The original draft had stated that an international meeting would be convened to determine final status on the basis of three criteria:

- The opinions of relevant authorities.
- Each party's efforts regarding the implementation of the agreement.
- The Helsinki Final Act (founding document of the OSCE, containing provisions on human rights – the so-called 'human dimension').

Throughout the conference the Kosovar Albanian delegation had insisted that they would only consider postponing their demand for independence if there was provision for a referendum at the end of the interim period. The mediators rejected these demands because they were primarily concerned with meeting Serb concerns. As the Serbs had refused to compromise on the key issues under discussion, Albright's team calculated that a small revision to the text could produce a Kosovar Albanian signature which could then be used as coercive leverage with the Serbs. The proposed alteration to Chapter 8, Article 1(3) added a fourth dimension to the final status decision. Now, the decision would be taken, 'on the basis of the expressed will of the people' as well as on the basis of the other three criteria, though there was no suggestion that the will of the people would be more important than any of the other criteria. Albright's team attached a note to the Kosovar Albanian delegation, instructing them that the Secretary of State understood this revision to mean that at the end of the interim period there would be a referendum on independence. Importantly, although the note contained Albright's name at its foot, the Secretary of State did not sign it as was reported.[66] Diplomats told the Kosovar Albanians that the letter would only be signed if they agreed to the interim settlement before the new 23 February deadline.

The proposed revision convinced most of the Kosovar Albanian delegation to sign. They now had a promise that NATO ground troops would enforce the settlement and that after a three-year interim period there would be a referendum on independence. Only Thaçi held out. On the morning 23 February, prior to the 2 p.m. deadline, a diplomatic impasse within the Contact Group almost derailed the process. Boris Mayorski rejected Albright's revisions, denouncing the idea that there should be a referendum. As a result the Contact Group failed to adopt the clause and efforts by other members of the Kosovar Albanian delegation to persuade Thaçi to sign began to flounder. Outside the châteaux, the pressure on the UÇK leader began to build. Both the Albanian government and the famous Albanian writer, Ismail Kadare, called upon the delegation to sign the agreement. Tim Judah reports that Florin Krasniqi (the UÇK's main fundraiser in the US) contacted Thaçi to inform him that failure to sign would prompt the American government to cut off the UÇK's supply of funds.[67] Still Thaçi held out. The person Demaçi claimed had replaced him, Sulejman Selimi, contacted him by telephone and told him not to sign.

An hour after the deadline passed, Christopher Hill invited the Kosovar Albanians to sign the interim settlement. This they were unable to do because of Thaçi's dissent and insistence that he would disown the agreement if the others signed it. At this point, Veton Surroi, the independent newspaper editor who had mediated between the different political factions throughout the conference, suggested a compromise. Surroi understood that it was vital not to be seen to be refusing to sign and proposed that the delegation would sign the agreement after a two-week period of consultation with the people.[68] This compromise suited Thaçi because it allowed him the opportunity to present the agreement in full to the UÇK's regional commanders, including the new provisions on the referendum and details on military implementation. Significantly, Hill reassured the UÇK representatives that whilst it would be demilitarised, NATO would create a civil protection role for a transformed army. Surroi therefore drafted a paper, which stated that:

> The Delegation of Kosova with consensus understands that it can sign the agreement in two weeks after consultation with the people of Kosova, political and military institutions.
> ... The delegation has voted in favour of this agreement, as presented in the negotiation of 23 February, which will undergo only technical review on the part of experts.[69]

The Serb delegation also agreed to the two-week moratorium. This gave them an opportunity to take stock and confer with the leadership in Belgrade. The Serbs welcomed the progress that had been made towards a political agreement and expressed hope for the next phase of the negotiations.[70]

Kosovo's 'last chance for peace' thus ended inconclusively. Three deadlines had passed and many revisions had been made to the proposed interim settlement yet neither side seemed to have moved very far on fundamental issues. The Kosovar Albanians had moved furthest. They had deferred their demand for independence and had accepted in principle the demilitarisation of the UÇK in return for a pledge that there would be a referendum on independence after three years. While the Serbs claimed to have accepted the political aspects of the agreement, there was no evidence of this when they finally got around to making concrete proposals when the parties reconvened in Paris.

From Rambouillet to Paris

Although Védrine and Cook insisted that Rambouillet represented a step in the process rather than the once-and-for-all summit it was described as at the outset, the failure to persuade either side to sign the agreement had a palpable effect on policy-makers. Madeleine Albright told the US Senate that Milošević had chosen war over peace and that NATO must be prepared to act should the Yugoslav troops massing in Kosovo be used.[71] However, the threat of force was much less resonant than it had been a month or so earlier in the aftermath of Racak. The *Washington Post*, for example, observed that, 'giving warnings is a sad substitute for policy'.[72] Most NATO members had assumed that issuing warnings would be enough to persuade the belligerents to accept the deal. The fact that neither of them had done so was a worst-case scenario for Western diplomats as it both halted political progress and prevented a clear identification of the cause of the blockage. All was not lost though. Both parties had agreed to return to Paris for further negotiations and there seemed to be a reasonable chance that agreement could be reached. The Kosovar Albanians had indicated that they agreed in principle and the Serbs had suggested that their difficulties lay only with implementation and not with the political aspects of the settlement. Given that James Rubin later noted that the US would have accepted re-badging KFOR as a UN operation had the political aspects been agreed to, there seemed to be reasonable hopes for success.

The chances of success were greatly enhanced by political machinations within the UÇK. Immediately after the Rambouillet talks, Veton Surroi publicly identified Adem Demaçi as being responsible for their failure and thus for the failure to secure an immediate KFOR deployment.[73] A few days later, Demaçi resigned after losing the support of the regional commanders and Hashim Thaçi was confirmed as the political head of army. The about turn was partly prompted by an American initiative to persuade the UÇK to accept the agreement. Some sources reported that the rebels were invited to send representatives to Washington for discussions about the army's transformation, others that is was offered military assistance by Military Professional Resources Incorporated (MPRI), an ostensibly private agency that had worked with both the Croatian and Bosnian armies. Jakup Krasniqi confirmed that the UÇK had been invited to Washington though in the end the visit did not take place. This may have been because of Serb opposition. After hearing news of the American–UÇK discussions, the Belgrade daily *Politika* accused the State Department of supporting genocide in the province.[74] The decision to move away from making more overt overtures to the UÇK may also have been influenced by a loss of consensus among the NATO allies. One Western diplomat in Belgrade told reporters that, 'the US does not have the support of its European allies, there's no longer the will to bomb'.[75]

There was little doubt in international circles about what the ousting of Demaçi meant for the peace process. The OSCE Chairman-in-Office reported that it 'appeared to be an indication of a shift within the KLA [UÇK] towards acceptance of the interim agreement advocated at Rambouillet'.[76] A further positive sign was the adoption of a statement by eight Kosovar Albanian parties, including those led by Ibrahim Rugova and Rexhep Qosja, which called upon all Kosovar Albanians to accept the Rambouillet accords.[77] The Contact Group proposed that the Kosovar Albanians delay the actual signing of the agreement to allow time for further pressure to be put on the Serbs.

The Serbs were becoming more, rather than less, intransigent. NATO's extraction force in Macedonia was almost called into action to free 21 KVM verifiers who were held against their will by Serb border guards after trying to enter Kosovo. There was also increasing evidence that the Serb forces that had been deployed in and around the province during the Rambouillet negotiations were being put to use. Police sealed off the Eshmiri suburb in Pristina. Using tactics that clearly resembled those used during the offensives of spring and summer 1998, the Serbs also launched a major attack near Kacanik, killing dozens and forcing over 500 out of their homes. KVM verifiers in Ivaja reported that 80 percent of the village was little more than rubble, that the mosque had been attacked with anti-aircraft guns and then vandalised, and – a forewarning of what was to come – the registration office, which contained identity papers, land deeds and such like, was ransacked.[78]

Tony Blair took the lead in trying to persuade reluctant allies that they should be prepared to actually use force against Yugoslavia. In a speech to the Royal United Services Institute he insisted that the 'lessons of Bosnia' be learned. He argued that 'we will not allow war to devastate part of our continent, bringing untold death, suffering and homelessness'.[79] He went on to insist that continuing prevarication was not an option and that the forthcoming negotiations in Paris should reach a swift conclusion. Reinforcing the view that NATO must provide the key component of the agreement's implementation Blair remarked that 'the Balkans are littered with agreements that are signed but not implemented. To make an agreement work, to bring stability in Kosovo, an international force is an indispensable element. Only NATO is equipped to lead it'.[80] Although there was now consensus that a robust NATO-led force, similar to the IFOR force that had been deployed in Bosnia, would be deployed, most European allies believed that there was a huge distinction between deploying a peace force in what was often referred to as a 'semi-permissive' environment and using air power against Yugoslavia to coerce compliance.

The German Defence Minister, Rudolf Scharping, argued that the peace-keeping plan for Kosovo represented the most dangerous mission that Germany had undertaken since the Second World War.[81] He toned down London and Washington's rhetoric by revealing that he believed that agreement would be forthcoming and that there would be no need to bomb. Said Scharping, 'the experience of the last ten years is that Milošević caves in only at the very last moment, so we need credible and intensive pressure'.[82] Even at this late stage, then, there was still a belief that the threat of force would be enough to coerce compliance. Such evidence of discord frustrated Klaus Naumann, chair of NATO's Military Committee. Naumann argued that the allies' different positions provided the Yugoslav president with diplomatic ammunition and reduced the credibility of the Alliance's coercive diplomacy.

On 8 March, Joschka Fischer, the German Foreign Minister and Hans Van den Broek, EU Commissioner for Foreign Affairs, visited Belgrade to take the argument directly to Milošević. Fischer and Van den Broek formally offered Milošević the opportunity to renegotiate the implementation aspects of the agreement. Christopher Hill had privately offered this to the Yugoslav president, but the Europeans put it firmly on the agenda without, of course, consulting the Kosovar Albanians. The fact that implementation was raised as an area of potential negotiation supports Ivo Daalder and Michael O'Hanlon's conclusion that had the Serbs accepted the political aspects of the agreement, NATO would have revisited the implementation aspects. As the State Department spokesman, James Rubin, later put it:

> Had President Milošević been prepared to accept a NATO force in Kosovo, and had [he] been prepared to work out the kind of military–technical agreement that was worked out at the end of the air war – without the silver bullet clause, without the ability to deploy anywhere in Yugoslavia – we would have accepted it.

A senior British diplomat supported this view insisting, 'you don't think we would have bombed Serbia for this reason alone, do you?'.[83]

Milošević revealed a subtle change of position in this meeting. He insisted that no state had the right to prevent Yugoslavia conducting an anti-terrorist campaign. A similar message was given to Richard Holbrooke and Christopher Hill when they visited Milošević a few days later. Although the Americans insisted that they would not offer any 'carrots', such as immunity from ICTY prosecution or a lifting of sanctions, there were many issues of interpretation that could be resolved in the Serbs favour. Milošević was also encouraged to outline a deal that might be acceptable to him. Although this presented the Yugoslav president with an opportunity to stall the allies, it was one he chose not to take. When the Serb counter proposals were unveiled in Paris they were so at odds with the plans that had been drawn up over the previous 18 months that even the Russian mediator, Boris Mayorski, was appalled. Rather than stalling the allies, the counter proposals tightened the noose around Milošević's neck by exposing his lack of interest in genuine negotiation and compromise.

There was therefore a confused atmosphere when the parties reconvened at the Centre Kléber near the Arc de Triomphe in Paris. All the Kosovar Albanian parties, including the UÇK, had indicated their intention to sign the interim settlement while the Serbs had reportedly moved six times as many soldiers into Kosovo as was allowed under the Holbrooke–Milošević agreement.[84] As happened at the beginning of the Rambouillet negotiations the commencement of talks in Paris was accompanied by a series of bomb explosions in Pristina. This time there was no joint statement of condemnation. Robin Cook and Hubert Védrine again chaired the talks. They opened proceedings by insisting that the negotiations must produce a quick result and would be wound up within a week if there were no agreement. Cook indicated on British television that he saw no reason why the talks should be prolonged because he presumed that both parties accepted the political aspects of the agreement and that the implementation aspects were non-negotiable.

The negotiations opened smoothly enough with the Kosovar Albanians delivering a letter to the Contact Group that formally expressed their intention to sign the agreement at a time and place of the Group's choosing. Hashim Thaçi's signature was included at the foot of the letter. It has been widely assumed that the UÇK's decision to accept the agreement was a cynical one taken to pit NATO against the Serbs. While it may appear logical, this assumption is ill founded. It was still not clear that the Serbs would not sign and indeed most commentators in Paris and Belgrade believed that there would be a deal. Moreover, implementing the interim settlement would have had a profound long-term impact on the UÇK. Finally, many in the organisation still did not believe NATO's rhetoric about the threat of airstrikes. As their London representative, Pleurat Sejdiu, put it when asked about the decision to sign, 'we know there will be no airstrikes if the Serbs do not sign and, in that case, if the Serbs keep on shelling, there will be trouble'.[85]

Because the Kosovar Albanians agreed to sign the diplomatic effort turned towards persuading the Serbs to do likewise. Clinton summed this up when he warned that 'the most important thing is that Milošević and the Serbs sign'.[86] The effort to persuade the Serbs was severely hampered by the Kosovar Albanians' swift agreement to sign. One Western diplomat suggested that the Serbs were 'rattled' by this and reported that a Serb negotiator had asked 'have you come to fuck us again?' when the talks began. Tim Judah argues that the reason for this response lay in the fact that the Serbs had been caught off-guard. A diplomat told him:

> At Rambouillet, I think that Serb Intelligence had picked up that they were not going to sign but it let them down over Paris. I was in the coffee bar in the Kléber Centre and the Yugoslav delegation were all there laughing. Then, a junior foreign ministry official, whom I recognised came running in and said: 'They are going to sign!' Their faces dropped and they all charged out.[87]

This certainly seems the most plausible explanation to account for the lack of Serb activity at Rambouillet. We have to ask though whether it is simply implausible to argue that by the time of the Paris conference the Serbs still believed that the Kosovar Albanians would refuse to sign. After all, although Thaçi had not openly declared his hand prior to arriving in Paris – to the extent that Judah reports that some of his own delegation was taken aback by the rapidity of his acquiescence – the removal of Demaçi had been enough of a gesture to persuade the OSCE that in all likelihood the Kosovar Albanians would sign. The fact that the OSCE picked this up and Serb intelligence had not is remarkable.

There are two possible reasons for this apparently catastrophic failure. First, the Serb security forces were in turmoil and not unconditionally loyal to Milošević. In November 1998 Milošević sacked General Momcilo Perišić, a well-respected soldier who was known to be uneasy with the tasks the VJ was being given in Kosovo. General Dragoljub Ojdanić, a hardline Milošević loyalist, replaced him. Two days before NATO launched Operation Allied Force, Milošević also sacked his intelligence chief, Aleksander Dimitrijević. Dimitrijević had repeatedly warned the president not to call NATO's bluff. Because of these changes of personnel the intelligence services and military either failed to pick up on the significance of Demaçi's resignation or failed to fully convey it back to Belgrade. The alternative possibility is that Milošević did know about the Kosovar Albanian position but had not briefed his negotiating team. He did not believe that NATO would attack him or rather he thought that if they did they would not be able to sustain that attack in the face of criticism from Russia and from within the allies' own electorates. It is likely that both factors played a part in shaping Serb responses in Paris and Milošević's subsequent refusal to compromise.

The Serbs did take up the opportunity to outline their own proposals. Rather than revealing a genuine desire for a negotiated solution, the proposals they presented at Paris revealed their intransigence and lack of interest in the diplomatic process. The Serbs refused to accept the basic principles for a Kosovo constitution. Instead, Chapter 1 Article 1(3) of their counter-proposals insisted that all Yugoslav federal laws apply across the whole territory of Yugoslavia, as should the Yugoslav constitution. This meant that no change to the constitutional status of Kosovo would be applicable unless that change emanated from a prior change in the Yugoslav and Serbian constitutions. The authors of this proposal calculated that the Serbian parliament would veto such changes thus derailing the entire first two chapters of the interim settlement.

Chapter 1 Article 1(4) of the counter-proposals reaffirmed this point by insisting that whereas the Rambouillet proposals curtailed Yugoslavia's jurisdiction over Kosovo, it should be the autonomy given to the province that be proscribed. The Serbian government thus revealed that it had an utterly different comprehension to that of the Contact Group about what Kosovan autonomy should mean. Rather than Kosovo holding general jurisdiction with the Belgrade government holding exceptions, the principle was reversed. Yugoslav rule would be total, except in areas that it delegated to Pristina. It conceived Kosovo's future as one of devolution rather than autonomy.

The Serbian counter-proposal also took the opt-out for national communities one step further. Their proposed Chapter 1 Article 1(6) demanded that 'each national community may enact separate rules for its members'. In essence, this clause envisaged a codification of apartheid. It reckoned that the Serbian community in Kosovo could legislate for itself, be subject to Serbian rather than Kosovan law (Chapter 1 Article 5(2)), and enjoy independent relations with Belgrade. All this was contrary to the spirit of autonomy envisaged in the interim settlement because it would not alter Kosovo's *de facto* status. The Kosovar Albanians would continue to have their state (previously the underground parallel system) and the Serbs theirs.

Most of the other core elements of the interim settlement were absent completely. Under the Serbian proposals, there would be no Kosovan judicial system, only limited local taxation powers, a largely continuous police force, and most crucially no significant international supervision of the implementation. The VJ and MUP would remain unrestricted.

These Serbian counter-proposals revealed just how little progress was made at Rambouillet. Given that the chapters regarding implementation were rejected in their entirety, it is difficult to see how an appendix (the military annex) to one of those chapters could have had much of an impact on Serb decision makers. The very concept of autonomy was substantially different to that envisaged by the Contact Group and there was only a token commitment to ceasing hostilities and respecting human rights. To put it in context, the Serbian counter-proposals, which were supposedly the result of many months of negotiation, did not even accord Kosovo the autonomy it had held for 15 years between 1974 and 1989. Even Boris Mayorski was shocked by the fact that 'whole chapters that had taken months of work were simply crossed out and replaced with other clearly unacceptable paragraphs or nothing at all'.[88]

For many diplomats, the Serb counter-proposals were evidence enough that force was going to have to be used if any mutually acceptable settlement was going to be agreed. According to State Department spokesman, Robert Foley, there were two triggers for launching airstrikes and Serb actions had activated both of them. These were non-acceptance of the interim settlement and evidence of breaches of the ceasefire agreed the previous October. Foley concluded that 'the Serbs, on the two triggers for the NATO decision, are out of compliance and the NATO decision is becoming more and more relevant given that Serb behaviour'.[89] Contrary to this relatively straightforward American reasoning, many European allies were not convinced that either of the triggers had been crossed. They believed that there remained scope for continuing negotiation and that the escalating violence in Kosovo did not necessarily indicate a general breakdown of the ceasefire. The French and Italian governments offered a cool response to Christopher Hill's announcement from Paris that there was very little prospect of making progress with the Serbs and it was certainly not self-evident that the North Atlantic Council would call for airstrikes.[90]

That decision moved closer on 18 March with a formal Serbian refusal to countenance the interim settlement. Serb President Milan Milutinovic denounced the proposals as 'fake' and warned that, 'if they attack us, we shall fight back. We are ready to defend our country'.[91] Meanwhile, the Kosovar Albanians formally signed the agreement in a ceremony witnessed by the American and European negotiators. Boris Mayorski refused to witness the signing. The Russian mediator was in a very difficult situation. On the one hand, he had patently failed to bring the Serbs into line and was at least as frustrated as the other Contact Group negotiators about the counter-proposals that the Serbs unveiled. On the other hand, however, he was only too aware that should NATO use force, Russia would be taken out of the diplomatic equation and given only a marginal role in any future agreement for the province. Furthermore, the Russian government's public position was one of vehement opposition to NATO. This resulted from the twin imperatives of having to be seen to be playing a leading part in the international diplomacy and the domestic imperative of having to be seen to be assisting their Orthodox brethren in Serbia. Trying to balance these imperatives led Mayorski into a confusing position. This resulted in him remaining engaged in the negotiating process – a process that was always underpinned by the threat of force – until the end but then when it became clear that the process had failed, he moved swiftly to distance himself from it.

Milošević had already decided that he would test NATO's resolve and go to war if necessary. Gauging the discord among allies and believing that he would receive material assistance from Russia, the Yugoslav president believed that he could outlast any NATO bombing campaign. There were several reasons for this belief:

- Bill Clinton categorically ruled out the use of ground troops to free Kosovo. Relying on airpower alone meant that the decision as to when to stop lay in Milošević's hands.
- The previous autumn, the allies had conducted a similar operation against Iraq in Operation Desert Fox. Alliance consensus about that attack withered away very quickly allowing Saddam Hussein to claim a diplomatic victory. Hardliners like General Ojdanić advised Milošević that it would be the same this time.
- The 18 months of negotiations that had just passed proved the point that there was no agreement amongst allies about the best way to proceed. Milošević calculated that Alliance consensus would quickly evaporate if he made it clear that the campaign would not be quick and painless.
- Milošević believed that it was not just Kosovo that was at stake but also his very regime. He believed that if he gave NATO a foothold in Yugoslavia they would use it to oust him. He also realised that the only way he could keep himself out of prison was by remaining in power.
- Although Russia had indicated to NATO some months earlier that it would not offer material assistance to Yugoslavia if it was attacked, it is clear that they had not conveyed this message to Milošević. The realisation that material assistance would not be forthcoming proved to be one of the turning points of the war.

On the day that the Paris negotiations collapsed, the VJ began to prepare itself for two wars: One against NATO and one against the Kosovar
Albanian population. It announced that it the event of an attack it
would launch counter-attacks against NATO targets in Bosnia, Albania,
Macedonia and in the Adriatic. General Ojdanić told young recruits to
prepare for martyrdom. A poll in the pro-government *Večernje Nevosti*
proclaimed that 93 percent of people supported the Generals.[92] Given
the nature of the publication one has to take the figure with a pinch of
salt, but it did indicate a general belief that the Serbs should use whatever means possible to defend themselves against NATO. It was not
Serbia's bellicose rhetoric that helped solidify NATO consensus on
whether to use force however. It was their activities in Kosovo.

The KVM began its withdrawal from Kosovo on 20 March. Learning
the lessons from Bosnia where airstrikes had been delayed because of fear
of reprisals against UNPROFOR peacekeepers, it was decided that the
KVM should be withdrawn to Albania and Macedonia. It was also hoped
that the withdrawal would send a signal of intent to Milošević leading to
the eleventh hour agreement that most people still thought was proba-
ble. Instead, the Serbs began a massive campaign of ethnic cleansing. By
20 March, the UNHCR estimated, 20,000 Kosovar Albanians had been
driven out of their homes since the beginning of the Paris meeting.
There were also the first indications that a well-organised campaign had
begun. Masked Serbs from special MUP units were reportedly systematically forcing people from their homes, indicating that the infamous
Operation Horseshoe was being implemented.[93] Ominously, President
Clinton observed that, 'I think that whatever threshold they need to
cross has been crossed' while Robin Cook indicated that there was still
time for Milošević to pull back from the brink.[94]

Even at this late stage it was still not clear what the precise trigger for
airstrikes would be. The US clearly thought that that the triggers had
been crossed on 21 March but many European allies did not. Richard
Holbrooke was summoned and despatched to Belgrade for his 41st
and final visit. If Milošević was ready to negotiate he would do it with
Holbrooke and the airstrikes would be put on hold, as they had been
the previous October. If he was not ready to negotiate, Holbrooke was the
man best placed to gauge the situation. The portents for success were
not good. On the day of Holbrooke's visit, the Serb parliament voted
overwhelmingly to reject the interim settlement. Serbian television
refused to admit that there was even a crisis and *Tanjug* reported that
the situation in Kosovo was calm. On arrival in Belgrade, Holbrooke
told the press that, 'we've reached the edge, time is running out', before

appealing for Serb television viewers to accept the proposals.[95] This time though Milošević had already made his mind up. There would be no eleventh hour agreement nor even the pretence of negotiation. This time he was going to test NATO's resolve.

It is worth quoting Holbrooke's account of what happened in Belgrade on 22 March at length:

> I said to him, 'you understand what will happen when I leave here today if you don't change your position, if you don't agree to negotiate and accept Rambouillet as the basis of the negotiation?' And he said, 'yes, you will bomb us'. And there was a dead silence in the room er ... uncharacteristic and I said, 'I want to be clear with you, it will be', and I used three words that I had worked out very carefully with the US military, 'it will be swift, it will be severe, it will be sustained'. And he said in a very matter-of-fact way, very flat, 'no more engagement, no more negotiation, I understand that, you will bomb us. You are a great and powerful country, there is nothing we can do about it'. And I said, 'it will start very soon after I leave', and there was, again, dead silence and I looked at my watch and I saw it was noon, and I said, 'you know it's 6 a.m. now in Washington, people are getting up. I have to report to Washington and to our allies in London and Paris and Bonn and Brussels, where we stand'. And I waited, last chance. And he said, 'there is nothing more I can say', so I got up and we left and exactly 34 hours later the bombing began.[96]

Tim Judah records that just as Holbrooke left, Milošević asked him, 'will I ever see you again?' The American diplomat replied, 'that's up to you, Mr. President'.[97]

There was a widespread belief that there would be a further delay of a week or so to ensure that the beginning of the bombing campaign did not coincide with the visit of Russian Prime Minister Primakov to Washington. This was not to be the case. Holbrooke left Belgrade for Brussels, briefing the State Department, Pentagon, and White House in Washington as he travelled. There was, he told the North Atlantic Council, no likelihood of Milošević agreeing to the peace plan or halting the escalating violence. It was now estimated that number of displaced people in Kosovo caused by the renewed violence had increased to 60,000. However, there was still time for diplomatic wrangling within the Alliance. The Italian Ambassador suggested that there be a brief period of bombing followed by a pause to give Milošević an opportunity to reassess his position. The American and British governments opposed this idea, arguing that a pause would only cement Milošević's determination to resist NATO. Holbrooke's report proved enough though to secure a minimal level of consensus. In the event though, rather than being swift, severe, and sustained, the campaign plan that the council agreed upon consisted of a three-day assault primarily against air defence targets.

At 10.30 p.m. after a day of consultations, Javier Solana authorised the SACEUR, General Wesley Clark, to begin the air campaign. It would last 78 days.

Summary

According to Madeleine Albright, the decision to use force on 24 March represented the end of diplomacy backed by force and the beginning of force backed by diplomacy.[98] The SACEUR, Wesley Clark, disagreed. For him, the shift was less fundamental. For Clark the shift was from diplomacy backed by the *threat* of force to diplomacy backed by force. At stake is more than semantics. For some, Operation Allied Force merely represented a new phase of coercive diplomacy. Actually, it represented its failure. At some point between the end of Rambouillet and the beginning of the Paris negotiations, Slobodan Milošević decided that there would be no deal and that he would fight a war with NATO if necessary. As Barry Posen puts it in his excellent account of Serbia's political-military strategy, Milošević had acquired 'a plausible theory of victory'.[99] That theory was not primarily based on an intelligence failure as suggested by Tim Judah, though it is clear that Milošević did not tell many people about his choice of strategy and certainly not his negotiators in Paris. The man most involved with the decision was General Ojdanić. Milošević's decision was influenced by NATO's inability to convey a credible threat. For coercive diplomacy to work, the target has to be made aware that the costs of non-compliance far outweigh the costs of compliance. In this case, NATO simply failed to persuade the Yugoslav president of this.

There were two principal reasons for this. Firstly, the strategy of coercive diplomacy was based on unilateral experiences. For a coalition of 19 states to achieve the necessary coherence is hugely problematic. The complexity of the situation was increased by the role of states such as Russia. At Rambouillet, the pinnacle of coercive summitry, the threat was carried to the Serbs by the Contact Group – including Russia – not by NATO. On occasion, Russia played the coercer. On other occasions, it rushed to the defence of the coerced. The ambiguity this created led

Milošević to believe that NATO would not be able to sustain military attacks that could inflict more pain than the pain that would be caused by what was being offered at Rambouillet.

Secondly, because NATO was standing at the cusp of creating a new norm in international relations many of its members were highly reticent about what they were doing. Some, such as the Italian and Greek governments were openly uncomfortable about what they were being asked to do and even hawkish allies were unsure of their footing. In an era of global communications these internal debates resonated in Belgrade. Milošević was only too well aware that over 90 per cent of Greeks opposed the war, that the coalition government in Italy would collapse if the communists withdrew their support as seemed likely at the outset, and that even the German government, which had been one of the more hawkish, would be threatened if pacifists in the Green Party (which was part of the ruling coalition) had their way. Furthermore, Milošević believed he could escalate the conflict in a way that would quickly erode alliance cohesion by threatening a regional imbroglio. He would cause instability in Bosnia and Montenegro, would solve his own Kosovar Albanian problem by expelling or killing them all, and in doing so would put pressure on Macedonia and Albania. NATO, he believed, would not be able to tolerate such escalation and would back down leaving Milošević with a Serb dominated Kosovo and a diplomatic triumph.

As with all the previous transitions from one phase of engagement to another, the shift from coercive diplomacy to war was incremental and unplanned. We noted earlier that back in October 1998 many allies had only agreed to the Activation Order because they believed that force would not be necessary. It was on the basis of that order that NATO was going to war six months later. There remained a considerable degree of disagreement about what sort of campaign NATO should fight. The Italian government, for example, believed that the Alliance was still in the coercive diplomacy phase and argued for an early pause in the bombing to allow for negotiations.

Throughout the book, we have seen how perceptions of political necessity shaped the international policy agenda. While in October 1998 the Alliance deemed it necessary to tie diplomacy and the threat of force together, learning – they believed – the lessons of Bosnia, this did not mean that allies believed it necessary to use force to coerce a political settlement. Even after the failures at Rambouillet and Paris many allies simply did not believe that Serbia's failure to sign was reason enough to bomb it. The political necessity was created by the commencement of a major Serbian campaign of ethnic cleansing during the Paris negotiations. Evidence had pointed towards a massive build-up of military power in and around Kosovo during the Rambouillet negotiations and the Serbs wasted no time getting to work. 20,000 people were ethnically cleansed during the Paris negotiations alone. That figure had more than doubled by 24 March. The West now had to confront its three syndromes discussed earlier – the 'Srebrenica syndrome', 'refugees syndrome' and the 'Balkan wars syndrome'. It was Serbian ethnic cleansing that created the sense of crisis in the North Atlantic Council in the final week of March. It was the overwhelming evidence that Milošević had passed the point of no return, both in international negotiations and on the ground in Kosovo, which provided the trigger. However, continuing disagreement about the air strategy meant that the first strikes were not as severe as Clark had promised. Ethnic cleansing and mass killing in Kosovo ensured that they were sustained, however.

6
NATO Goes to War

NATO's decision to go to war contained two elements. First, there was agreement on the principle of using force. This agreement was reached in October 1998 with the North Atlantic Council's decision to pass the Activation Order. There remained, however, considerable disagreement about what the trigger for military action should be. Hawks like Tony Blair and Madeleine Albright believed that a phased bombing campaign was a proportionate response to the Racak massacre. Subsequently, they argued that the failure of the Rambouillet and Paris negotiations made the use of force necessary. Most commentators argue that it was the diplomatic failure in France and Richard Holbrooke's subsequent inability to persuade Milošević to accept the terms on offer that triggered the airstrikes. In fact, the perceived need to move from *coercive diplomacy* to *limited war* was triggered by the dramatic increase of Serb oppression and ethnic cleansing in Kosovo during, and immediately after, the Paris negotiations. In all likelihood, Operation Allied Force would not have begun had the Serbs not launched a massive campaign of ethnic cleansing. The disagreements within the Alliance shaped the war, a period of engagement characterised by:

- Constant debate about the appropriate military strategy and compromises between different alternatives.
- Disagreement about the way the war should be ended.
- Lack of clarity caused by the multiple channels of political and military decision-making.
- Uncertainty about the political and military objectives.
- Complex diplomatic processes aimed at ending the war.[1]

General Clark, who directed the campaign, provides an excellent portrait of the uncertainty and lack of direction that characterised the war.

Clark recalls that after a meeting with President Gligorov of Macedonia in early 1998 he faxed the Pentagon warning them of potential trouble in Kosovo. The response came swiftly in the form of a telephone call from Joe Ralston:

'Look Wes' Ralston continued, 'we've got a lot on our plates back here. We've got our defence bill to get through and NATO enlargement coming up in the Senate. We can't deal with any more problems. And' he continued, 'the Secretary's [of State for Defence, William Cohen] concerned that Madeleine Albright might get a copy of this'.[2]

Operation Allied Force was a new kind of post-Clausewitzian war; one where the military means agreed upon by the Alliance (a phased air campaign) dictated the political objectives. In theory, Clausewitzian war leaves military commanders fitting military means to political ends. In Kosovo, the exact nature of the military campaign had little effect on the outcome. Milošević's decision to negotiate depended more on the perception that NATO was not going to go away and that help from Serbia's Slav brothers in Russia or sympathisers in China was not coming over the horizon than it did on the bombardment *per se*. At the outset of the war alliance leaders insisted that the aim was to *prevent* ethnic cleansing in Kosovo. However, the means agreed upon by the North Atlantic Council in October 1998 (phased air strikes) could not achieve the very different objectives asked of them in March 1999. Once this became clear, the Alliance simply changed its political objectives.[3]

War aims

In a statement to the House of Commons on the day the campaign began, Tony Blair told MPs that the aim of the airstrikes was to, 'avert a humanitarian catastrophe' by stopping Serb forces continuing their 'violent oppression' and ethnic cleansing of Kosovar Albanians.[4] A day later, Blair told an EU summit in Berlin that the military action had a specific task: 'To damage Serb forces sufficiently to prevent Mr. Milošević from continuing to perpetuate his vile oppression against Kosovar Albanian civilians.'[5] The military mission identified by Wesley Clark echoed Tony Blair's understanding of NATO's war aims. Clark told his subordinates that the military mission:

Is to attack Yugoslav military and security forces and associated facilities with sufficient effect to degrade its capacity to continue repression of the civilian population and to deter further military actions against its own people.[6]

There was substantial disagreement within NATO's military command about the virtue of this mission. Upon retirement at the end of May, the Chairman of the Military Committee, General Klaus Naumann, told newspapers that the campaign had been lengthened by a lack of political and military resolve at the outset.[7] Naumann wrote:

> We need to find a way to reconcile the conditions of coalition war with the principle of the use of surprise and the overwhelming use of force. We did not apply either in Operation Allied Force and this cost time and effort and potentially additional casualties.[8]

Moreover, General Mike Short, the commander of NATO's air campaign, believed that only a strategic campaign directed against the Yugoslav elite would prevail. Such a strategic campaign would maximise the effect of NATO's air power he thought. Short argued that contrary to Clark's assessment, the Serb army was not the centre of gravity.[9] For Short, that was Milošević's ability to exercise power and draw authority from the Serb elite. Clark's assessment, though, was based on the belief that the objective was to prevent a humanitarian catastrophe. To do this, NATO had to be seen to be attacking the cause of that catastrophe. Furthermore, Alliance heads of government expected to see NATO attacking forces in Kosovo. Attacking bridges in Novi Sad at the outset would have raised huge questions about the legitimacy of the war. However, as the war continued Short persuaded Clark to redirect resources away from Kosovo towards strategic targets in Serbia proper.[10]

After discussing the military strategy on the telephone with Tony Blair, Bill Clinton issued a statement calling on Americans to look at their world maps and find Kosovo. The American President compared Serb oppression in Kosovo with Nazi activities in the Second World War before asking how many lives would have been saved 'if people had listened to Churchill and stood up to Hitler earlier.'[11] However, he went on to tell Americans that 'I do not intend to put our troops in Kosovo to fight a war.' According to Tim Judah this was 'one of the cardinal errors of the campaign'.[12] Wesley Clark was not forewarned about this severe limitation on the means at his disposal. Ever the diplomat, Clark reasoned that, 'a series of painful national debates about the ground option at this point would have added no coercive pressure to the NATO air campaign'[13] before recognising that the lack of a ground option was a serious impediment.

Although Clinton's statement informed Milošević that if he could withstand airstrikes he would prevail, making NATO's military task much more difficult, the President was speaking to three wider audiences and in each his reassurance that ground troops would not be used had a positive impact. First, the President was speaking to the American public, many of whom did not know where Kosovo was. Ruling out ground troops ruled out the danger that Kosovo could become a new Vietnam imbroglio and helped shore up public support for the air campaign. Secondly, he was speaking to the Republican dominated Senate and Congress. Although prominent Republicans, such as Bob Dole, had long supported the Kosovar Albanian cause, the majority of Republicans in both houses were driven primarily by an urge to depose Clinton as the Monica Lewinsky affair rumbled on. The prospect of a land invasion would have increased Clinton's problems and may have jeopardised congressional support for the air campaign. Finally, Clinton was speaking to reluctant allies such as Greece and Italy. Back in October 1998, Greece had almost vetoed the Activation Order and allowed it to pass only once the Security Council passed Resolution 1199 and Holbrooke had advised them that his diplomatic mission to Belgrade would be successful. Had Clinton left open the possibility of a land invasion, persuading Greece and Italy to accept the air war would have been much more difficult. Clinton's statement proved vital in shoring up the US' commitment to the air campaign and Alliance unity. It was the persistence of Alliance unity that ultimately won the war.

The lack of a ground option meant that NATO was unable to prevent the humanitarian catastrophe. One of the lessons learnt during the Deliberate Force operation in Bosnia was that it is very difficult to hit individual 'smoking gun' targets engaged in operations on the ground from the air.[14] An issue we will deal with later is whether NATO knew about the likely scale of the catastrophe and whether its actions exacerbated the problem, as many of its critics have claimed. By week two of the campaign, with half a million Kosovar Albanian refugees seeking shelter in Macedonia and Albania, NATO began to reformulate its war aims. The new aims identified by the North Atlantic Council on 12 April were concerned with *reversing* the consequences of a catastrophe that the Alliance had failed to prevent. Summarised by Tony Blair as, 'Serbs out, NATO in, refugees home', NATO's five objectives were:

1. A verifiable halt to all Serb military action and an immediate halt to violence and oppression.
2. The withdrawal of all Serb military, police and paramilitary forces.

3. The stationing of an international military force in Kosovo.
4. The unconditional and safe return of all refugees and displaced persons and unhindered access to them by humanitarian aid organisations.
5. Credible assurance of work towards a political settlement based upon the Rambouillet accords.[15]

Wesley Clark devised his own so-called 'measures of merit' to evaluate the success of the air campaign. These three measures tell us more about the nature of the campaign than any amount of political rhetoric. Clark's first measure of merit was to minimise the loss of NATO aircraft. This, Clark tells us, 'drove our decisions on tactics, targets, and which airplanes could participate'.[16] The second measure was to have an impact on Yugoslav ground forces and police activities as rapidly and effectively as possible. The third was to protect NATO ground forces based in Bosnia, Macedonia and northern Albania. While Clark noted that the key political imperative was to attack Yugoslavia's fielded forces it is illuminating that two of his three 'measures of merit' concerned the protection of NATO forces. Interesting omissions were the protection of the Kosovar Albanian victims or the achievement of effects through the strategic attack of bridges, oil refineries, army barracks, and even television studios throughout the length and breadth of Yugoslavia, which became the campaign's key characteristics. While the importance of protecting NATO forces is not surprising, and spoke directly to the need to preserve NATO unity, the two omissions are important. They meant, for example, that the wholesale ethnic cleansing and mass murder of Kosovar Albanians did not alter Clark's understanding of success and failure.

What sort of war?

The war for Kosovo in 1999 consisted of two separate but interlinked conflicts. In the first, the Serbs confronted the massively superior air and naval force of NATO. In the other, the Serbs confronted the massively inferior forces of the UÇK and Kosovar Albanian civilian population. Ivo Daalder and Michael O'Hanlon correctly point out that NATO did not expect a long war. They argue out that when Allied Force began, the Alliance had only 350 aircraft in the region, some 60 less that it had in the region in October 1998.[17] This was only ten percent of the aircraft available to the allies at the beginning of the Gulf War and only one-fifth the necessary aircraft identified by the Pentagon for one of the two 'regional wars' that the US reckons it should be able to fight simultaneously.[18] Furthermore, the US withdrew the carrier *Enterprise* shortly before the beginning of the campaign, greatly irritating Wesley Clark and clearly indicating Washington's lack of will to Slobodan Milošević. The North Atlantic Council only authorised Phase One of the air campaign, which included some 50 targets the great majority of which were air defence targets. The British Harrier pilots who took part in the first few days of the campaign were expressly told at the outset that it would last only three days.[19] Indeed, two of the most hawkish NATO leaders, Madeleine Albright and Javier Solana publicly stated before the war that they expected it to be a short one.[20] This meant that the Alliance lacked the firepower it needed to have a devastating effect on Yugoslavia (dropping fewer bombs in two weeks than had been dropped on the first night of Desert Storm) and repeatedly revisited targets regardless of whether they had been hit or not.[21]

NATO allies were divided on the question of how targets would be selected and approved. Throughout the whole process of target selection and approval military lawyers offered legal justifications and objections for each target set and weapon selection.[22] During the course of the air strikes the allies delegated their prerogative to scrutinise targets to Javier Solana, who in turn allowed an informal process of on-going consultation principally involving the US, UK and France.[23] This took into account the fact that some NATO members, most notably Greece, did not want their pilots involved in the campaign at all and that others wanted to restrict the geographical scope of their aircraft's participation (the French government, for example, did not want its aircraft to attack targets in neutral Montenegro). Initially, only Tony Blair and Bill Clinton took decisions about whether to bomb particular civilian targets. This greatly alarmed the French president, Jacques Chirac, particularly after American Tomahawk missiles struck the Serb Interior Ministry on 2 April without the French having prior knowledge. Chirac demanded direct personal involvement in target selection and the three leaders agreed a set of guidelines that gave each direct input on the selection of civilian targets. Later on, this process was extended to include the German and Italian governments. Each day the leaders (or their representatives) teleconferenced with Wesley Clark on the subject of target selection.[24] This delegation of authority allowed targeting decisions to be taken more quickly than could otherwise have been had all 19 members been consulted about each target set. This political process slowed down the acquisition of new targets, causing NATO to frequently return to targets it had already hit because there were not enough new targets to strike. As Clark put it:

> What was becoming increasingly clear to me … was just how difficult the process of target approval was going to become. Once we moved

past the obvious air defence target set, every target ... was, in one way or another, likely to become controversial.[25]

The recriminations began to fly after the war. The French and Dutch accused the US of using its national chain of command to authorise particular strikes outside the NATO system. Both pointed to the bombing of the Chinese Embassy as a case in point, though this interpretation may not be wholly accurate, as we will see later. Americans such as General Short believe that the campaign was unnecessarily lengthened by the allies' reluctance to strike swiftly and massively as they had done prior to the liberation of Kuwait.

Allowing all NATO members to participate in targeting decision-making would also have made information security virtually impossible, with literally hundreds of people having access to NATO's campaign plan. Even with limited consultation there was evidence that the Serbs were gathering a great deal of information from within NATO headquarters. Suspicions were aroused in April when on three occasions military installations in Serbia were cleared of men and materiel shortly before being bombed. On one occasion, a Serb barracks was evacuated when an urgent radio message was received only 'minutes' before being hit.[26] It subsequently transpired that Commandant Pierre-Henri Bunel had shown details of NATO's strike plan to a Yugoslav diplomat in October 1998. Writing in *Libération*, Bunel insisted that he had done so in order to show the Serbs 'the scope of the destruction that was envisaged' and persuade them to participate in the peace process.[27] NATO had to tread a difficult path between maintaining operational security, democratic transparency and input from anxious member governments.

Given the ambiguity of the political objectives, the limitations on targeting, scarcity of military resources, and widespread belief that ethnic cleansing on the ground could not be abated by air strikes, it is not surprising that Milošević believed he could prevail.[28] To do so the Serbs devised a strategy of promoting regional instability, carrying out reprisals against the Kosovar Albanians, defeating the UÇK, and dividing NATO.

The first strand of Milošević's strategy was to provoke regional instability, threatening to raise the stakes higher than he believed NATO was prepared to go. The Serb regime planned to ferment conflict in Macedonia, Montenegro and Bosnia. Two attempts were made to derail the Bosnian peace process. At the beginning of March, SFOR soldiers seized two civilian trucks that were carrying illegal weapons including anti-aircraft weapons. The international force disbanded the Bosnian Serb infantry brigade that had been responsible for this arms importing.

Shortly before the launch of Operation Allied Force, SFOR encircled Bosnian Serb arms dumps and threatened to destroy them if any attempt was made to seize arms. It was then that the commander of the Bosnian Serb army, Momir Talić, admitted to British General Mike Willcocks that he had been instructed by Milošević to launch a guerrilla war against SFOR in Bosnia and that, given the position his weapons were in, he had refused to carry out the order.[29] Talić himself was later indicted for war crimes by the ICTY and was arrested when attending a conference in Vienna.

Having failed to secure support on the ground, Milošević attempted to destabilise Bosnia from the air. Two days into Operation Allied Force, two Serb MiG29 aircraft entered Bosnian airspace and were shot down by American F15 fighters over the Bosnian Serb border around Teocak. SFOR sources reported that they believed that the aircraft had flown into Bosnia with the intention of attacking them, a point seemingly confirmed when Zivadin Jovanović told *Tanjug* that the Serbs had not lost two aircraft but that NATO had lost several over Bosnia.[30]

The Serbs failed to cause trouble in Bosnia thanks to liaison between different NATO elements in South Eastern Europe. After falling short in Bosnia, the Serbs turned their attention onto Montenegro where the republic's president, Milo Djukanović, was pursuing an independent anti-Belgrade policy. At the beginning of April, Milošević installed a stout loyalist, Milorad Obradović, as head of the military in Montenegro.[31] This raised fears that Djukanović's government would be confronted with a coup. Again, NATO acted swiftly, using informal channels to warn Milošević that any attempt to oust the Montenegrin president would be resisted with NATO ground troops if necessary.[32]

The third element of Milošević's strategy was an attempt to split NATO. Milošević made frequent concessions to carefully chosen politicians and diplomats in an attempt to persuade states like Greece, Italy and Germany to baulk at the continuation of airstrikes. There is plenty of evidence to suggest that the diplomatic machinations between the allies were well understood in Belgrade. The VJ's own weekly newspaper, *Vojska*, reported that, 'NATO's aggression against Yugoslavia has greatly divided the alliance' and that the atmosphere at NATO headquarters in Brussels was, 'highly strained'. It continued, 'in all NATO military establishments except for the US, the position prevails that the aggression on Yugoslavia has only caused great problems failing to bring about the desired effects'.[33] However, Milošević's fourth strategy, which aimed to defeat the UÇK, re-establish Serb dominance in Kosovo and destabilise Macedonia lead to the failure of this third strategy. The mass murder and ethnic cleansing of Kosovar Albanians that accompanied Operation Horseshoe stiffened NATO's resolve and ensured that Milošević was ultimately fighting a war he could not win.

Operation Horseshoe

The first that Western publics heard about Operation Horseshoe was when Joschka Fischer told the *Berliner Zeitung* newspaper that on 26 February the Serbs had put the plan into effect and that its aim was to expel Kosovo's Albanian population. Fischer went on to say that he regretted not taking Milošević at his word when the Serb leader had told him that he would empty Kosovo within a week.[34] Germany's Defence Minister, Rudolf Scharping then told *Le Monde* that the document was passed on to Germany by a country bordering Yugoslavia (later thought to be Austria) and was believed to have been stolen.[35] Operation Horseshoe was so named because it envisaged the ethnic cleansing of Kosovar Albanians through a massive offensive around the province's borders in a horseshoe shape, suffocating the UÇK's supply chain and draining the province of Kosovar Albanians. Although British diplomats told Tim Judah that this public revelation was the first that they had heard of Operation Horseshoe,[36] causing anti-war critics such as Eric Herring to doubt its credibility,[37] there are two principal reasons for believing its existence.

First, it provides a good description of what actually happened in Kosovo during and immediately after the Paris negotiations. Recall that Milošević had placed hardline loyalists as head of the MUP forces and the VJ in preparation for his assault. Less than a week into Allied Force over 100,000 Kosovar Albanians found themselves as refugees outside the province and hundreds of thousands more were internally displaced.[38] Kosovar Albanians were systematically 'cleansed', street-by-street. Within five days of the campaign having begun, the Serbs had created a tight *cordon sanitaire* in the western corner of Kosovo, concentrating their forces there. This was foreseen by the Operation Horseshoe plan. Typically, Kosovar Albanians were given 30 minutes to leave their homes, their personal documents were destroyed and the Serbs often even laid on transport to near the border.[39] It is simply not possible to coordinate and manage such a rapid rate of expulsion without pre-planning. Furthermore, given that Milošević had told international diplomats of his intention to 'kill them all' and 'empty Kosovo within a week' and that the Serbs began conducting ethnic cleansing in border areas, the circumstantial evidence points very clearly to the Operation

Horseshoe plan. The fact that no written evidence has been disclosed is not surprising given that Milošević's decisions were always delivered orally.[40]

The second indicator that Operation Horseshoe existed is that despite the protestations of Western leaders to the opposite, their intelligence agencies knew about the likelihood of widespread ethnic cleansing. Two points of clarification need to be made though. The ethnic cleansing began some time before Operation Allied Force began and in fact provided the trigger for its launch. To say that NATO intelligence agencies knew about Operation Horseshoe is not to say that the Alliance knowingly provoked the ethnic cleansing. The Serbian operation began several days *before* NATO began its air campaign. In fact, knowledge of Operation Horseshoe would have added to rather than detracted from the case for employing military force as swiftly as possible. What is clear is that nobody expected the murder and ethnic cleansing to be so swift and large scale. The American press reported that Bill Clinton had been advised that a bombing campaign would provoke a Serb killing spree. General Hugh Shelton, chairman of the Joint Chiefs of Staff, and George Tenet, Director of the CIA, had both told the president this, it later emerged.[41] Furthermore, several senior military figures had told him that air power alone could not prevent or halt this ethnic cleansing. There is an important question that remains unanswered. If Operation Horseshoe was known about, why was so little done to prepare the UNHCR and other agencies to receive refugees in Albania and Macedonia? British politicians tended to defend themselves by arguing that the ethnic cleansing was not foreseen. After making a statement to this effect, Robin Cook came in for severe criticism from former Irish Prime Minister, John Bruton. He said of Cook, 'he is wrong. The present refugee crisis was not only foreseeable, it was foreseen. It is profoundly dishonest to pretend otherwise'.[42]

Phase One

Phase One of Operation Allied Force lasted only three days but exposed key disagreements within the Alliance. The first night of bombing made use of only 80 aircraft and cruise missiles. Eleven NATO members participated in the first night of the campaign and the British submarine, *HMS Trafalgar*, fired several Tomahawk missiles. Although targets in Kosovo, Serbia and Montenegro were hit they were confined to air defence and communications sites, command and control bunkers, missile batteries and army barracks. In an effort to isolate Yugoslavia, NATO combined military force with a diplomatic guarantee to the 'frontline' states. Javier

Solana effectively told these states that NATO would protect their territorial integrity from potential attack by Yugoslavia.[43]

Despite the very limited nature of phase one of the campaign, divisions within the Alliance were evident within hours. In Italy, the government's Communist coalition partners led by Armando Cossutta threatened to withdraw from the government. Cossutta argued that Italian forces could only be used in self-defence. In response, Prime Minister Massimo D'Alema insisted that although Italian aircraft were playing their 'full role' in the campaign (at the peak of the campaign, Italy had 54 aircraft committed to it) they were not involved in strikes on Yugoslavia and were instead deployed to protect other NATO aircraft.[44] D'Alema also promised to make every effort to bring about peace as soon as possible, though in mid-April he again faced domestic pressure when the Communists introduced a parliamentary motion demanding an immediate cessation of hostilities, which the government narrowly survived thanks to support from the opposition.[45] The Italian media raised concerns about Italy's vulnerability to Serb counter-attack. *La Republica* wrote that, 'southern Italy is living in fear' of terrorist reprisals, while *La Gazzetta del Mezzogiorno* observed with some alarm that Serbian warplanes could be over Italian airspace within 15 minutes.[46]

The Italian government and its counterpart in Athens, where 98 per cent of the population opposed the airstrikes, came under immediate pressure to oppose the campaign once phase one got under way. This prompted both governments to call immediately for a bombing pause and further negotiations with Belgrade. D'Alema insisted that the first night of bombing had been so successful that they had caused the Serbs to stop their offensives. There was little evidence to support this claim.[47] Meanwhile, the Greek government insisted that military operations would not resolve the conflict and called for more negotiation.[48]

Outside NATO the campaign came in for severe criticism particularly from the Russian, Chinese and Indian governments. Igor Ivanov was on his way to Washington believing that NATO would not begin airstrikes until after his visit when he was informed that they had begun. He immediately turned his aircraft around and headed back to Russia. He later called the attack, 'a strike against Russia' and instructed Ambassador Lavrov to summon an emergency Security Council meeting.[49] China condemned the strikes, as did India. A passage from the *Hindustan Times* aptly summed up the Indian response:

> The foreign policy of the world's most powerful nation and its allies can be summed up in one word: bomb. It is a ludicrous sight to watch

the mighty NATO war machine preparing to tame a tiny nation whose only lapse has been its refusal to pawn its sovereignty.[50]

States such as Indonesia, South Korea, and Japan, usually staunch supporters of NATO, were mute in their response to the bombing campaign. On the one hand, Tito's Yugoslavia had been a leading member of the Non-Aligned Movement and there remained a considerable amount of sympathy for the state, particularly in Asia and Africa. On the other, states acknowledged the conundrum between concern for human rights and support for sovereignty and territorial integrity that confronted NATO.[51]

The concern that was expressed by both allies and other states caused immediate problems for NATO. After all, the North Atlantic Council had only authorised phase one of the operation, a phase that was scheduled to last three days.

The purpose of phase one of the campaign was to eliminate Yugoslavia's integrated air defence system and establish the Alliance's air superiority.[52] However, with the Serbs carrying out Operation Horseshoe in Kosovo, Wesley Clark perceived a need to respond to it directly by attacking military targets in the province. The North Atlantic Council therefore moved rapidly to authorise phase two of the plan on 27 March. This decision marked an escalation and showed that the mounting evidence of ethnic cleansing and mass murder in Kosovo and perceived need to respond directly was overriding the concerns of states like Italy and Greece who had initially intended a bombing pause between phases. By deciding to move to phase two some time before all the phase one targets had been hit and its objectives reached, the North Atlantic Council departed from the initial idea of the phased air campaign.[53] NATO began to attack phase one and phase two targets simultaneously. Political concerns in the Council meant that NATO never officially moved beyond phase two but the 27 March decision gave the military significant flexibility to decide target sets, for example allowing Clark to attack targets in Montenegro while assuaging French concerns by not using their aircraft in such attacks.

Phase Two – widening the air war

NATO's second phase only lasted two days before being widened into the so-called 'phase two-plus', which remained in place for the rest of the war. Recognition in the West that Milošević was not planning to capitulate without a fight and the on-going ethnic cleansing in Kosovo prompted the Alliance to abandon its military plans. Phase two targets included targets in downtown Belgrade, the sorts of targets that Mike Short thought that the Alliance should have been attacking from the outset. However, the start of phase two was met almost immediately with NATO's first loss. On 27 March an American F117-A 'Stealth' aircraft was shot down by a Serb anti-aircraft missile about 35 miles northwest of Belgrade. The pilot was able to eject and was recovered within 12 hours by American Special Forces.[54] While the recovery of the pilot from under the nose of the Serbs was a major success, the loss of what was considered to be a virtually 'undownable' aircraft was a huge blow.

Towards the end of March an important disagreement emerged about the direction of the air war. Some states, particularly the US and UK wanted to increase the overall number of targets and bring more firepower to bear on the Serb forces reeking havoc in Kosovo.[55] The need to target these forces, even if it meant increasing the threat to NATO aircraft by flying lower and engaging the Serbs more closely, was a constant theme in the British approach to targeting debates. Having insisted that NATO's action was aimed at preventing or reversing Serb atrocities in Kosovo, Blair and Cook were keen to be seen to be attacking the perpetrators directly. At the other end of the spectrum, the Greek and Italian governments tried to persuade the North Atlantic Council about the need for a bombing pause between phases particularly as Easter approached.[56] It was clear that the Council would not be able to authorise a further widening of the war beyond phase two and that Wesley Clark would soon be running out of targets to hit. A compromise was reached that allowed the Alliance to put the target selection process outlined earlier into effect. Under 'phase two-plus' the Council did not explicitly authorise the widening of the air war but relaxed the geographic restrictions of phases one and two, allowing Clark to strike targets throughout Yugoslavia. In return, Javier Solana undertook a continuous consultation process with allies about potentially controversial targets and Wesley Clark was instructed to take national concerns into consideration when ordering a nation's aircraft to strike a particular target.[57]

This new phase reflected the emerging view that the air war would be a protracted affair and that striking at a limited selection of targets would not inhibit Serb activities in Kosovo. Operation Horseshoe made it virtually impossible for reluctant allies to demand a halt to Allied Force and reinforced the hawkish allies' belief in the rightness and necessity of their cause. Phase two-plus recognised the differences of opinion within the Alliance but delegated a degree of flexibility to Solana and Clark that would allow them to navigate through the different positions while maintaining military effectiveness. From Milošević's point of view the decision made the job of splitting the Alliance much harder. Allies could buy-in or out of different aspects of the air campaign, could maintain different diplomatic positions, and launch individual and collective political initiatives without directly affecting the military campaign. This compromise, therefore, was far more important than has been generally acknowledged.

Wesley Clark now called for the deployment of Apache helicopters to strike directly at Serbia's fielded forces in Kosovo. From the NATO military point of view, the first three weeks of the campaign had been very slow. Of 21 days of bombing only seven had enjoyed good weather. On ten of the days, half of all strikes had been cancelled due to lack of visibility.[58] Add to that the shortage of agreed targets and desire to protect allied pilots, it was becoming clear to Clark that he was not having a decisive impact on Serb forces. Indeed, on 17 April NATO estimated that it had only destroyed around a dozen Serb tanks.[59] Clark asked the Chairman of the Chiefs of Staff, Hugh Shelton, for Apache helicopters to be deployed in northern Albania beginning a saga that continued for the rest of the operation. In the end, the US lost two helicopters without ever engaging the Serbs.

Clark argued that the Apaches would be able to engage Serb forces in Kosovo directly. Given the helicopter's range of fire they could do this without actually entering Kosovo, thus minimising the potential danger to American Apache crews, which would be considerably greater than the threat to crews of fixed wing aircraft operating at much higher altitude. Persuading the Pentagon and the American Army to allow him to use Apache proved to be difficult. Clark's own account of the war is littered with requests for the helicopters to be deployed and used. After receiving authorisation to deploy some 24 Apaches in northern Albania, Clark instructed his staff to begin planning for their use and conducting training. The real planning began on 5 April with the decision to deploy Task Force Hawk in Albania. About 8,000 NATO soldiers from the Allied Command Europe Mobile Force joined Task Force Hawk in Albania, commanded by General John Reith. These troops formed Operation Allied Harbour, which took over responsibility for dealing with the tens of thousands of Kosovar Albanian refugees pouring over the border into northern Albania. The announcement of the deployment of the helicopters themselves, along with the arrival of Operation Allied Harbour prompted debate about the potential for, and likelihood of, the use of ground forces against the Serbs in Kosovo. This debate rumbled on throughout the war and hijacked NATO's fiftieth anniversary meeting in Washington.

The initial deployment of Task Force Hawk suggested that the Alliance was beginning to seriously consider its land options. This image was reinforced in two ways. First, by the beginning of April there was a pronounced feeling amongst NATO militaries that given the failure to coerce an immediate Serb capitulation ground forces would have to be employed if the Alliance was to achieve its political objectives. Wesley Clark's desire to use Apache helicopters, and the Pentagon's reluctance to allow him do so was well covered by the media.[60] Kenneth Bacon, the Pentagon's chief spokesman, even went as far as commenting in mid-April that Task Force Hawk would be expanded in line with the well known wishes of Clark.[61] Presidential candidate, George W. Bush, insisted that he would back the use of ground troops if the military thought that they were necessary, though he chose not to criticise Clinton for ruling out the ground option.[62] In Britain, General Michael Rose, former military head of UNPROFOR, wrote that:

> I believe that we should reinforce NATO's troops already on the ground in Albania and Macedonia – something that would threaten Milošević with a ground offensive in Kosovo. The purpose of any ground offensive would be to seize territory that could ultimately be traded for peace.[63]

The key concern for these figures was that if the refugees were to be returned home before the winter snow arrived, and they calculated that the humanitarian catastrophe would be greatly worsened if they were not, the use of ground troops might be necessary because by mid April there were few signs of Serb capitulation. As one NATO source argued, 'we really want to get the refugees back inside Yugoslavia and in homes by the winter. Any land campaign would have to take place well before then to secure the ground for their return'.[64] If a land campaign was to be contemplated, a political decision would need to be taken as early as possible to allow the military to begin detailed planning and build up the estimated 200,000 troops that were thought to be needed.

This emerging military advice went in tandem with strengthening political resolve amongst the allies provoked by Serbian ethnic cleansing. In particular, the French political scene underwent an important sea change with the usually vitriolic anti-American Socialists and Greens offering support for NATO. The Green representatives in Lionel Jospin's coalition government even went as far as to call for a land invasion.[65] There was also evidence of increasing public support in the West for a land invasion, with polls in April showed 66 per cent in favour of the war in the UK, compared with 60 per cent in both France and Germany. The Italian public, usually seen as the least hawkish after Greece, was divided almost 50–50 on the issue of support for the war.[66]

At the same time, the Alliance deployed ground forces into Macedonia as part of Operation Agricola. This was a preparation for the deployment of the KFOR peacekeeping force into Kosovo itself that was envisaged both at Rambouillet and Paris. Tony Blair announced the despatch of the aircraft carrier, *HMS Invincible* and the deployment of 2,000 troops in Macedonia, bringing the number of British troops there up to 8,000.[67] Operation Agricola was led by the multinational Allied Rapid Reaction Corps, commanded by the British General, Mike Jackson. Supporting this military build-up, Petro Koci, the Albanian interior minister called upon the Alliance to respond more robustly to the repeated shelling of targets inside Albania by the VJ.[68]

Wesley Clark began to plan for a ground element to the campaign at the beginning of April. It soon became clear, however, that the circumstantial evidence of mounting support for a ground campaign was misleading. The confidence exuded above by NATO leaders was wafer thin. The West was shocked to wake up on 8 April and discover that the 30,000 Kosovar Albanian refugees in the Blace camp in Macedonia had been moved to Albania by the Macedonian army. Most of the allies rigidly distinguished between troops deployed in preparation for an entry into Kosovo after a ceasefire and the possibility of using them to force their way into the province. When this latter issue was raised before the Washington summit not a single leader called for a land invasion. Jamie Shea, NATO's spokesman, insisted that, 'for the moment, troops will only go in when we have a ceasefire agreement', and General Ferenc Vegh, stated that, 'Hungary will not send ground troops because it would not be in our national interest. I believe air power alone is not sufficient, but I don't think it is a correct answer to send ground troops.'[69] Even General Charles Guthrie, Chief of Staff of hawkish Britain explained that, 'neither NATO nor the UK have any plans for an opposed invasion of Kosovo'.[70]

NATO began planning a land operation at the beginning of April but had to be imaginative about the way that it went about doing so. The planners considered two ideas in particular. First, a limited invasion taking part of Kosovo to act as a sanctuary for refugees and give NATO a foothold from which to negotiate. The key problem with this approach was that it would create a *de facto* partition of Kosovo. Partition was widely thought to have been Milošević's preferred end state (behind

NATO simply disappearing) and ran contrary to the Alliance's humanitarian goals. The second idea, pushed by the British, was the idea of an invasion into a 'semi-permissive' environment. The 'semi-permissive' environment was somewhere between the permissive environment envisaged for the entry of KFOR where the Serbs gave their consent, and an all-out land invasion against hostile VJ and MUP forces. It was a condition in which there was no invitation but where organised opposition at the operational level had collapsed, giving KFOR the role of 'mopping up' pockets of uncoordinated resistance. The problem with this approach was that it would be difficult to guarantee a specific level of damage from the air and that if an invasion was launched on the semi-permissive assumption and resistance proved to be much better organised than thought NATO forces could sustain substantial casualties.[71] Because of these concerns, Clark's preferred plan was to follow the Gulf War model and attack with decisive force. However, there was little support in Washington for such an approach let alone amongst allies. Several of the Service Chiefs argued that minimising NATO casualties was more important than attacking Serb forces in Kosovo because casualties would discredit the campaign and bring about its premature termination.[72]

Clark was able to secure more aircraft with which to strike at the expanded target list he had been granted by the North Atlantic Council. The total number of aircraft available to him rose from 350 to 600. Clark also used his new authority to begin striking strategic targets and Milošević's sources of power and wealth.[73] However, the expansion of the air war increased the number of civilian casualties caused by NATO's mistakes. On 6 April, NATO attacked the town of Aleksinac in southern Serbia. Two bombs struck the centre of the town, damaging its hospital and killing 12 civilians.[74] Worse followed on 12 April when an aircraft attacked a railway bridge over the Morava River in the town of Leskovac. Two missiles struck a train that was on the bridge, killing 16 civilians. Two days later came one of the worst mistakes of the campaign, which resulted in the death of around 75 Kosovar Albanian refugees.

Because Clark and the Alliance's political leaders were keen to be seen to be attacking Serbia's fielded forces in Kosovo, NATO aircraft maintained a permanent presence over the province on 'search and destroy' type missions. Having observed the use of vehicles in the destruction of a village, an American F16 pilot spotted what he believed to be a military convoy on the Prizren to Djakovica road. Several aircraft then attacked the convoy. After initially denying that the attack had happened, believing that they had attacked only military targets, NATO later admitted that it had indeed accidentally attacked a civilian convoy though continued to claim, with some plausibility, that military vehicles were using the convoy for cover. The attack on the Djakovica road greatly shook the Alliance and caused widespread public concern in the West, principally because NATO was seen to be attacking the very people it was supposed to be protecting. Moreover, the confusion with which NATO imparted information about the attack, only fully explaining events some five days later, made many believe that it was trying to cover up its mistakes.

One possible explanation for the attack was suggested to the author by people inside American Special Forces. To help identify Serb military targets in Kosovo, US agents handed mobile phones to UÇK fighters and gave each an individual code. This enabled the UÇK to inform the American Air Force about troop movements. One such UÇK fighter was captured by the Serbs and had the code beaten out of him. The Serbs then called NATO and informed them that the Djakovica road convoy was a Serbian military convoy. NATO aircraft duly struck the convoy several times. General Clark would never admit to this explanation because that would mean admitting a much higher degree of cooperation with the UÇK than has hitherto been acknowledged but it does help to explain why American pilots were so convinced that this refugee column was actually a military one and why NATO first denied the attack, believing that they had attacked a Serb military convoy.

There were other controversial attacks, such as the mistaken attack on the Chinese Embassy and the attack on the Belgrade television station. This latter attack, on 23 April, prompted criticism from the European Broadcasting Union and caused Italian Foreign Minister Lamberto Dini to publicly break allied unity for the first time. Dini described the television station bombing as 'terrible', adding, 'I disapprove ... the question of television wasn't, I believe, part of the plan'.[75] However, the Djakovica road attack stands out as the lowest point of Operation Allied Force. Its plans changed irrevocably and lacking agreement about how to proceed, NATO was now making mistakes that cost the lives of the very people it was supposed to be helping. There also seemed little hope of manufacturing a political solution that would be acceptable to the warring parties and all the permanent members of the Security Council.

The search for a settlement

As we will see in Chapter 7, the Russian mediator Viktor Chernomyrdin played a crucial role in bringing the war to a close. For the first month of the campaign, though, Russia was bellicose in its opposition to NATO. It withdrew its military mission from the Alliance's Brussels headquarters, suspended its participation in Partnership for Peace, and severed diplomatic ties. This bellicose response represented a significant shift away from Russia's previously cooperative approach, and Chernomyrdin's appointment was more of a return to Russia's pre-war stance than a change of policy. At the beginning of April, Russia despatched a warship to the Adriatic to fulfil two roles: Force the Alliance to take notice of Russia by asserting a military presence in the region and intercept NATO's radio traffic. Western–Russian relations worsened immediately after, with Russia threatening to re-target its nuclear weapons on Western cities, bring Yugoslavia into a union with Russia and Belarus, and provide material assistance to the Serbs.

On 9 April, Yeltsin gave an extraordinary speech in which he argued that, 'they [NATO] want to bring in ground troops ... they want simply to seize Yugoslavia to make it their protectorate ... we cannot allow that to happen'.[76] A foreign ministry official explained that Yeltsin had ordered the papers for a union with Yugoslavia to be drawn up and that this would result in Russia providing military assistance to the Serbs. Yeltsin also reportedly ordered the re-targeting of Russia's strategic nuclear missiles, causing alarm in the West. On the same day, however, Igor Ivanov, the Foreign Minister denied both that the missiles had been re-targeted and that Russia was about to join a union with Yugoslavia and Belarus. Indeed, both threats turned out to be something of a distraction. Nuclear experts pointed out that as it took less than two minutes to target a missile the idea of re-targeting was something of a misnomer. Furthermore, a poll in *Sergodnya* found that 76 per cent of the population thought that targeting the West was a bad idea.[77] The Monday following Yeltsin's dramatic speech saw the Yugoslav parliament vote overwhelmingly in favour of the proposed union, believing that military assistance would be forthcoming. The truth of the matter, however, was that Yeltsin had already got cold feet about the plan and the suggestion did not go any further. As the war progressed, it also became clear that Russia was not even supplying small arms covertly let alone supplying the sophisticated anti-aircraft weaponry sought by the Serbs.[78]

The explanation for Yeltsin's extreme initial response to NATO, which was at odds with the earlier political signals that the Russians had sent out, lies in domestic Russian politics. At the same time as Yeltsin was making his extraordinary threats, he was himself coming under the threat of impeachment by the Communist led Duma (parliament), which was unhappy with the President's handling of the economy and the endemic corruption in public life. Yeltsin's bellicose nationalism persuaded the Duma to indefinitely postpone the impeachment vote on 12 April, allowing the president to reinforce his position by subsequently sacking the powerful Prime Minister, Yevgeny Primakov. According to Russian political analysts, 'all this populist talk about a union between Russia, Belarus and Yugoslavia has ruined the Duma's plans for getting rid of Yeltsin'.[79] It was only two days after this vote in the Duma that Yeltsin appointed Viktor Chernomyrdin as his special envoy to Yugoslavia. This appointment fundamentally changed Russia's relations with NATO and Yugoslavia. Chernomyrdin essentially agreed with NATO's demands and took on a key role in the search for a mutually acceptable settlement.

The effort to find a diplomatic solution to the conflict began at the beginning of April when Boris Yeltsin identified the G-8 industrialised states as an appropriate forum for the world's major powers to discuss and resolve the problem. However, the first peace overtures came from Belgrade a few days before NATO outlined its five objectives outlined at the beginning of the chapter. The first sign that the air strikes were hurting Belgrade and that the Serb government was interested in doing a deal with NATO came on 6 April when it offered to begin a unilateral ceasefire.[80] The ceasefire offer coincided with the arrival of Yevgeny Primakov in Belgrade and stated that all Kosovar Albanian refugees would be allowed to return to their homes. That evening, Vuk Drašković, the maverick Serb nationalist leader who had led opposition to Milošević in the past but who now found himself in the government,[81] intimated on Serb television that the government would also be prepared allow some form of international presence in Kosovo to assist with implementing the peace settlement. Unsurprisingly, NATO leaders swiftly rejected the peace offer. British Foreign Office officials correctly pointed out that Drašković had no authority within the Serb government. Interestingly, Primakov's efforts in Belgrade – his last role in the conflict – were not adopted as official Russian policy by either Yeltsin or Igor Ivanov.

A week later, Madeleine Albright and Igor Ivanov met in Oslo. Following Yeltsin's successful avoidance of impeachment proceedings, the Oslo meeting gave birth to a more cooperative Russian approach. The meeting secured three important achievements. Firstly, it marked the end of the acrimony that had accompanied Russia's initial response to the air strikes. Secondly, it began a process of negotiation on substantive issues that eventually led to the G-8 statement that informed the demands made in Security Council Resolution 1244 at the end of the war. Finally, it gave Russia the role of interlocutor between NATO and Yugoslavia. It was immediately after this meeting that Yeltsin announced Chernomyrdin's appointment. In Oslo, Ivanov told Albright that Milošević still opposed the idea of foreign troops being deployed in Kosovo without his consent but that there might be scope for a UN peacekeeping deployment with the consent of the Serbs.[82]

At around the same time, the German government responded to the hawkish British position on the use of ground troops at an EU meeting it was chairing in Bonn. As we saw, the British government argued that NATO should begin planning and preparing for a possible ground invasion and was determined than NATO should lead an eventual KFOR peace implementation force. Thinking about the practicalities of ending the war and offering an alternative to the 'semi-permissive' approach favoured by the British, the German plan called for a 24-hour suspension of the bombing once Milošević began to withdraw his forces, that the bombing would cease permanently once the withdrawal was complete and that a UN-authorised military force would be despatched to the province.

The German plan repeated the Russian suggestion that the G-8 provide the forum for negotiating an agreement to present to the Security Council. However, the idea of a bombing pause was rejected by the EU Council of Ministers. A day after Joschka Fischer unveiled the plan, German Chancellor Gerhard Shröder was forced to insist that:

> It goes without saying that military action will continue unabated. It is crystal clear and not called into question by the by the non-NATO members of the EU, that the points set forward by the [NATO] Secretary-General have to be met before we can consider reducing our military activity.[83]

At the EU meeting in Bonn, both Tony Blair and Jacques Chirac distanced themselves from the plan because of the bombing pause passage. Chirac went as far as to say that the German plan was not even discussed. The US administration also dismissed the idea of a bombing pause, with White House spokesperson Joe Lockhart pointing out that 'the important thing to note is that there will be no cessation of the air campaign until demands are met'.[84] At the heart of this disagreement was confusion over the nature of the bombing pause. Several states had advocated a bombing pause at the end of phase one to create an opportunity for further negotiation. The Americans, British and French had vigorously opposed this idea, pointing out that such a pause would diminish the overall impact of the campaign and, once stopped, it would be difficult to resume the bombing. There was thus some confusion between this idea, put forward most forcefully by Italy and Greece, and the German plan that called for a suspension of bombing only after the Serbs began to withdraw. Although the US rejected the German plan, this idea was actually taken up by the American–Russian diplomatic process and became part of the functional modalities of the peace plan that was eventually implemented.

The German plan proposed that Kosovo be placed under UN administration and that KFOR be authorised by the Security Council. Although it was always envisaged that KFOR would have UN authorisation the idea of creating a UN administration was qualitatively different from the Rambouillet peace settlement, which had envisaged a tightly supervised form of self-rule. However, EU leaders chose instead to give partial support to a French plan to bring the province under temporary EU administration.[85] The UN option came out on top once the European and American–Russian diplomatic processes came together after the Washington summit.

NATO's fiftieth birthday: the Washington summit

As befitted this type of war, the decisive turning point came not on the battlefield but around the negotiating table. Uniquely, sitting around the negotiating table were the representatives of only one the belligerents. NATO's fiftieth anniversary summit held in Washington between 23–25 April has generally been noted for two things. First, the toning down of the proposed celebrations to take into consideration the fact that NATO was conducting a campaign that most Alliance leaders thought would have been over several weeks earlier. Secondly, journalists and diplomats tend to focus on one key issue that was raised at Washington – the possibility of a land campaign. Tony Blair went to Washington hoping to persuade the American public and Bill Clinton that NATO should start to think the unthinkable and plan and deploy for a ground operation aimed at getting the refugees home before the snow arrived. The British Prime Minister found himself to be utterly isolated, with the US, France, Germany, Italy and others all arguing against the idea.

Prior to the summit, Blair used his American visit to take his case directly to the American people and policy-makers. At a now famous speech in Chicago he called for a new internationalism, warning Americans about the dangers of isolationism. He told them that 'we cannot turn our backs on conflicts and the violation of human rights within other countries if we want still to be secure'.[86] Joining Blair, Robin Cook observed that the issue was not *if* ground forces would be used but *when* and in what circumstances. It was soon clear, however, that Blair and Cook had few allies at Washington. As William Cohen, the American Secretary of State for Defence put it:

> There's no consensus for ground troops in the NATO Alliance. There's no consensus in the Congress of the country at this point, and there's no need according to our commanding officers, those who are in charge of carrying out and executing the military campaign. So until such time as that changes, we would not even consider it.[87]

Wesley Clark's memoirs show that this was not an entirely accurate representation of the military position. While Clark believed that the air strikes were working and would succeed in forcing a Serb capitulation he also believed that army capabilities such as the Apache helicopters should be used and that the Alliance should plan seriously for a land invasion and begin preparatory deployments to the region if only to add to the coercive pressure on Milošević.

Other Americans were more hostile to the British idea than Cohen. Pat Buchanan, former presidential candidate, described Blair as 'the mouse who roared', adding, 'it isn't British troops who are going to be humping up the road to Belgrade'.[88] Buchanan was quite wrong. At the time of the summit, the British Ministry of Defence was already contemplating the despatch of 50,000 troops to the region and by the end of May it was drawing up call-up letters for reservists.[89] Massimo D'Alema and Gerhard Schröder were similarly hostile to British hawkishness. They had enough trouble winning parliamentary support for the air campaign as it was so there was little chance that either would win domestic support for a land campaign. Thus, the very idea put Alliance unity at risk. Schröder, whose position was being challenged by the former Finance Minister and senior Social Democratic Party activist Oskar Lafontaine, lambasted the idea of a land war and described Blair as 'totally isolated'.[90]

These, though, we not the reasons why the Washington summit was a turning point. Instead, two important decisions were taken that reinforced the Alliance's resolve and instructed Milošević that his attempts to break NATO's unity would fail. The leaders at Washington first agreed to provide Wesley Clark with greater authority to expand the target list, including new targets and increasing the number of aircraft available to him. They also rubber-stamped the routine use of daytime attacks, significantly increasing the number of assaults that Clark could make on Yugoslavia each day.[91] The summit also provided a forum for the US to take soundings on an overall strategic campaign plan that it was working on. The plan, put into practice immediately after the summit, combined military, political, and economic objectives. The crucial sea-change in this new strategy was that Russia now lay at the heart of diplomatic effort.[92]

Summary

NATO had envisaged a brief and limited war reminiscent of Operation Deliberate Force four years earlier in Bosnia. However, the 12 months of threat and prevarication that preceded it persuaded Milošević that NATO unity was weak and that he could withstand the air bombardment for longer than the Alliance could. This proposition had much merit. However, Milošević attempted to escalate the conflict and deal with his UÇK problem once and for all by draining Kosovo of Kosovar Albanians. This was a fatal mistake. By unleashing Operation Horseshoe, Milošević solidified Alliance unity and made it more difficult for potential supporters such as Russia to denounce NATO. Although the Alliance continued to rule out a land campaign, Tony Blair placed the prospect of such a campaign firmly on the agenda. Moreover, as the winter snow drew nearer, Alliance members began to come around to the idea. NATO leaders delegated more authority and aircraft to Wesley Clark and the daily sortie rate increased sharply after the Washington summit. Finally, Yeltsin's success in deferring an impending impeachment allowed Russia to resume the constructive role it had played for the previous 12 months through its bilateral relations with Yugoslavia and through the Contact Group, after a three week impasse at the beginning of the war. Although things continued to look bleak for the Alliance when its leaders gathered at Washington, they had in fact turned the corner. Victory was now inevitable.

7
The Triumph of Diplomacy

The immediate aftermath of the Washington summit saw the widening and deepening of NATO's air campaign, a marked increase in diplomatic activity and continued disagreement within the Alliance about the need to employ ground forces. As part of the widening and deepening of the campaign new targets were approved, Wesley Clark was given greater discretion about which targets to hit, and the Alliance added a maritime dimension to support an EU oil embargo against Yugoslavia. The targeting of oil production facilities was one of NATO's most successful operations and by the end of April, Serb access to refined oil was severely reduced leading to reports that oil rationing was commonplace in the VJ and MUP, restricting their on-going programme of ethnic cleansing. Indeed, NATO intelligence sources suggested that whereas before the war Yugoslavia had access to 60,000 barrels of oil per day, by the end of April it could only count on 32,000.[1] However, despite the embargo Yugoslavia was still able to acquire oil through the Montenegrin port of Bar and the Danube route, though the importation potential of that route was greatly reduced by NATO's destruction of bridges along the river. The third route for oil was a pipeline running through Hungary and Croatia to two refineries in Pancevo and Novi Sad (both of which were damaged or destroyed by air strikes). This pipeline was shut off.

Although NATO indicated that it would enforce the EU's oil embargo with a maritime 'stop and search' strategy it soon became clear that it had no legal authority to turn back tankers that were carrying fuel to Yugoslavia.[2] This problem emerged after several Alliance and EU members, including France, Italy, Greece and Ireland, objected to the idea of directing a naval blockade against Montenegro. These states also objected to the plan to isolate Bar by attacking its road and rail connections. Because of these objections, NATO's Military Committee had to devise a compromise strategy that would allow some form of enforcement while falling short of an all-out naval blockade. The solution, put together by Klaus Naumman, was a 'visit and search' regime aimed at deterring oil shipments rather than preventing them. NATO warships would visit and search tankers but not turn them around if they were found to be carrying oil. This plan sounded like a fudge. After all, what was the point of 'visiting' and searching ships if you had no authority to do anything about it if they were carrying oil? However, its architect believed that it would have a profound effect. Revealing the plans, Naumann told reporters:

> I think we will see a certain impact from the visit and search regime, third nations' ships will get very, very cautious, they will think twice whether they will take this route, because no one likes to be stopped at sea by a warship.[3]

The Russian government insisted that it would not respect the embargo. Igor Ivanov argued that it would increase the suffering of Yugoslav civilians and that complying with it would mean reneging on international export commitments.[4] However, both Russia and China dramatically reduced the number of oil shipments to Yugoslavia albeit citing non-payment for previous deliveries rather than compliance with the EU embargo as the principle reason.[5]

Renewed diplomacy

The aftermath of the Washington summit saw almost two weeks of frenetic diplomatic activity intimating that the war could be coming to an end. The fact that it took another seven weeks to end can be largely put down to the accidental bombing of the Chinese Embassy in Belgrade on 7 May. The post-Washington diplomacy was based upon the German plan outlined in the previous chapter. The initiative was supported not only by Russian participation through Viktor Chenomyrdin but also by signs of splits in the Yugoslav government. Vuk Drasković told state television that the Serbian government should start 'telling the truth' about what was happening in Kosovo and make people aware that the VJ and MUP were engaged in wholesale ethnic cleansing and that this was the reason why they were being bombed.[6] Drasković was promptly sacked from his position within the government. There were also signs of divisions within the VJ, with mounting evidence of resistance to the compulsory draft and riots in southern Serbian towns and cities, including Niš, when local VJ detachments were ordered to Kosovo.[7]

The first suggestion that agreement with Russia on a mutually acceptable form of words to present to the Yugoslav government would be possible came with an indication from the UK that contrary to its earlier pronouncements it would approve a Security Council Resolution that made no reference to NATO. While maintaining that KFOR should be 'NATO-led' the British concession was clearly aimed at Russia.[8] The actual job of finding an appropriate form of words with Viktor Chernomyrdin was given to the US administration's primary Russian expert, Strobe Talbott. On the first of many visits to Moscow, Talbott arrived on 26 April for intensive negotiations with Chernomyrdin and Ivanov. The Russians maintained their view that there would have to be a halt to the bombing before there could be talks with Belgrade. However, progress was made on the nature of the post-conflict KFOR force with the Russians accepting the idea of such a force in principle. This was a departure from their previous insistence that KFOR should be a lightly armed observer mission. From here on in the bulk of the negotiations focused on the modalities of implementation rather than the basic principles.[9]

Almost immediately after his meeting with Talbott, Chernomyrdin visited Belgrade again. On his way to the Serb capital, the Russian envoy stopped off in Bonn and Rome for talks with Schröder and D'Alema, in which he outlined the basis of a peace proposal. Although there was now considerable agreement on the basic principles there were three key points of disagreement between NATO and Russia, and considerable disagreement within the Alliance about how rigidly it should stick to its demands. The three areas of disagreement were:

- The modalities for ending the war. This was the issue of when the air strikes should stop. The British and Americans insisted that the campaign should continue until the Serbs had completed a verifiable withdrawal from Kosovo. Other allies, most notably the Italians and Germans, argued that the air strikes be suspended once the Yugoslav withdrawal had begun. They could then be resumed if the withdrawal was not completed. Russia and Greece argued that the air strikes should stop once NATO and Russia had agreed a form of words that they could take to the Security Council and then offer to Belgrade.
- The nature of KFOR. Whilst there was an emerging agreement that an eventual Security Council resolution would not make reference to NATO but that it would create a militarily capable force, the Russians still opposed the idea that the force should be NATO led with its command structure following the model set by IFOR/SFOR in Bosnia.

Instead, Russia favoured a blue helmeted UN peacekeeping force. Later, after agreeing that KFOR would be NATO led, Russia insisted that it should have its own sector. This insistence delayed the KFOR's deployment by a week and caused the standoff at Pristina airport discussed later.

- The presence of Yugoslav troops. NATO insisted that *all* VJ and MUP forces should leave Kosovo. Russia, however, argued that as Kosovo was part of Yugoslavia the Serbs should be allowed to retain armed forces there, albeit at a reduced level.

There was enough agreement about the basic principles to allow Chernomyrdin to travel to Belgrade and offer terms to Milošević. Indeed, it is testament to the amount of consensus that had emerged between NATO and Russia that the Yugoslav president dismissed Chernomyrdin's proposals out of hand. Whilst the Russian envoy suggested that an agreement was likely, Milošević insisted not only that KFOR be a UN force but also that it be unarmed and contain no representatives from NATO countries.[10] However, within the space of a few days the Serbs did make two important conciliatory gestures. Following a visit by Reverend Jesse Jackson, they released three American soldiers that had been taken prisoner along the Macedonian border at the beginning of the war.[11] A few days later they released Ibrahim Rugova from a house arrest during which he had been paraded on Serbian television in purported 'peace negotiations' with Milošević. Rugova was released to Italy, following a month of bilateral negotiation between the Italians and Yugoslavs. Italian Prime Minister, Massimo D'Alema insisted that Rugova's release created the potential for genuine negotiations between the Serbs and Kosovar Albanians.[12]

At around the same time, the US witnessed two important votes in the Congress and Senate. These votes effectively endorsed the conclusions of the Washington summit, on the one hand curtailing the president's ability to launch a ground war while offering greater resources for the air campaign.[13] In the first vote, on 28 April, Congress voted by 249 to 180 (with five abstentions) to assert its right to decide upon the allocation of funds for any potential ground campaign. At the same time it also approved a request from the president for more funds to support the on-going operation.[14] Importantly, although many Democrats opposed the clauses restricting funds for a land campaign, arguing of the need to retain flexibility,[15] the White House actually lobbied in favour of the full package. Clinton himself argued that, 'Congress should resist the temptation to add unrelated expenditures, even important ones, which could delay the process, because that would undermine the very goals that this funding is intended to meet'.[16] While it may seem odd for a president to argue in favour of curtailing his powers as Commander-in-Chief of the armed forces his reasoning was impeccable: Congress would authorise an increase in funding for on-going operations if the president accepted that the House would have to be consulted before the campaign was widened to include a land invasion. Although some of the extra funds were needed to sustain the build-up of American ground forces in Albania and Macedonia, the decision as to whether to use them in an invasion would be taken by Congress. A similar pattern was followed a week later when a motion was tabled in the Senate to authorise the president, 'to use all necessary forces and other means' in order to prevail over the Serbs.[17] Again, although the motion would have technically strengthened Clinton's position and would undoubtedly have made the threat of a land invasion more resonant, the White House argued that the motion be shelved to avoid a divisive debate on the ground option.[18] The Senate concurred, voting by 78 votes to 22 to shelve the resolution.

The effort to find a formula for peace that both Russia and NATO could agree upon was given impetus at a G-8 meeting held in Bonn on 6 May. Three days earlier Chernomyrdin had visited Washington for a 90 minute meeting with Clinton. After the meeting, the Russian envoy met his old friend, American Vice-President Al Gore, along with Strobe Talbott, Sandy Berger and others. At this meeting, Chernomyrdin suggested a 'hammer and anvil' plan. According to Tim Judah, Chernomyrdin told Gore and Talbott that, 'I represent Russia and will go and pound away, but I want someone else to pound against'.[19] The Russian mediator thus proposed that he have a negotiating partner representing the West so that a united and more credible front could be presented to Belgrade.

Several names were discussed. One suggestion was Carl Bildt, the former Swedish Prime Minister who had previously served as UN envoy in Bosnia. The Americans and British torpedoed Bildt's candidature because of his outspoken criticism of Operation Allied Force at the outset of the campaign. On 22 March he had written that:

> For NATO to initiate acts of war against Serbia is only justifiable if the initial air operation can be followed directly by comprehensive ground operations. Otherwise there is the risk that the effect will be that we leave millions of people defenceless on the ground in the conflict that will rapidly escalate. And to believe that a war fought with Kalashnikovs between ruins can be stopped by means of cruise missiles and B-52's is naïve and dangerous.[20]

Bildt subsequently became a UN envoy for Kosovo, much to NATO's irritation, though he was never able to play a leading role because of the dominance of the Russian–NATO diplomatic axis during the war and the role of Kosovo's international administrator, Bernard Kouchner and the head of KFOR, General Mike Jackson, immediately after. Another suggestion was Kofi Annan, the UN Secretary-General. This proposition was rejected by Albright who insisted that Chernomyrdin's partner be linked to NATO or the West in some way. It was then that Albright proposed Martti Ahtisaari, the Finnish President. Ahtisaari was ideal for the job. On the one hand he had impeccable personal credentials. He had served the UN as a mediator in Namibia for 13 years and had also served the organisation in Bosnia, gaining a reputation as a skilled and judicious diplomat. On the other hand, he was ideally placed as President of Finland. Finland was not a member of NATO (making life easier for Chernomyrdin) but supported its cause (placating Albright). Finland was also tied to the West as a member of the EU and was scheduled to take over its presidency in July. When Albright suggested Ahtisaari, Chernomyrdin reportedly retorted 'voht!' (That's it!) And the deal was done.[21] Ahtisaari was formally appointed EU envoy on 11 May.

The principal aim of the G-8 meeting in Bonn was to ratify the Chernomyrdin–Ahtisaari partnership and continue work towards a mutually acceptable settlement that the mediators could put before the Serbs. Indeed, one of the conditions Ahtisaari insisted on before he accepted his new role was that he would not travel to Belgrade until NATO and Russia had reached an accommodation. The Finn made this demand after it became clear that Strobe Talbott and Viktor Chernomyrdin envisaged different roles for him. Talbott wanted Ahtisaari to travel to Belgrade alone to take NATO's demands to Milošević whereas Chernomyrdin saw his role as a partner in the process that he had begun.

The Bonn summit saw Russia make two important concessions, which brought it much closer to accepting NATO's five war aims and reflected the key points of the German proposals that the Alliance had publicly rejected. First, Ivanov implicitly accepted for the first time that *all* VJ and MUP forces, as well as irregular Serb paramilitaries, would have to leave Kosovo[22] though the word 'all' was actually left out of the G-8 statement issued at the end of the meeting.[23] This left the possibilities of total or partial withdrawal open, a circle that was squared by a later agreement to accept only a total withdrawal followed by, in principle if not in practice, a limited redeployment of Serb forces to man the borders and protect Serbian cultural heritage in Kosovo. Some two years after the deployment of KFOR such a return has not happened and is unlikely to happen in the foreseeable future.

The second key agreement secured at Bonn was agreement with Russia that an international military force sanctioned by the UN would have to be deployed into Kosovo after the war. Getting Russian agreement on this was vital as without it there could be no UN authorisation. In return, and again in line with the German plan, NATO dropped its insistence that the relevant Security Council resolution explicitly authorise the Alliance to act, agreeing instead that such a force would only have to be 'NATO led' and that this criteria need not be present in the resolution. Moreover, as an indication of how close to agreement the sides had come and how prescient the earlier German initiative had been, Bill Clinton even suggested that NATO would consider a 24 hour bombing pause if Milošević accepted the G-8 proposals.[24]

The Bonn agreement effectively endorsed NATO's five demands while making the language more general to secure Russian acquiescence. Chernomyrdin and Ahtisaari were to be despatched the following week to deliver the G-8 terms to Milošević and underline the fact that Russia and NATO had reached a consensus. I have argued throughout that the appearance of Russian-Serbian unity, at least at the governmental level, was a chimera. However, it was only the Bonn agreement that made it absolutely clear to the Serbs that Russia would not support Yugoslavia or offer it material assistance. On the evening of 6 May, therefore, peace looked close at hand. One night later, as Chernomyrdin prepared to deliver the G-8 terms to Milošević, NATO launched a disastrous mistaken attack on the Chinese Embassy in Belgrade.

The Chinese Embassy bombing

On the night of 7 May, NATO aircraft attacked the Chinese Embassy in Belgrade, killing three Chinese journalists. The attack was carried out by American B-2 bombers flying from Whitman Air Force Base in Missouri. The threefold impact of the attack was immediate. Firstly, and most publicly, demonstrators in Beijing and around the world attacked British and American embassies and the Chinese government swiftly condemned the Alliance. NATO members issued immediate apologies but Chinese premier Jiang Zemin refused to receive Clinton's verbal telephone apology for over a week. Secondly, the mistake increased opposition to Operation Allied Force in the West. In Britain, for example, the Conservative Party defence spokesman, Michael Howard, lambasted NATO for its 'gross incompetence'.[25] Only four days after the attack, the coalition governments in both Italy and Germany came under threat and the Greek government stepped up its campaign for a bombing pause to allow time for a negotiated settlement to take shape. Finally, the G-8 process was derailed and Milošević given hope of finally splitting NATO and thus cause to prolong the war.

The Chinese Embassy bombing attracted a great deal of public scrutiny and provoked a number of conspiracy theories. Some, such as Peter Gowan's idea that the bombing was a deliberate attempt to antagonise China and prompt Taiwan to purchase more arms from the US were plainly nonsensical.[26] A team of British and Danish journalists offered another, more credible, theory. They argued that contrary to NATO's claims that the bombing was a mistake the Embassy had been deliberately targeted because it was being used by the Belgrade government to communicate with its armed forces in Kosovo. Because of the sensitivity of the mission, the US acted unilaterally using the most sophisticated technology possible. Not only did the bombs hit the right building, the journalists argued, they even hit the right room in the right building. The dead Chinese were not journalists, it was suggested, they were secret service agents.[27] There is much to commend this theory, which is why many in academic and public circles have tended to accept it. In particular, the fact that the aircraft was a B-2 flying out of the US and a startling picture that showed the damaged embassy with an undamaged Mercedes car parked in front suggested that this was a deliberate and immaculately targeted operation.

There are several flaws and contradictions in the theory and there is now plenty of evidence to suggest that the attack was a mistake, the intended target being the Federal Procurement and Supply Directorate. The main flaw is that the theory rests upon an assumption that a particular room in the Embassy was deliberately targeted, a room that was being used to communicate with Serb forces inside Kosovo. Had it been a genuine attack against a presumed Yugoslav building, surely NATO would have ensured its destruction rather than launching a pinprick attack that only partially damaged the building. Had it, however, been a deliberate attack on the Embassy the restraint and careful targeting would have been perfectly logical. There are two problems with this. First, both the Yugoslav and Chinese authorities insisted that three bombs were dropped on the Embassy but that only one had exploded. Had all three exploded the Embassy would have been completely destroyed and the death toll would have been much higher. Secondly, the photograph that accompanied the Anglo-Danish story was slightly misleading. Other photos of the damaged Embassy showed a much greater degree of devastation. Taking these two factors into consideration, it seems clear that the intention had been to destroy the targeted building and not merely to destroy a room in that building, a premise on which the theory rests.

The second debate revolves around the issue of whether the attack was a unilateral American action or a NATO approved action. According to Leurdijk and Zandee 'nobody in NATO had any knowledge about this attack in advance'.[28] They also point out that both the French and Dutch 'lessons learned' reports criticised the US for acting alone on occasions, with the French citing the Chinese Embassy incident as a case in point.[29] If this were the case, the argument that the attack was deliberate would seem to carry weight. However, Wesley Clark tells us that he personally authorised the attack believing it to be aimed at the Federal Directorate, on 5 May. It is worth quoting Clark at length here:

> On the 5th [May] we received the completed target sheets for several more targets, including the headquarters for the Federal Directorate of Supply and Procurement in Belgrade. According to the target sheet, this agency was responsible for the coordination of arms trafficking. I looked at it and saw what looked like a three-storey building with long rows of warehouse-like structures behind it. It was the same once-over I gave all the targets in my review – I was principally checking the risks of civilian casualties if we went ahead, and the proximity of any other significant structures. Along with the targets, we also maintained a comprehensive 'no strike' list, which we used to avoid strikes that might damage churches, hospitals, schools, embassies and so forth. As I looked at this target, number 493, it seemed significant in isolating Serbia from arms imports.[30]

The mission to strike the Federal Directorate was therefore approved by the SACEUR. Moreover, the fact that the mission was assigned to a B-2 operating from the US can be explained by the fact that the target was in downtown Belgrade making it essential for NATO to ensure the utmost accuracy, hence the employment of the most accurate weapons delivered by the most accurate aircraft available to the Alliance. How, though, did the people responsible for finding the Federal Directorate find the Chinese Embassy instead?

The answer to this conundrum lies in bureaucratic politics. The problem lay in the use of outdated maps that failed to show the 'new' purpose built Chinese Embassy that had begun service in 1997. The map used by the CIA was a 1992 'city plan of Belgrade', which did not identify many buildings by name or number. The agency updated its map in July 1998 but failed to indicate the embassy's move across the river. Furthermore, the two buildings (the embassy and the directorate) were only separated by around 200 yards across Lenjinova and looked very similar from satellite imagery.

The mistake was further compounded by the fact that the CIA's imagery intelligence and human intelligence were separated. The imagery, maps, and precise coordinates came from the National Imagery and Mapping Agency, which was formed from a number of Pentagon and CIA agencies in 1996. Before the Chinese Embassy catastrophe, its analysts had failed to map the Italian ski-lift cable that an American Air Force pilot flew into killing 20 people and had failed to spot India's preparations for testing a nuclear device.[31] The reorganisation led many experienced intelligence staff to join other agencies, with the Imagery and Mapping Agents being described by some as glorified cartographers. The separation of tasks meant that human intelligence was not used in the selection of target 493. Thus, when agency analysts found a building that looked like the directorate in the vicinity of where the directorate was supposed to be, they were convinced that they had the right target. Moreover, because NATO did not have enough targets at the outset of the war the agency had to find new targets rapidly. Any number of people in the Pentagon and State Department could have identified the Chinese Embassy because they had been there. Furthermore, other sources of human intelligence such as telephone books with embassy addresses and information about the renaming and renumbering of streets and buildings were overlooked. That bureaucratic processes led to the disaster was evidenced by Walter Jertz's comments to the press. Jertz, NATO's military spokesman argued that NATO had, 'no reason to know the locations of all the embassies in Belgrade ... particularly as we were not going to attack the Chinese Embassy, we were not trying to find out where it was'.[32]

The Embassy bombing damaged the political momentum that had gathered behind the G-8 process. The Chinese reaction threatened the whole process. They insisted that the air campaign halt before there could be any consideration of the peace plan in the Security Council. This demand challenged NATO's preferred approach of suspending the air campaign once Yugoslav forces had begun their withdrawal.[33] However, NATO's cause received an unlikely supporter when Viktor Chernomyrdin travelling to Beijing to persuade the Chinese government to at least accept the continuation of the peace process. This mission proved to be successful and the process continued.[34]

The search for peace resumed

Although the Chinese Embassy bombing delayed the Ahtisaari–Chernomyrdin process by up to five days, the intangible elements of the delay were much more profound. Not only did the mistaken attack bolster ailing Serb beliefs that NATO unity was not immutable but like the misguided attack on the refugee convoy on the Djakovica road it had a significant impact on the allies' self-confidence, providing succour to the anti-war movement in the West. The Serbs attempted to exploit this impasse by offering a unilateral ceasefire.[35] The offer, which came from the VJ, was based on the premise that the UÇK had been defeated and that as a result the army no longer needed to maintain such high force levels in the province. The VJ thus stated that it would reduce its number in Kosovo to pre-war levels and strive towards reaching an agreement on the deployment of a UN mission.[36] Although significant, in that the offer publicly accepted the principle of a UN mission for Kosovo, it was immediately rejected by NATO because it did not address core elements of the G-8 demands.

The damaging effect of the Chinese Embassy incident was felt almost immediately in Germany, where Foreign Minister Joschka Fischer came under intense pressure from his own Green Party. The seeds of discontent within the German Green Party had been sown at the beginning of the war. On 9 April, the Greens' Berlin regional committee passed a motion calling for an immediate halt to the bombing and a return to negotiations.[37] The crisis came to a head on 13 May when the Party came together in Bielefeld for its annual conference. Conference delegates put forward a series of resolutions demanding an immediate end to the bombing and Fischer's resignation. Once again the assault was led by Greens from Berlin. They put forward a resolution which demanded that 'if the Green members of the government, in particular Foreign Minister Joschka Fischer, are not ready to push in a determined, credible way for the immediate and unconditional end to NATO combat operations, we demand that they resign from office'.[38] The Party was deeply divided on the issue. There were even divisions between Green government ministers. Jürgen Tritten, the Environment Minister, told the media that, 'I am outraged at the increasing number of innocent victims of the airstrikes … I find it unacceptable that NATO planes are dropping splinter bombs and bombarding civilian targets'.[39]

During a heated debate delegates pelted Fischer with red paint. Others chanted 'murderer, murderer' and posters depicted Fischer and Chancellor Schröder as Adolf Hitler. Fischer's defence of the air strikes was based on three key arguments. Firstly, he threatened to resign form the party but remain as Foreign Minister if the Greens failed to back him. Being by far the most senior and prominent Green politician the threat promised to cut the Greens out of the policy making process altogether. Secondly, Fischer reiterated the moral and functional case for the air strikes. Finally, he pointed out that Germany was fulfilling an important role in the search for peace and that were it to withdraw from the war the chances of finding a swift end to it would be greatly diminished. The weekly newspaper, *Der Speigel*, reported that the progress that was being made on the diplomatic front was down to the opening of a 'back channel' to Milošević by the German government in April. That channel was apparently opened through Peter Carstenfeldt, a businessman with a Swedish passport and good relations with Moscow. Carstenfeldt was reportedly briefed by the German government before travelling to Belgrade. *Der Speigel* and German government sources claimed that this channel had 'far-reaching consequences' though neither went into detail on precisely how.[40] Although 318 delegates supported a motion calling for an immediate ceasefire and Germany's withdrawal from the war, 444 supported a compromise motion that pressed the Foreign Minister to strive towards a peaceful settlement as soon as possible but stopped short of demanding an immediate cessation of the war.[41]

It was not only the German government that came under pressure. Walter Veltroni, head of the ruling Party of the Democratic Left argued that Italy should take the initiative in the UN by exploring whether a bombing pause would reinvigorate the diplomatic process.[42] Green and Communist members of the coalition went one step further by calling for a unilateral ceasefire. Unlike Joschka Fischer, who was able to avoid defeat in his party without departing from NATO's core demands, Massimo D'Alema responded by shifting from NATO's line on when a suspension of the air campaign might happen. The Italian Prime Minister argued that:

> We are convinced that a pause in the bombing would become necessary at the time when an agreed draft resolution for the UN Security Council were available ... that is needed to enable the convening of such a meeting, the adoption of such a resolution and the communication to Belgrade of the resolution itself, and to receive an immediate answer by the Belgrade government.[43]

This idea marked a significant departure from the G-8 formula, which suggested that the air strikes would stop only once the Serbs had actually begun to verifiably comply with the demands. Although Javier Solana, who was with D'Alema when he made the proposal public, attempted to downplay the problem by arguing that the Security Council was still a long way from passing a resolution, there can be little doubting the significance of this first breach of NATO solidarity. Fortunately for the Alliance the breach came almost two weeks after the Chinese Embassy incident at a time when the G-8 process was beginning to gain momentum once again. Moreover, D'Alema's statement proved enough to save his government. The lower house of the Italian parliament accepted a compromise resolution echoing the new line that there would be a suspension of the air campaign but only after an appropriate Security Council Resolution was adopted.

On 19 May, the G-8 process reconvened with a series of meetings held in Bonn, Helsinki and Moscow. The talks centred on the three envoys, Strobe Talbott, Viktor Chernomyrdin, and Martti Ahtisaari. They took place just as the possibility of a land war began to raise its head once again. Back in April, Wesley Clark had written a letter to his superiors in which he argued that if there was to be a land campaign aimed at returning the refugees to their homes before the winter snow a national decision to begin preparations would have to be taken by 1 May at the latest.[44] He had been persuaded to put his deadline back by two weeks by the Chairman of the Joint Chiefs of Staff, Hugh Shelton, which meant that as the G-8 gathered in Bonn, its NATO members were being pushed by the military to make a decision on whether ground forces would be used. What is more, after over a year of attempting to limit the American military's role in the Balkans, the Pentagon, whilst continuing to maintain that the airstrikes were working, began to lobby in favour of a positive decision on a land operation. *Newsweek* magazine reported that the Joint Chiefs had collectively advised Defence Secretary William Cohen that only the use of ground troops would guarantee the successful achievement of NATO's objectives.[45] Unsurprisingly, Tony Blair reiterated his view that the ground option should be considered telling journalists in Bulgaria that 'at some point troops will have to go in and NATO, not Milošević, will decide when that will be'.[46] However, although there was a discernable shift in American thinking, NATO did not move any closer to consensus. A ground war would have been unthinkable to the Italian and Greek governments. The French and Germans were also adamant at this point that there could be no intervention on the ground without Belgrade's consent.

Wesley Clark supported his case for a decision by presenting new plans for a ground invasion. The plan, which involved the use of overwhelming force, called for the deployment of around 175,000 troops. The main thrust would be a drive north from Macedonia and a 'right-hook' through the Presevo valley in southern Serbia into Kosovo through its eastern border. This would be accompanied by simultaneous drives directly north from Macedonia and east from Albania. There were two advantages to the 'right hook'. There would be an element of surprise and a multi-pronged attack would throw the VJ and MUP into disarray. Moreover, the Presevo valley route offered the best terrain, avoided the mountains, and would allow NATO to bring its superior firepower to bear. Clark also presented a timetable for action. The SACEUR believed that it would take three months to deploy the necessary forces into the theatre and that the operations could take one month to complete and secure the environment for the return of the refugees. For a land war to be at all feasible, therefore, Clark warned that the North Atlantic Council would have to pass the Activation Order by mid-June at the absolute latest.[47] There is now a considerable body of informal evidence to suggest that, given the unlikelihood of such an order being passed by the North Atlantic Council, the UK and US at this point started to consider a land campaign conducted outside the NATO chain of command by a 'coalition of the willing', probably consisting only of American, British, and possibly Dutch forces.[48]

As the G-8 met in Bonn important new sounds were coming out of Washington, sounds that must have greatly alarmed Milošević. Although NATO and Russia had clearly moved much closer together, the three bones of contention outlined earlier remained. However, the negotiations came to focus on more specific issues, and one in particular. Issues such as the modalities of halting the war and whether Yugoslavia had to withdraw all its forces, though far from resolved, could be sidelined by ambiguous language. The new issue that now divided NATO and Russia was the composition of KFOR. NATO acknowledged that Russian involvement was vital and Chernomyrdin committed Russia to participating. However, the NATO leadership wanted KFOR to resemble the successful IFOR/SFOR missions in Bosnia where Russian peacekeepers came under the Alliance's operational command whilst retaining tactical autonomy and its national chain of command. Chernomyrdin had quite a different view. The Russian mediator insisted that the Russian contingent be quite separate from the NATO contingent (indeed, persuading Chernomyrdin to accept the principle of a NATO contingent at all had been quite a feat for Strobe Talbott) and that Russia should have its own zone in the province, in the north where most of the Kosovar Serbs lived. Both these proposals were unacceptable to Talbott, who feared that granting Russia operational autonomy would diminish KFOR's effectiveness and that granting it a zone of its own would lead to a de facto partition.

On 19 May, Chernomyrdin returned to Belgrade to present the G-8 terms to Milošević. The Russian mediator described the talks as 'tense', leading Barry Posen to conclude that 'it seems likely that it was at this meeting that Milošević first learned that the Russians had gone as far as they could and would on Yugoslavia's behalf'.[49] Although Posen is probably correct to identify this meeting as being the first time that a Russian had told the Serb leader that Moscow's rhetorical and diplomatic support had withered away, Milošević must have seen this coming prior to the Chinese Embassy bombing when the Russian government first acquiesced to a G-8 plan that accepted all of NATO's five demands in principle.

Ending the war

At the end of May four events combined to bring about the end of Milošević's stubborn resistance to NATO:

- A further escalation of the air campaign combined with an UÇK offensive.
- A meeting in Cologne that increased the likelihood of a land campaign.
- Milošević's indictment for war crimes by the ICTY.
- Agreement between Chernonmyrdin and Talbott about the basis for a Security Council Resolution.

On 26 May, the UÇK launched a major offensive aimed at breaking out of the small Kosare enclave on Kosovo's eastern border. There was intense fighting on Mount Pastrik with the Kosovar Albanian rebels receiving artillery support from the Albanian army over the border. Ominously for the Serbs, Wesley Clark decided that it was crucially important for NATO's land invasion plans for the UÇK to retain their foothold on the mountain. According to Clark:

> The battle to protect the KLA [UÇK] toehold over the crest of Mount Pastrik continued for the next two days. Our airmen were flying repeated strikes against Serb forces and areas throughout western Kosovo...And we were sending B-52 strikes in against border posts and staging areas.[50]

Although NATO had been using information from the UÇK about Serb forces in Kosovo throughout most of the war, the fighting and bombardment on Mount Pastrik signalled a worrying escalation for the Serbs. Not only did it indicate that the guerrillas had not been defeated, by launching an offensive the UÇK drew Serb heavy forces – which had been cleverly hidden from NATO's prying eyes – into the open. Almost overnight this increased the amount of heavy armour destroyed by the Alliance. This three-way battle came to a head on 7 June when Serbian forces engaged on Mount Pastrik were intensively targeted by B-52's. Agim Çeku, the military head of the UÇK, told Tim Judah that:

> One of the reasons why Milošević had to end the war was because we were attacking from the border and he was obliged to bring in many units who made good targets [for NATO]. Before, they had been dug in, but our attack made them come out. NATO enjoyed *that* bombing! The Serbs were faced with low morale and no one wanted to go to Pastrik or Kosare. Milošević was in danger of losing his army. One B-52 killed 224 soldiers.[51]

The stepping up of NATO and UÇK activity in Kosovo had a profound effect in Belgrade, not only because of the dramatically increased number of military casualties it produced but also because for months Milošević had been advised that the Kosovar Albanian guerrillas were a vanquished force. Having emptied Kosovo of the bulk of its Albanian population, the Serbs had failed to permanently curtail the UÇK's activities. Furthermore, despite numerous damaging mistakes, NATO's general appetite for destruction was undiminished and the strategic bombing campaign against downtown Belgrade intensified. At the end of May, Clark was even given permission by the targeting 'troika' to attack Belgrade's power stations, regularly shutting off power to the capital. According to Mike Short, the head of the air campaign, it was these attacks that finally brought the message home to Milošević. He recalled how at the beginning of the Gulf War, the allies had gone 'downtown Baghdad' from the outset, shutting off the city's power 'in the first thirty seconds of the war'. Short recalls that at that moment he knew that the allies could not lose the Gulf War and argues that NATO should have launched a similarly overwhelming attack against Belgrade at the outset of Allied Force.[52] It was only at the end of May, Short believes, that the air strikes reached a sufficient intensity to cause the Serb leadership to rethink its strategy.

The military pressure on the Serbs increased when the possibility of a land invasion was placed firmly on the agenda at a meeting of Defence

Ministers on 27 May in Cologne. Heeding Clark's advice that the time for a final decision was approaching the ministers met to discuss the invasion plans and offer troop contributions. The British pressed the case for a positive decision on the land invasion. George Robertson reportedly argued that any land campaign would have to start before 15 September to guarantee victory before the onset of winter. One of the participants to the discussion told Louise Richardson that William Cohen turned to Robertson and asked him, 'well, how many troops are you prepared to commit?'[53] Richardson continues:

> Robertson calmly replied, 'Fifty thousand'.
> The participant describes a sharp intake of breath around the room, followed by long silence. Then Cohen followed up: 'For how long?'
> 'For as long as it takes', Robertson replied.[54]

It is now widely known that the British Ministry of Defence had got to an advanced stage of planning such a contribution.[55] Importantly, because of the mounting military advice and the widely understood need to get the refugees home before the snow arrived, both the French and Italians agreed to the idea of a land invasion and pledged to contribute troops, though on a much smaller scale than the British contribution. Only Germany and the US remained uncommitted, but the pledges of troops from NATO's three main European military powers and the sheer scale of Britain's pledge meant that American participation was now more likely as it would only have to bear approximately half of the overall burden, contributing around 100,000 troops.[56]

The Cologne meeting raised the stakes in a number of ways. In a context where NATO was escalating its air campaign and having a significant impact on Serb ground forces the meeting indicated that the Alliance would do whatever it took to prevail before winter. Continuing Serb resistance prompted states to look at alternative strategies and the meeting saw something that had been an idea with little substance take on an air of credibility. Moreover, the pressure from the military for a decision was intensifying very publicly. Finally, NATO had an invasion plan and the existence of such a plan had been disseminated to the Western press and must have been known in Belgrade, further increasing the credibility of the ground threat.

The threat of a ground war offered the worst of all worlds to Milošević. Despite the rhetoric that he would turn Kosovo into a 'second Vietnam'[57] he knew that all would be lost should NATO launch a ground attack. Damage to bridges throughout Yugoslavia had been deliberately designed to cut off military and logistic support to the forces inside Kosovo. Command and control was starting to falter and oil was running in short supply. Moreover, the Mount Pastrik attacks showed that standing up and fighting presented NATO air power with an opportunity to wreak havoc on the VJ. What is more, Milošević believed that a land invasion would be directed against him personally and that NATO would try to oust him from the presidency. The resonance of this fear increased dramatically on 24 May when the ICTY confirmed that it had indicted Milošević along with his close allies, Milan Milutinović (President of Serbia), Nikola Sainović (Yugoslav Deputy Prime Minister), General Dragljub Ojdanić (Chief of Staff of the VJ), and Vlajko Stojiljković (Ministry of Interior of Serbia). The tribunal accused them of planning, instigating, committing or aiding, 'the campaign of violence conducted by the forces of the FRY and Serbia in Kosovo'.[58] The indictees were accused of instigating 16 particular attacks that constituted either a war crime or crime against humanity.

Initial responses to the indictments were mixed. Both the Yugoslav and Russian governments denounced them as a propaganda trick that exposed the ICTY as little more than a Western puppet.[59] Seasoned Western diplomats such as Henry Kissinger argued that the indictments were unhelpful to NATO because they would make negotiating with the Yugoslavs much more problematic.[60] This latter view was widely expressed, though the proposition did underline the fact that the ICTY was acting independently of NATO. With hindsight the indictments can be seen as adding to the very real diplomatic and economic pressure being exerted on Milošević. They reinforced NATO's insistence that there could be no negotiation on its five demands in a context where discussion of a land war was taking on new impetus; Milošević must have feared that NATO would seek him out for arrest. The president was also aware that the best way for him to beat arrest was to remain in power and that both the continuation of the airstrikes and the possibility of a ground invasion could put his position in jeopardy. Thus, although they were initially seen as an impediment to ending the war, the indictments contributed to the atmosphere of isolation felt by the political leadership in Belgrade.

The final strand in concluding the war was the Talbott– Chernomyrdin negotiating marathon that led to agreement on a form of words for the Security Council Resolution that was passed on 10 June. On 26 May, Talbott travelled to Moscow for talks with the Russian interlocutor. According to Talbott, this meeting had two important effects on Russian thinking. First, Talbott argued that Chernomyrdin finally accepted that NATO would not compromise on its key demands; something that we know Chernomyrdin had already told Milošević a week earlier. Until this point, however, Chernomyrdin had continued to insist that Yugoslavia be allowed to maintain an armed presence in Kosovo. Secondly, Chernomyrdin came to believe that there were no differences between the US and its European allies that Russia could exploit.[61] It was here that Chernomyrdin took two important decisions; to accept that NATO's demands were non-negotiable and that in order to maintain Russia's input into the proceedings it would have to play a key role in their implementation.

On 1 June, Talbott, Chernomyrdin and Ahtisaari met again in Bonn, amidst reports that Belgrade had accepted the G-8 terms. Milošević wrote to Joschka Fischer confirming that he was willing to accept the demands. Despite intensive negotiations there remained no agreement on the two issues of whether Yugoslav troops would be allowed to remain in Kosovo and what the precise nature of Russia's participation in KFOR would be. Chernomyrdin continued to insist that it be separate from NATO and that Russia be given its own zone in the north of the province. Two days later in Petersberg, however, the Russian negotiator made a series of important and unexpected concessions. After reportedly speaking with Boris Yeltsin on the telephone, Chernomyrdin accepted that *all* Serb forces would have to leave the province. In return, Talbott formally accepted that some would be allowed back into Kosovo after an unspecified amount of time. This formulation had been arrived at almost a month earlier with the initial G-8 plan but the Chinese Embassy bombing had so weakened NATO that the Russian and Yugoslav governments believed that they could get a better deal. There was still no agreement about the precise nature of KFOR and Russia's role within it. However, the negotiators agreed on a form of words that could be presented to Milošević, leaving the modalities of the operation to a later date. They agreed on the 'deployment in Kosovo under United Nations auspices of effective international civil and security presences, acting as may be decided under Chapter VII of the Charter'.[62] Moreover, the plan called for an interim administration and a 'military–technical' agreement between Yugoslavia and NATO that would facilitate the VJ and MUP's withdrawal from Kosovo.

Martti Ahtisaari and Viktor Chernomyrdin set off for Belgrade armed with a comprehensive peace plan agreed upon by NATO, the EU, and Russia. Their meeting with Milošević was to contain no negotiation. He could either accept the plan and begin to comply with it or reject it. Ahtisaari read out the plan and Milošević asked whether adjustments could be made. Ahtisaari and Chernomyrdin made it clear that there could be no adjustments or negotiations. Milošević then spoke to

General Ojdanić and instructed him to telephone Wesley Clark and make arrangements for negotiating the military–technical agreement. On the same day, the Serbian parliament voted by 136 to 74 to accept the plan.

The military–technical agreement

NATO now confronted two final obstacles on the path to peace: Negotiating a 'military–technical' agreement with the VJ and agreeing KFOR's modalities with Russia. As instructed by Milošević, General Ojdanić contacted Wesley Clark and proposed a meeting on Sunday 9 June.[63] Given that Chernomyrdin had implicitly accepted that NATO would not cease its bombardment until the Serbs actually began their withdrawal the proposed delay of five days surprised Clark. What is clear now is that Milošević hoped to use the delay to 'tidy up' the province by both removing damaged military equipment (masking just how effective NATO had been towards the end of the campaign) and relocating the corpses of murdered Kosovar Albanians. Since Milošević's demise in 2000, graves have been discovered throughout Serbia including a refrigerated lorry full of Kosovar Albanian corpses that was driven into the Danube. This put the figure of Kosovar Albanians murdered during Operation Horseshoe at much closer to the 10,000 figure originally estimated by NATO and others than the 2,000 frequently claimed by NATO's critics.[64] Most interesting is the fact that although under pressure from Clark, Ojdanić agreed to begin the talks almost immediately near the Macedonian town of Kumanovo, agreement was not reached until 9 June, the date originally preferred by the Serb General.

Although the G-8 principles had been delivered to Belgrade on a take them or leave them basis, the Serbs wanted to continue negotiating. The first meeting was delayed when Ojdanić refused to travel into Macdeonia and asked instead that the NATO negotiators, led by General Mike Jackson, move north into Yugoslavia for the meeting. This suggestion was unacceptable for an alliance that was supposed to be dictating terms rather than negotiating but as well as wanting to delay the proceedings for as long as possible, Ojdanić also feared that if he crossed the border into Macedonia he would be arrested because of his indictment by the ICTY. Nevertheless, NATO refused to compromise and Ojdanić decided that he would send a team to Kumanovo rather than go himself. When the meeting did begin, the Serb delegation immediately questioned the content of the agreement by arguing that it contained political elements that they had no authority to agree to. The Serbs also objected to the seven-day timetable for withdrawal, arguing instead that they would need at least 15 days if they were to avoid creating a security vacuum in the province.

Although the Kumanovo discussions were not supposed to be negotiations, the Pentagon did slightly revise the agreement to make it more acceptable to the Serbs. Although the timetable remained in tact, all reference to NATO was removed and a clause demanding that the Serbs account for all missing Kosovar Albanians was dropped. Moreover, a 20-kilometre demilitarised zone that the allies demanded the Serbs create on their side of the Kosovo–Serbia border was reduced to five kilometres. These limited concessions encouraged the Serbs to harden their position and demand that they be allowed to retain the pre-war number of VJ and MUP personnel in the province. The Alliance responded by publicly announcing that the talks were faltering and stepping up the air campaign, which had been reduced considerably at the beginning of the meeting. The renewed bombing helped to persuade the Serb delegation that NATO would not accept any deviation from the G-8's demands and on 9 June they signed the slightly revised military–technical agreement detailing an immediate commencement of a total withdrawal. In response, the North Atlantic Council ordered the immediate suspension of Operation Allied Force though importantly it did not order its end, allowing Clark to retain the option of resuming the bombardment if the Serbs failed to comply with the agreement.

A day later, the UN Security Council passed Resolution 1244 with 14 votes in favour and a Chinese abstention. The Russians played a vital role in persuading the Chinese not to use their veto. Ambassador Lavrov argued that it was better to create a UN administration than to force NATO to create a protectorate outside UN auspices. Resolution 1244 placed Kosovo under UN administration (UNMIK) and authorised a KFOR intervention, though it named neither KFOR nor NATO and spoke only of an 'international security presence'.[65]

The problem of how to organise KFOR remained, however. Chernomyrdin continued to demand that Russia have its own sector, something that NATO had consistently opposed because they feared it would lead to a de facto partition of the province. Meanwhile, NATO planners created five multinational zones, with each led by one of the five key contributors, UK, US, France, Italy, and Germany. The Alliance proposed that Russia contribute forces to one of these zones, with the French zone in the north and west, centred on Mitrovica where many Serbs lived, as the most likely possibility. Although Chernomyrdin and Igor Ivanov accepted that NATO would not back down on this issue, elements within the Russian military argued that it should take the initiative. Around 200 Russian soldiers and 30 armoured personnel carriers deployed in Bosnia as part of SFOR were rapidly repainted with the 'KFOR' ensign and departed for Kosovo, driving through Serbia to Pristina where they were received as saviours by the Serb population. The forces then moved to Pristina airport to prepare for the expected landing of Russian paratroopers who would be flown from Russia proper. All this before NATO elements of KFOR had begun to deploy.

The Russian deployment threw NATO into confusion, not least because Ivanov continued to insist that the forces leaving Bosnia would not enter Kosovo itself. This confusion indicated that there was no coherence to Russia's policy and that there was considerable disagreement between foreign policy makers and defence policy makers. When the first indications that Russia would try to get to Pristina airport before NATO became apparent the French government suggested that Clark use French paratroopers based in Macedonia as part of Operation Agricola to get to the airport first. That plan had been rejected at the outset because Clark feared that he may be unable to get support to the airport quickly enough and that the paratroopers would become isolated. However, once the Russians had reached the airport Clark began to consider the options for seizing it. One option was to make an airborne landing and another was to use KFOR ground forces. Whilst this was happening both Hungary and Romania denied Russia access to their airspace for the airborne element of their gambit, effectively cutting off support for the 200 troops already at the airport. It was at this point that Clark and Mike Jackson had their infamous disagreement. Clark believed that control of the airfield was vital and that KFOR should take it over as swiftly as possible. Jackson, the KFOR commander, refused to carry out this order, arguing that the airport was not vital to the early stages of the deployment, that the Russian troops were isolated and lacked supplies and would therefore need NATO support, and that provoking conflict with Russia would be disastrous to the overall mission. Jackson used his national chain of command to change the orders he was given by the SACEUR, bringing Blair and Clinton into the debate on its way. As it was, Jackson's perception proved correct, and whilst the Russians still hold the airport today it is administered by the Italian KFOR contingent. Jackson accurately calculated that given a NATO force some 200 times bigger than the Russian contingent the Russians could be brought into line through cooperation and dialogue. Indeed, the Russians later accepted that they would operate within one of NATO's zones rather than having one of their own. However, this episode also revealed for the final time the impotence of the SACEUR when faced with competing national chains of command.

The VJ and MUP completed their withdrawal virtually on time. The refugees began to flood back to their homes and the great majority of those that still had homes returned to them well before winter arrived.[66]

Summary

A question that many people have asked is did NATO win the war? If we consider the Alliance's five demands and Wesley Clark's 'measures of merit' the answer seems positive. Moreover, if we place the limited war in the wider context of many phases of international engagement it can be seen as the only phase in a decade of diplomacy that had the desired effect to the extent that the phase that succeeded it was one envisaged and shaped by the engagement beforehand. On the other side of the coin, however, Operation Allied Force had originally been justified as 'preventing' a humanitarian catastrophe. This it clearly failed to do though that is not to say that NATO provoked the wave of murder and ethnic cleansing unleashed by the Serbs or that Operation Allied Force had no effect in limiting it. Indeed, one can imagine how much worse things may have been had the Serbs been able to fully use the firepower at their disposal. When they tried to do that, as they did in the battle for Mount Pastrik, they sustained heavy casualties. Nevertheless, the argument that the means chosen (airstrikes) could not achieve the desired end state (preventing a humanitarian catastrophe) is a powerful one. The important issue though is not whether a land campaign would have been more successful but given that had the decision to use force at all contained the possibility of a land invasion the North Atlantic Council would not have authorised it, were airstrikes better than nothing at all? The evidence of ten years of diplomacy suggests that negotiation, sanctions, limited initiatives, and comprehensive but unarmed verification would have neither prevented nor mitigated the effects of Operation Horseshoe. Given that, not only was the use of air power necessary but the public denunciation of the land option at the outset of the war was vital to ensure its success.

There are two ways of arguing that NATO did not win the war. The first is to argue that the military–technical agreement was a considerably better deal for Milošević than the Rambouillet terms.[67] The second argument is that the war's end was not brought about by military force. The first argument is based on the view that Rambouillet was rejected because of the military annex. I have argued earlier that this perspective is fundamentally flawed. Although under the military–technical agreement KFOR cannot transit through Yugoslavia the effect of this has been to cut Kosovo off from Serbia because the province's supplies are garnered through Albania and Macedonia. Whereas Rambouillet created an autonomous province within Yugoslavia's constitutional ambit, the entity created by Resolution 1244 is completely separate. Whereas Rambouillet allowed Serbia to maintain a security presence in Kosovo, the military–technical agreement demanded their full withdrawal and although they would be allowed in principle to send a token force this would only be done at the behest of the KFOR commander and remains a highly improbable proposition today. Although KFOR faced, and continues to face numerous challenges,[68] Javier Solana was right to point out that 'the situation in Kosovo today is better than it was before the alliance intervened, and it continues to improve'.[69]

The argument that the bombing was not successful because it did not bring about the end of the war is much more resonant, though misses the point about what strategic air campaigns are all about.[70] Because this was a limited war, the transition from *coercive diplomacy* to *limited war* can be understood, as Wesley Clark did, as a transition from diplomacy backed by threat of force to diplomacy backed by force. In both, the aim was not to force Milošević to alter his course of action by altering it for him but rather to persuade him to alter his course of action by making it too costly. The use of force in this way always works in tandem with diplomatic and economic levers. The extensive use of a Russian mediator was a triumph rather than an admission of failure by NATO. In particular, persuading Russia to accept all of NATO's key demands was an important aspect of the war, though as I have argued throughout, Russia's decision should not have surprised us. Alliance members had prepared the ground with Russia well and understood that Russian policy was driven more by a desire to maintain a pivotal role in the world than by sentiments of pan-Slavism or liking of Milošević. Indeed, on a personal level, Yeltsin disliked Milošević more than most Western leaders. The Serb leader had lied to him in 1998 rapidly turning a diplomatic coup into an international embarrassment and in 1991 Milošević had been the only world leader to recognise the hardline communist conspirators that had overthrown Mikhail Gorbachev.

Conclusion

How did NATO come to launch Operation Allied Force? This is the question I posed at the beginning of the book and the one to which we return at the end. The rise of the UÇK changed international perceptions about the need to act in Kosovo. The failure of Rugova's non-violent strategy tells us important things about contemporary global politics. It questions the notion that the power of the elite depends on the consent of the majority, a notion that underpins much of the thought about the politics of resistance.[1] In this case the vast majority of people in Kosovo withdrew their consent to being governed by Belgrade to the extent that they rejected the possibility of ousting Milošević by voting for Milan Panić in 1992. They subverted Serb rule by establishing a complex parallel state with its own health, education, law and order, and taxation systems. However, in doing so they did not manage to prevail on the Serb authorities. There were two principal reasons for this.

First, Kosovo was by far the poorest part of Yugoslavia and the Serb economy was not dependent on Kosovar Albanian labour. The withdrawal of that labour and retreat from the formal state did not significantly worsen the Serbian economy. In fact, the Serb political elite profited in the short term. It removed a potential million or so hostile voters from the political scene, allowed Milošević to continue legitimising his rule with nationalist rhetoric, and thus more importantly, to shore up his regime from extreme nationalist opponents such as Vojislav Šešelj and others like Zoran Djindjić who questioned his nationalist credentials.

Secondly, and more importantly for the purposes of this volume, events in Kosovo were shaped by the international engagement. Rugova's non-violent strategy failed largely because he failed to persuade international society of the legitimacy of his cause. Moreover, the strategy of non-violence failed to persuade outsiders of that legitimacy. Although David Owen argues that he greatly admired Rugova's strategy the fact that it was non-violent allowed international engagement with the conflict to be delayed until after Dayton.[2] However, having delayed tackling the issue because of the perceived damage it would do to the cause of persuading Milošević to accept peace in Bosnia, Western states then decided that preserving the peace required continuing Serb consent. This prolonged the period of non-engagement and delegitimised Rugova's strategy in the eyes of his constituents. The rise of the UÇK prompted the West to confront three syndromes: the Srebrenica (humanitarian) syndrome, the refugees (national interests) syndrome, and the 'Balkan Wars' (geopolitics) syndrome. In the debates that ensued, different actors emphasised different aspects of these syndromes.

Two relevant features of contemporary global politics emerge from the way that NATO came to launch Operation Allied Force. On the one hand, for those without statehood non-violent resistance will not, by itself, win legitimacy for a cause that challenges dominant ideas about who holds sovereignty. It is worth pointing out that at the outset international society supported the application of Serb force against the UÇK and that it was only once that reaction caused a humanitarian disaster with wider consequences that this stance began to shift. On the other hand, recourse to violence can alter calculations of political necessity in rapid and dramatic ways. By threatening to precipitate a humanitarian disaster that confounded Western national interests and raised geopolitical concerns the UÇK was able to do something that Rugova was never able to do – prompt international engagement. At the outset, of course, there was no agreement about what that engagement should consist of, but by mid-1998 a consensus began to form around the idea of a comprehensive negotiated settlement supported by the threat of force. Two recurring problems then confronted the prospective interveners: How to fashion an agreement that both sides could accept and how to decide when the threat of force should be acted upon?

The main problem with devising an agreement that both sides could accept was that international society agreed with Serbia's basic premise that Kosovo was part of Serbia. I argued in Chapter 1 that this understanding was based on a flawed reading of the Yugoslav constitution. Even more unhelpful was the fact that for reasons of political expediency the Badinter arbitration commission that had been created to evaluate the competing legal claims made by all of Yugoslavia's interested parties chose not to assess the legal quality of Kosovo's claim. This only

exacerbated the problem by informally closing the possibility of independence without ever providing the reasoning as to why. Given the
almost universal agreement in Kosovar Albanian society about the need
for independence, a negotiated settlement based upon Yugoslav constitutional reform alone was never likely to succeed. For most of 1998,
negotiations were conducted on a bilateral basis between different elements of international society and the Serb government. Although
Christopher Hill engaged the Kosovar Albanian leadership in the
process of putting a peace plan together, they were not formally
involved in international negotiation until the Rambouillet conference
in 1999. As a result of this, there was very little movement between the
parties throughout the period, making the chances of success at
Rambouillet most unlikely. The Contact Group negotiators were able to
extract two important concessions from the Kosovar Albanians at
Rambouillet: An agreement to disband the UÇK and delay the demand
for independence for three years. In return, the Contact Group promised that a NATO led peacekeeping force would ensure that the Serb
forces complied with a ceasefire and would withdraw. It also promised
that after an interim period an international conference to decide on
the future status of the province would take 'the will of the people' into
account. Although this amounted to the promise of a referendum,
famously articulated in a note from Madeleine Albright to the Kosovar
Albanian delegation, it did not amount to an effective granting of independence after three years. Rather, the Contact Group would only take
the results into account, and given that Yugoslavia's territorial integrity
was one of the basic principles adhered to by the Group and repeatedly
by the UN Security Council it is unthinkable that independence would
have been recognised without the acquiescence of Belgrade. Russia's
position in both these bodies would have ensured that.

Rambouillet failed because NATO, which was not represented there,
was unable to persuade the Serbs that the threat of force would manifest
itself in sustained and severe air strikes. In detailing the international
debates that took place, Chapters 3–6 provide ample evidence of how
Milošević came to believe this. The Alliance was divided. Greece and
Italy in particular were deeply reticent, and even the Alliance's most
hawkish leaders ruled out the use of ground forces. Whilst in the days
running up to Operation Allied Force most people in Serbia believed
that their president would reach an eleventh hour agreement, a belief
that I and most Western leaders shared, Milošević had already decided
to go to war. He did not believe NATO's threats and saw an opportunity
to deal with the UÇK once and for all.

The failure to prepare for a land war meant that once the conflict started the Alliance was physically unable to achieve its primary aim: the prevention of a humanitarian catastrophe. According to Nicholas Wheeler, 'what has to be explained in the case of Kosovo is why the most powerful military alliance in history could not furnish a credible ground option'.[3] The answer he provides to his own question is only partially correct. Wheeler argues that 'the answer is that no Alliance government argued for such a strategy, because they believed that casualties would undermine public support at home'[4] and:

> The reply to those who argue that bombing was the only strategy that could ensure Alliance cohesion is that, by ruling out the ground option, NATO governments demonstrated that their commitment to defending the human rights of Kosovars did not extend to accepting the risks to soldiers' lives of deploying ground forces.[5]

As we saw in Chapters 7 and 8, some states and other key actors did argue for a ground option. The British government and General Clark both believed that such an option should be made available and used if necessary, and one of the key turning points of the war came when George Robertson told his allied partners that the British planned to commit 50,000 troops (around one-third of the total thought necessary) for such an operation. It was not, as Wheeler argues, the need for a 'casualty free' campaign that prompted NATO to adopt a particular strategy, it was rather the need to maintain Alliance cohesion that drove the nature of the war though limiting casualties clearly played a role in maintaining cohesion. Both the German and Italian governments were threatened because of Green and Socialist opposition to the war, prompting both to support the idea of a bombing pause as a way of deflecting parliamentary censure. The Greek government would have come under similar pressure had the possibility of a ground war been on the table at the outset. Without explicit UN legitimisation the UK and US placed great emphasis on winning North Atlantic Council legitimisation. The question, as I said earlier, is not whether a ground campaign would have been better than an air campaign. There would have been no air campaign at all had their been serious talk of a ground campaign at the outset. Instead, the question is, was the air campaign a better strategy than choosing not to act? Throughout the book I have argued that it was.

One can learn much about NATO's reluctance to act and the imperative of maintaining allied cohesion by looking at the North Atlantic Council's decisions. The original Activation Order, passed in October 1998, was only agreed after Holbrooke briefed the Council that his negotiations with Milošević were heading towards a successful conclusion (and that airstrikes would therefore not be necessary) and the Greek government won an assurance that the Order would only be issued if a Resolution being discussed concurrently by the UN Security Council (Resolution 1199) was passed. Germany, Italy, France and the UK remained deeply concerned about acting without explicit UN authorisation, which also helps to explain why the Activation Order only authorised the first phase of a limited air campaign. It is also worth noting that although the planned campaign contained three phases, the North Atlantic Council only ever authorised the first two. It was states such as Italy, Germany, and Greece who drove the agenda of moderation and there is very little evidence to suggest that they were primarily prompted by a desire to protect NATO pilots. That said, once the Alliance had chosen air and missile strikes as its preferred strategy two further considerations came into play. First, the American administration placed a premium on protecting its forces and striking strategic targets. This was greatly at odds with what General Clark wanted to do, leading to the Apache saga that was discussed earlier. Secondly, Alliance leaders continued to wield an important influence over targeting. For some this represented a triumph of political control over the military whilst for others, particularly American Air Force planners, the level of control prevented them from conducting an effective war.

Does the intervention in Kosovo represent a fundamental shift in the function of international institutions like NATO? The complex interaction between NATO members suggests that it is contributing towards the deepening of the European 'security community' and that it is moving away from its function as a defensive alliance. According to Karl Deutsch a security community can be understood as a group of sovereign actors who enjoy a sense of community that is able to, 'assure, for a long time ... the resolution of social problems without recourse to force'.[6] The formation of a security community depends on shared values, mutual economic benefit, increased transactions across borders, and high levels of communication. This concept was more recently refined by Emanuel Adler and Michael Barnett. For them, a security community exists where states have a 'dependable expectation of peaceful change'.[7] They also indicated that such communities differ between 'nascent', 'ascendant' and 'mature' types, with the latter involving considerable degrees of integration at a variety of levels. It is clear that NATO began its life as the institutional embodiment of a 'nascent' North Atlantic security community. According to Adler and Barnett, in this phase, 'governments do not explicitly seek to create a security community', but instead begin to, 'consider how they might coordinate their relations in order to: Increase their mutual security; lower the transaction costs associated with their exchanges; and/or encourage further exchanges and interactions'.[8] With NATO in mind, one trigger for the establishment of a security community that is often cited is the existence of a common threat. By contrast, members of a 'mature' security community, 'share an identity', so that, 'mutual-aid becomes a matter of habit'.[9] Moreover, 'the right to use force shifts from the units to the collectivity'.[10]

According to Stephen Walt, an 'institutionalized alliance may also create capacities that are worth keeping even after their original rationale are gone'.[11] Throughout the diplomacy and war fighting recounted earlier the 19 NATO members behaved as if they were part of a mature security community. The achievement of a consensus was not, therefore, the result of American hegemonic power nor was it produced by the forcible cajoling of the weak by the powerful in the Alliance. The most reluctant ally, Greece, recognised itself to be part of a mature security community underpinned by shared values. Those shared values were repeatedly evident and were manifested in an appreciation of the three 'syndromes' discussed earlier.

For example, the Greek government recognised that being part of this community entailed responsibilities as well as rewards. Even so, being part of a community does not mean accepting the will of another imposed upon you. The Greek government was able to define a particular role for itself, making a worthwhile contribution to the wider NATO effort by providing a great deal of humanitarian support. Furthermore, on numerous occasions it helped shape the Alliance's strategic policy. The same could also be said for most of the other member states. What is also interesting is the extent to which governments showed an appreciation for the difficulties confronted by their partners. The near toppling of the Italian government and the troubles that confronted the German government prompted the Alliance to look again at the idea of a bombing pause, a policy that was ultimately incorporated despite the grave reservations of the Americans and British. Targeting and the matching of aircraft to task was fashioned in such a way as to ameliorate national concerns. Of course, there were moments of intense disagreement. The Anglo-German argument about the ground option was one such case in point, though even here the idea of a coalition of the willing within the Alliance was proposed as a way of mediating the problem, allowing states to contribute to the broad aim while opting out of particular aspects of the operation.

NATO's engagement with Kosovo during and after 1998 therefore points towards its development from a defensive alliance into a fundamental pillar of Western Europe's mature security community. The Alliance is underpinned by shared values and common interests and its continued existence and proper functioning is perceived to be in the interests of its members even when it decides to act in a way that particular governments do not feel entirely comfortable with. The crucial point, and the role that only NATO plays in this security community, is that the use of force by members of that community takes place only with the community's blessing. It was the existence of a mature security community in Western Europe that on the one hand allowed NATO to justify its actions without having explicit UN Security Council but on the other ruled out the possibility of its members using force unilaterally. The existence of the mature security community shaped the Alliance's diplomacy and military strategy. We have seen this trend continue after Allied Force with the Alliance's involvement with conflict prevention initiatives in Macedonia.

Some critical writers have gone as far as to suggest that the whole purpose of Allied Force was to assert NATO's dominance over other European security institutions such as the OSCE and EU.[12] Although its transition into a fundamental part of a mature security community points towards a wider and deeper alliance, the engagement with Kosovo revealed that this is not at the expense of other European organisations who also play a vital role within the community. Throughout the 1990s, the EC/EU played a role in the engagement, using the civilian instruments at its disposal. The war itself was brought to an end by a joint Russian–EU diplomatic initiative after substantial consultation between these two parties and NATO. Significantly, the overlap and differences between the EU and NATO strengthened the diplomatic effort. As the President of Finland, a country that was a member of the EU and supported NATO but was not a member, Martti Ahtisaari was widely viewed as the ideal candidate for the position of EU envoy to Yugoslavia. Both the EU and OSCE offered policy alternatives to those offered by NATO and both were utilised both before and during Allied Force. In Chapter 4, I argued that it was the OSCE's unique status that allowed it to fulfil its role, supported by NATO. However, it was that same status that made it an inappropriate policy tool once Milošević had decided that his 'Albanian problem' required a military solution. That said, it was OSCE reporting that provided the tripwire that persuaded Western states to move from a strategy of *limited engagement* to one of *coercive diplomacy* at the beginning of 1999. What was striking, therefore, was not the competition between different European institutions but their complementary and mutually supportive relations. Different organisations contributed to the institutional affiliation that states felt towards NATO.

Does Kosovo therefore provide evidence of the emergence of a fortress Western Europe, one that refuses to tolerate humanitarian catastrophe on its borders but which also refuses to accept international norms of behaviour and the jurisdiction of more inclusive international institutions such as the UN? There are those who argue that Allied Force points towards a dangerous regionalism that can only make international society more unstable by challenging basic norms of international behaviour such as the principle of non-interference in the internal affairs of states or the primacy of the Security Council in matters concerning international peace and security. However, one of the most interesting things about the story of international engagement is that the tentacles of international institutionalism reached out beyond Western Europe in both formal and informal ways. A wide range of organisations were involved including the G-7, G-8, Contact Group and UN. Russia played a vital role in the latter three. Whilst many in the International Relations field have pointed to the Kosovo conflict as a dangerous moment in Western–Russian relations what is remarkable is the extent of Russian involvement in an ostensibly Western engagement.

The Russian government joined NATO in condemning Serb actions through the Security Council. It endorsed both the C/OSCE mission and contributed to the planning of the OSCE mission in 1998–99. In 1998, Boris Yeltsin pursued a bilateral path with Milošević and reached a ceasefire agreement that was welcomed by NATO until the Yugoslav president reneged on it. Russian ministers indicated that a bombing campaign would not damage NATO–Russian relations. And, although Yeltsin vehemently opposed NATO at the outset of Allied Force his position changed dramatically after he successfully fought off impeachment and he later despatched his special representative to Belgrade to press home NATO's case. This happened not because the West coerced Russia but because of the complex association of international institutions and elite networks through which common norms are developed and mutual interests supported. Some of these were formal institutions (such as the UN), others were informal and ad hoc arrangements (such as the Chernomyrdin–Ahtisaari–Talbott troika), and others made use of regimes not originally intended for such crisis management (the G-8).

It may be that the international diplomacy that preceded the Kosovo war and managed it once it began points towards the development of a heightened degree of liberal institutionalism in global politics. However, is this not a selective institutionalism, one in which the powerful select whichever institution suits them to legitimise actions that they decide to take anyway, regardless of the prevalent view of international society or the court of world opinion? Justin Morris raised this question with regards to American use of the UN as a 'rubber stamp' legitimising body for essentially unilateral acts in Haiti.[13] Morris argued that the emerging tendency to use the UN to legitimise unilateral state action risked undermining the global institution. In the case of Kosovo, it could be argued, NATO took this one step further by not even seeking the legitimisation of the UN. Instead, the North Atlantic Council, OSCE, EU, and even G-8 acted as legitimising institutions. We saw, for example, that in 1998 the American administration argued that UN legitimisation was not necessary because of the democratic deficit in many of its member states, particularly in China and Russia. Why, it was asked, should undemocratic states with poor human rights records prevent a group of democratic states from protecting people in foreign countries?

This was a powerful argument that is not easily addressed; yet it was not one shared by the majority of NATO members. While remaining convinced of the legitimacy of their cause, most Alliance members were concerned about accusations that they were guilty of 'selective indignation' as one book put it, of shedding 'crocodile tears' for 'fashionable' refugees whilst doing little to remedy truly global problems. For many people, Allied Force was not about humanitarianism at all but simply about pursuing Western interests, with some going as far as arguing that it was about asserting American hegemony in a region where a small state dared to challenge it.[14] The American ambivalence towards the UN was a sure sign of this, they argued. At least two points can be made in response. First, there is little doubt that the US did want to bypass the UN but it does not directly follow that this was because they were only concerned with pursuing narrow own interests. Indeed, Madeleine Albright appeared as concerned about the humanitarian situation and the possibility of a repeat of Srebrenica as Tony Blair. Secondly, returning to the theme of NATO as a security community the US did not, in fact, sideline the UN. It came under pressure not to do so from both its allies and from its formal and informal links with Russia. Throughout 1998, the UN Security Council played a pivotal role in efforts to prevent the conflict. Once war began it continued to play a role by providing the forum for global debate and authorising a significant UNHCR operation to assist the refugees. Furthermore, after the war the Security Council legitimised the war's outcome and the UN established Kosovo's administration, despite some states arguing that the EU or OSCE should have this role. The UN, therefore, fulfilled more than the legitimisation role. It provided practical assistance, endorsed the aims and outcomes of the operation, and provided the court of world opinion against which NATO tested its argument. Just because that court, which sat in both the Security Council and General Assembly, failed to condemn NATO and even though the Alliance did not have explicit authorisation, it does not mean that the UN was marginalised. Far from it.

The UN, recognising the problem of the competing claims of sovereignty and human rights, opted to defer the matter. On the one hand its decision-making bodies refused to condemn the Alliance but on the other also refused to endorse the proposition that there exists a general right of humanitarian intervention in world politics. What this suggests is that given the absence of agreed criteria outlining when humanitarian interventions may be launched the court of world opinion may scrutinise such claims according to their merits on a case-by-case basis.

But what about the charge that Allied Force was not about protecting the Kosovar Albanians but was instead motivated by age old concerns about the national interests and *realpolitik*? Surely, two of the three syndromes that I suggested prompted the West to jettison its strategy of non-engagement owed more to this realist logic than a so-called humanitarian logic. At a time when public opinion in many Western states believes that governments should take robust action against economic migrants and 'bogus' asylum seekers, the 'refugees syndrome' can be directly related to traditional national interests. As Jim Whitman put it:

> NATO humanitarianism was an emergency response to an unantici-pated refugee crisis of historic proportions, in which the rights of the refugees themselves and the larger issue of human rights in Kosovo did not interfere with the strategic and political concerns of Western European states.[15]

Moreover, the 'Balkan wars syndrome' revealed the prevalence of geopolitical concerns. Hence, it was the desire the preserve NATO (by protecting Greek–Turkish relations) and maintain stability on its borders that prompted action, rather than a humanitarian impulse. What these two syndromes also explain, of course, is why the Alliance remained uninterested in Kosovo prior to 1999.

By themselves neither the 'refugees syndrome' nor the 'Balkan wars syndrome' can explain why NATO acted as it did and when it did. If national interests and geopolitics were the primary motives why did

NATO not simply seal off Kosovo's borders, preventing a refugee crisis and greatly reducing the threat of the war escalating? What we need to appreciate is that in today's globalising world, and particularly in a deeply integrated Europe, injustice and brutality in one place will invariably affect places separated by increasingly permeable borders. Remember that whilst international society attempted to persuade both sides to accept a comprehensive peace plan under the threat of force, the failure to win that acceptance did not provoke the launch of Allied Force. Even British Foreign Office officials, usually most hawkish on such questions, suggested that the Rambouillet and Paris failures alone would not have provided a sufficient trigger for war. It was the launch of a massive campaign of ethnic cleansing and evidence that the campaign would intensify that provided the trigger. It was, then, all three syndromes together with the latter two being prompted by the 'Srebrenica syndrome'. After all, the Serbs only threatened perceived national interests and geopolitical stability because of their commission of war crimes and crimes against humanity.

In his speech to the Economic Club of Chicago, Blair pointed towards the inception of a new international community arguing that in Kosovo 'our actions are guided by a...subtle blend of mutual self-interest and moral purpose in defending the values we cherish...values and interests merge'.[16] Not only does the maturing of the Western European security community point towards this merger, so to does the complex web of formal and informal political, social, and economic networks that spanned the globe and framed the international engagement with the Kosovo conflict. The extent to which international values and interests have begun to come together during the 1990s and the processes by which that merger took place was revealed as our engagement with Kosovo shifted from ambivalence to war.

Notes

Introduction

1. The term 'humanitarian war' was first coined by Adam Roberts. See his, 'Humanitarian War: Intervention and Human Rights', *International Affairs*, 69(2), 1993 and, 'NATO's Humanitarian War Over Kosovo', *Survival*, 41(3), 1999.
2. The issue of intra-alliance politics is discussed throughout Pierre Martin and Mark R. Brawley (eds), *Alliance Politics, Kosovo, and NATO's War: Allied Force or Forced Allies?* (New York: Palgrave Macmillan, 2000).
3. Formally recognised by the EU and UN as the Former Yugoslav Republic of Macedonia (FYROM) but referred to as Macedonia throughout.
4. The idea of the 'court of world opinion' was put to me by Nicholas Wheeler. See Nicholas J. Wheeler, *Saving Strangers: Humanitarian Intervention in International Society* (Oxford: Oxford University Press, 2000).
5. Trotsky is cited by Noel Malcolm, *Kosovo: A Short History* (London: Papermac, 1999), p. 253.
6. Ibid.
7. Ibid., pp. 324–6. For a general overview of the key aspects of the conflict see Arshi Pipa and Sami Repishti, *Studies on Kosova* (New York: Columbia University Press, 1984), Robert Elsie (ed.), *Kosovo: In the Heart of the Powder Keg* (New York: Columbia University Press, 1997).
8. See Lenard J. Cohen, *Broken Bonds: Yugoslavia's Disintegration and Balkan Politics in Transition*, 2nd edn (Oxford: Westview, 1995), p. 33.
9. Article 4 of the Constitution of the Socialist Autonomous Province of Kosovo, 1974. See Marc Weller, *The Crisis in Kosovo 1989–1999: From the Dissolution of Yugoslavia to Rambouillet and the Outbreak of Hostilities* (Cambridge: International Documents and Analysis, 1999), p. 58.
10. Article 6 of the Kosovo Constitution, 1974.
11. Article 217 of the Kosovo Constitution, 1974.
12. Provisions for economic autonomy can be found in Article 292 of the Kosovo Constitution, 1974. The political status of Kosovo is principally articulated in Articles 300, 301 and 339.
13. Gazmend Zajmi, 'Kosova's Constitutional Position in the Former Yugoslavia', in Ger Duijzings, Dusan Janjic, and Shkelzen Maliqi (eds), *Kosovo/Kosova: Confrontation or Coexistence* (Nijmegen: Peace Research Centre of the University of Nijmegen, 1996), p. 98.
14. See Mihailo Crnobrnja, *The Yugoslav Drama*, 2nd edn (London: I. B. Tauris, 1994), pp. 75–6, 225. Crnobrnja was formerly Ambassador of Yugoslavia to the European Communities.
15. Miranda Vickers, *Between Serb and Albanian: A History of Kosovo* (London: Hurst and Co., 1998), p. 181.
16. See Amnesty International, *Yugoslavia: Prisoners of Conscience* (London: Amnesty International, 1985), p. 6.

17. Vickers, *Between Serb and Albanian*, p. 182.
18. See Ivanka Nedeva, 'Kosovo/a: Different Perspectives', in Thanos Veremis and Evangelos Kofos (eds), *Kosovo: Avoiding Another Balkan War* (Athens: Hellenic Foundation for European and Foreign Policy, 1998), p. 104.
19. Branka Magas, 'Yugoslavia: The Spectre of Balkanization', *New Left Review*, 174, March–April 1974.
20. Dennison Rusinow, *Yugoslavia: A Fractured Federalism* (Washington, DC: Wilson Centre Press, 1988), p. 70.
21. Ivanka Nedeva, 'Kosovo/a: Different Perspectives', p. 104.
22. Fred Singleton, *A Short History of the Yugoslav Peoples* (Cambridge: Cambridge University Press, 1985), p. 273.
23. For a detailed analysis on the student unrest in 1981 see Julie A. Mertus, *Kosovo: How Myths and Truths Started a War* (Berkeley: University of California Press, 1999), pp. 17–95.
24. Malcolm, *Kosovo*, p. 335.
25. *Vjesnik* (Zagreb), 16 April 1981.
26. Mertus, *Kosovo*, p. 33.
27. Ibid., p. 33.
28. *Tanjug* cited by Vickers, *Between Serb and Albanian*, p. 201.
29. Vickers, *Between Serb and Albanian*, p. 198.
30. See Mertus, *Kosovo*, pp. 56–91.
31. Pajazit Nushi, 'The Phenomenon of Military-Police Violence in Kosova in the Years 1981–1992', in Jusuf Bajraktari, Lefter Nasi, Kristaq Prifti, Fatmir Sejdiu, Edi Shukriu and Pellumb Xhufi (eds), *The Kosova Issue – a Historic and Current Problem* (Tirana: Institute of History – Pristina and Institute of History – Tirana, 1996), p. 150.
32. Amnesty International, *Yugoslavia: Prisoners of Conscience* (London: Amnesty International, 1985), p. 12.
33. Christine von Kohl and Wolfgang Libal, 'Kosovo: The Gordian Knot of the Balkans', in Robert Elsie (ed.), *Kosovo: In the Heart of the Powderkeg* (Boulder: East European Monographs, 1997), p. 75.
34. Mertus, *Kosovo*, p. 43.
35. Oskar Gruenwald, 'Yugoslavia's Gulag Archipelago and Human Rights', in Oskar Gruenwald and Karen Rosenblum-Cale (eds), *Human Rights in Yugoslavia* (New York: Irvington Publishers, 1986), p. 19
36. Malcolm, *Kosovo*, p. 339.
37. Ibid., p. 339.
38. Mertus, *Kosovo*, p. 107. A favoured Ottoman method of execution was to impale the victim on a stake driven through the anus, up the back and out again at the neck. The victim would be impaled in public and would die a slow and painful death. Most Serbs are very familiar with the horrors of impalement thanks to the graphic description of such an execution in Ivo Andric, *The Bridge on the Drina* (London: The Harvill Press, 1995).
39. Speech by Vuk Draskovic, 7 April 1986. Cited by Robert Thomas, *Serbia under Milošević: Politics in the 1990s* (London: Hurst and Co., 1999), p. 39.
40. Cited in ibid., p. 41.
41. Malcolm, *Kosovo*, pp. 344–5.
42. Esat Stavileci, 'Constitutional Changes and the Abolition of Autonomy', in Jusuf Bajraktari *et al.* (eds), *The Kosova Issue*, p. 155.

43. On the extent of the parallel state see: Richard Caplan, 'International Diplomacy and the Crisis in Kosovo', *International Affairs*, 74(2), p. 451.
44. *Guardian*, 26 July 1994. For more on Rugova's political platform see: Ibrahim Rugova, *La Question du Kosovo* (Paris: Fayard, 1994).
45. von Kohl and Libal, 'Kosovo', p. 93.
46. Ibid.
47. See International Crisis Group, *Kosovo Briefing*, 17 February 1998, p. 5.
48. von Kohl and Libal, 'Kosovo', p. 93.
49. Ibid., p. 94.
50. Behlull Beqaj cited by International Crisis Group, *Kosovo Spring*, part 1, 20 March 1998.
51. Elez Biberaj, 'Kosova: The Balkan Powder Keg', *Conflict Studies*, 258, February 1993, p. 7.
52. Human Rights Watch, *Humanitarian Law Violations in Kosovo* (London: Human Rights Watch, 1999), p. 66.
53. International Crisis Group, *Kosovo Spring*, p. 8.
54. Vickers, *Between Serb and Albanian*, p. 284.
55. See International Crisis Group, *Kosovo Spring*, p. 9.
56. Amnesty International, *Kosovo: The Evidence* (London: Amnesty International, 1998), p. 29.
57. Ibid.
58. These observations and figures are cited in International Crisis Group, *Kosovo Briefing*, pp. 16–17.
59. *Rilindja*, 12 November 1995.
60. Malcolm, *Kosovo*, p. 345.
61. International Crisis Group, *Kosovo Briefing*, p. 6.
62. International Crisis Group, *Kosovo Spring*, p. 34.
63. Ibid.
64. *International Herald Tribune*, 20 January 1994.
65. *Guardian*, 19 September 1994.
66. Ibid.
67. Ibrahim Rugova, *Impact International*, 10 April–7 May 1992, p. 10.

Chapter 1: Kosovo and the Dissolution of Yugoslavia

1. See Patrick F. R. Artisien and R. A. Howells, 'Kosovo, Albania and the Kosovo Riots', *The World Today*, November 1981; Mark Baskin, 'Crisis in Kosovo', *Problems of Communism*, March–April 1983; and Viktor Meier, 'Yugoslavia's National Question', *Problems of Communism*, March–April 1983. Specifically on the 1981 student riots see Jens Reuter, *Die Albaner in Jugoslawien* (Munich: R. Oldenbourg, 1992); Kjell Magnusson, 'The Serbian Reaction: Kosovo and Ethnic Mobilization Among the Serbs', *Nordic Journal of Soviet and East European Studies*, 4(3), 1987.
2. *Daily Telegraph*, 27 February 1990.
3. *The Times*, 23 March 1990; *The Daily Telegraph*, 7 September 1990; *The Financial Times*, 6 September 1990.
4. On the European Parliament visit see FBIS, *Daily Survey: Eastern Europe* (FBIS-EEU-89-125), 30 June 1989, pp. 74–6.

5. EC Bulletin 3-1991, p. 70.
6. *International Herald Tribune*, 24 November 1991.
7. Section 862 of House Resolution 2655, 29 June 1989. *Congressional Record*, 29 June 1989.
8. For example see, Laura Silber and Allan Little, *The Death of Yugoslavia* (London: Penguin for the BBC, 1995); Viktor Meier, *Yugoslavia: A History of Its Demise* (London: Routledge, 1999); Mihailo Crnobrnja, *The Yugoslav Drama* (London: IB Tauris, 1994).
9. FBIS, *Daily Report: Eastern Europe* (FBIS-EEU-89-131), 11 July 1989, p. 61.
10. *The Times*, 13 April 1990.
11. *The Financial Times*, 4 September 1990.
12. See Susan Woodward, *Balkan tragedy: Chaos and Dissolution after the Cold War* (Washington: The Brookings Institution, 1995), p. 151.
13. *International Herald Tribune*, 29 November 1990.
14. Woodward, *Balkan Tragedy*, pp. 160–1.
15. *The Financial Times*, 22 May 1991.
16. Wayne Bert, *The Reluctant Superpower: United States' Policy in Bosnia, 1991–95* (London: Macmillan – now Palgrave Macmillan, 1997), p. 136.
17. *Independent*, 29 March 1991.
18. *The Times*, 7 December 1991.
19. Željan Šušter, *Historical Dictionary of the Federal Republic of Yugoslavia* (Lanham: Scarecrow, 1999), p. 392.
20. For a persuasive critique of Resolution 713 and its impact on the war in Bosnia see, Michael A. Sells, *The Bridge Betrayed: Religion and Genocide in Bosnia* (London: University of California, 1996); and Ed Vulliamy, *Seasons in Hell: Understanding Bosnia's War* (New York: St. Martin's Press, 1994).
21. *USIA: European Wireless File*, 9 December 1991.
22. Ibid.
23. *International Herald Tribune*, 19 March 1991.
24. *USIA: European Wireless Brief*, 18 October 1991.
25. See Thomas Halverson, 'American Perspectives', in Alex Danchev and Thomas Halverson (eds), *International Perspectives on the Yugoslav Conflict* (London: Macmillan – now Palgrave Macmillan, 1996), pp. 4–6.
26. The German position is well documented. For example see, Jean-Marie Calic, 'German Perspectives', in Danchev and Halverson (eds), *International Perspectives on the Yugoslav Conflict* for a first-hand perspective on this see Michael Libal, *Limits of Persuasion: Germany and the Yugoslav Crisis: 1991–1992* (London: Praeger, 1997). For a xenophobic Serbian view of the Austrian and Hungarian positions see John Zametica, 'The Dissolution of Yugoslavia', *Adelphi Paper*, 270, 1992. For a more judicious assessment see Christopher Cviić, *Remaking the Balkans* (London: Royal Institute of International Affairs, 1991), pp. 97–9.
27. *The Financial Times*, 31 May 1990.
28. *The Financial Times*, 20 March 1990.
29. *Independent*, 20 March 1991.
30. See Lenard J. Cohen, *Broken Bonds: Yugoslavia's Disintegration and Balkan Politics in Transition*, 2nd edn (Boulder: Westview, 1995), p. 72.
31. *International Herald Tribune*, 6 and 9 November 1991, *International Herald Tribune*, 3 December 1991.

32. See James Gow, *Triumph of the Lack of Will: International Diplomacy and the Yugoslav Wars* (London: Hurst and Co., 1997), p. 53.
33. EPC Statement, 3 September 1991, EC Bulletin 9-91, p. 63.
34. Ibid., p. 65.
35. Paragraph Four of the Introductory Part of the Constitution of the Socialist Autonomous Province of Kosovo, 1974. Like many documents used in this book, I take this from Marc Weller, *The Crisis in Kosovo 1989–1999: From the Dissolution of Yugoslavia to Rambouillet and the Outbreak of Hostilities* (Cambridge: Cambridge Documents and Analysis Part 1, 1999), p. 58.
36. See Steve Terrett, *The Dissolution of Yugoslavia and the Badinter Arbitration Commission: A Contextual Study of Peace-Making Efforts in the Post-Cold War World* (Dartmouth: Ashgate, 2000), pp. 78–9.
37. European Parliament Resolution, 11 September 1991, EC Bulletin 9-1991, p. 48.
38. For an excellent account of Kosovar Albanian responses to Serb oppression see Howard Clark, *Civil Resistance in Kosovo* (London: Pluto, 2000)
39. Author's interview with Lord Carrington, Bledlow, 15 December 2000.
40. Author's interview with Lord Owen, London, 5 October 2000.
41. Cited by Laura Silber and Allan Little, *The Death of Yugoslavia* (London: Penguin for the BBC, 1995), p. 213.
42. *IWPR Balkan Crisis Report*, No. 209, 15 January 2001, p. 4.
43. Libal, *Limits of Persuasion*, pp. 29–30.
44. EPC Press Release, P. 128/91
45. *Uti Posseditis* is a legal principle formulated during the decolonisation process. It states that existing borders cannot be changed during the decolonisation process, unless by consent of the parties involved. See SKN Blay, 'Self-Determination Versus Territorial Integrity in Decolonisation', *New York University Journal of International Law and Politics*, 18, 1985–86.
46. See Marc Weller, 'The International Response to the Dissolution of the SFRY', *American Journal of International Law*, 86, 1992.
47. *Guardian*, 18 January 1992.
48. See ibid.
49. For an outline of the principle of territoriality as a basic element of statehood see Joseph Frankel, *International Relations in a Changing World* (Oxford: Oxford University Press, 1988), p. 20.
50. Declaration by the Twelve on Yugoslavia (Extraordinary EPC Ministerial meeting, Brussels, 16 December 1991), Sp. St/LON/164/91. Text from the French Embassy in London.
51. See Vickers, *Between Serb and Albanian*, p. 251.
52. Letter from Dr Ibrahim Rugova to Lord Carrington, Peace Conference on Yugoslavia, 22 December 1991. Reproduced in Weller, *The Crisis in Kosovo 1989–1999*, p. 81.
53. Interview with Lord Carrington, Bledlow, 15 December 2000.
54. Terrett, *The Dissolution of Yugoslavia*, p. 121.
55. Ibid., p. 124.
56. Ibid., p. 125.
57. See Michael Craven, 'The European Community Arbitration Commission on Yugoslavia', *British Yearbook of International Law*, 66, 1995.
58. Terrett, *The Dissolution of Yugoslavia*, p. 125.

59. Quoted by ibid., p. 143.
60. Para. 2c of Opinion no. 1 of the Arbitration Commission on the former Yugoslavia, 11 January 1992.
61. Para 3, ibid.
62. First opinion of Opinion no. 2 of the Arbitration Commission on the former Yugoslavia, 11 January 1992.
63. Opinion 2, ibid.
64. Tim Judah, *Kosovo: War and Revenge* (London: Yale University Press, 2000), p. 92.
65. Letter from Lord Carrington, Chairman, Conference on Yugoslavia, to Cr. I. Rugova, 17 August 1992. From Weller, *The Kosovo Crisis*, p. 86.
66. Robert Thomas, *Serbia under Milošević: Politics in the 1990s* (London: Hurst and Co., 1999), pp. 121–9.
67. Silber and Little, *The Death of Yugoslavia*, p. 289.
68. More on the Mission's terms of reference are included below. The expulsion of the Mission is dealt with in the following chapter.
69. Weller, *The Kosovo Crisis*, pp. 76–7.
70. London International Conference on the Former Yugoslavia, Work Programme, 27 August 1992. From Weller, *The Kosovo Crisis*, p. 89.
71. *RFE/RL* Research Reports, 2(44), 1993.
72. Report of the Secretary-General on the International Conference on the Former Yugoslavia, 11 November 1992. From Weller, *The Kosovo Crisis*, p. 90.
73. Author's interview with Hydajet Hyseni, former political prisoner, LDK activist and subsequent Kosovar delegate at Rambouillet, Pristina, 7 January 2001.
74. For the reaction of the Serbian delegation see Miodrag Perišić, 'On the State of Affairs in Kosovo and Metohija', CSCE/91-07-17.DOC/3. The report of the CSCE meeting of experts is reprinted in Arie Bloed, *The Conference on Security and Cooperation in Europe: Analysis and Basic Documents* (London: Kluwer Law International, 1993), pp. 593–602.
75. See Stefan Troebst, *Conflict in Kosovo: Failure of Prevention? An Analytical Documentation, 1992–1998* (Brussels: ECMI Working Paper 1, 1998), p. 12.
76. Committee of Senior Officials Statement on the Former Yugoslavia, 20 May 1992. The Yugoslav response is included in this text as an interpretive statement. From Weller, *The Crisis in Kosovo*, p. 94.
77. Report of the Conflict Prevention Centre Fact-Finding Mission to Kosovo, 5 June 1992. From Weller, *The Crisis in Kosovo*, pp. 102–4.
78. Decisions of the Committee of Senior Officials, Helsinki, 8/10 June 1992. From Weller, *The Crisis in Kosovo*, pp. 94–5.
79. Declaration on the Yugoslav Crisis, Adopted by the CSCE Summit, Helsinki, 10 July 1992. From Snezana Trifunovska, *Yugoslavia Through Documents: From Its Creation to Its Dissolution* (London: Martinus Nijhoff, 1994), p. 648.
80. The Helsinki Final Act, which is a statement of common principles that underlie the CSCE consists of three 'baskets' on politico-military aspects of security (basket 1), co-operation in economics, sciences etc. (basket 2), and co-operation in humanitarian affairs, including human rights (basket 3). See *Organisation for Security and Cooperation in Europe Handbook*, 3rd edn (Vienna: OSCE, 2000), p. 10.
81. Decisions of the Committee of Senior Officials, Prague, 13–14 August 1992.

82. Tore Bøgh, 'Interim Report from the Head of Mission to Kosovo, Sandžak and Vojvodina', Belgrade, 27 September 1992.
83. Ibid.
84. Interim Report from the Head of the Mission of Long Duration, 27 September 1992.
85. Philip E. Auerswald and David P. Auerswald (eds), *The Kosovo Conflict: A Diplomatic History Through Documents* (The Hague: Kluwer Law International, 2000), p. 65.
86. Text from the *Washington Post*, 18 April 1999.
87. Written answers from Thomas Niles, Assistant Secretary, Bureau of European and Canadian Affairs (1991–March 1993) to the author, 28 December 2000.
88. Author's interview with Sylejman Selimi, Priština, 7 January 2001.
89. A similar previous attempt to confiscate arms by the Yugoslav authorities had provoked conflict in Kosovo immediately after the Second World War. Malcolm, *Kosovo: A Short History*, pp. 320–1.
90. Supplemental written answer to the author by Thomas Niles, 29 December 2000.
91. Written answers to the author by Thomas Niles, 28 December 2000.
92. Ibid., and written answers to the author from Nicholas Rostow, National Security Committee Member at the time, 15 December 2000.
93. Judah, *Kosovo: War and Revenge*, pp. 73–4.

Chapter 2: The Absence of Prevention

1. Cited in *The Times*, 13 May 1993.
2. See Abiodun Williams, *Preventing War: The United Nations and Macedonia* (Lanham: Rowman and Littlefield, 2000).
3. A body that did not survive the transition from CSCE to OSCE. See the *OSCE Handbook 2000* (Vienna: OSCE, 2000), p. 194.
4. Testimony of Daniel Plesch, Director of the British–American Security Information Council, to the United States Congress Armed Services Committee, House of Representatives, on 'Bosnia and the former Yugoslavia', 26 May 1993.
5. CSCE Office for Democratic Institutions and Human Rights, 'Final Report of the CSCE Elections Mission to Yugoslavia (Serbia and Montenegro)', 7 January 1993, p. 1.
6. Ibid., p. 4.
7. CSCE Mission to Kosovo, Sandžak, and Vojvodina, 'Special Report: Kosovo: – Problems and Prospects', 29 June 1993.
8. Ibid.
9. *International Herald Tribune*, 19 May 1993.
10. Other NGOs involved included Médecins du Monde, Médecins sans Frontières, and Mercy Corps. See Clark, *Civil Resistance in Kosovo*, p. 90.
11. United Kingdom House of Commons Select Committee on Foreign Affairs, Appendices to the Minutes of Evidence. Supplementary Memorandum submitted by the British Council, 7 June 2000.
12. Author's interview with Lord Owen, 5 October 2001 and Geert Ahrens, 27 October 2001.

13. Lenard J. Cohen, *Serpent in the Bosom: The Rise and Fall of Slobodan Milošević* (Boulder, Westview, 2000), p. 167.
14. Ibid. and Thomas, *Serbia under Milošević*, p. 143.
15. Savović reported by *Tanjug*. Recorded in *BASIC Reports*, 32, 9 July 1993, p. 1.
16. Quoted in Ibid.
17. Ibid.
18. Ibid.
19. I am grateful to Stuart Griffin for bringing this to my attention. See Arie Bloed (ed.), *The Conference on Security and Cooperation in Europe: Basic Documents 1993–1995* (The Hague: Martinus Nijhoff, 1997), pp. 57–9.
20. *Independent*, 15 October 1993.
21. Ibid.
22. *Guardian*, 8 December 1993.
23. *Frankfurter Allgemeine Zeitung*, 11 August 1993.
24. *Guardian*, 2 September 1993.
25. Ibid.
26. *Guardian*, 8 December 1993.
27. *The Times*, 10 April 1993.
28. USIS Reference Center, European Wireless File, 14 April 1993.
29. *The Times*, 8 October 1993.
30. *Daily Telegraph*, 5 November 1993.
31. See Holbrooke, *To End a War*, p. 88.
32. According to Holbrooke, '... Milosevic hated the sanctions. They hurt his country, and he wanted them lifted' ibid. Also see Thomas, *Serbia under Milošević*, ch. 17 in particular, pp. 176–87.
33. See, 'Working Group on Ethnic and National Communities and Minorities', Background Briefing on 6 October 1992 by Ambassador Geert Ahrens, in B. G. Ramcharan (ed.), *The International Conference on the Former Yugoslavia: Official Papers* (The Hague: Kluwer International Law, 1997), Volume 2, p. 1603.
34. Chairman's report of 14 September 1993 to the steering committee on the former Yugoslav Republic of Macedonia, in ibid., p. 1607.
35. Ibid., p. 1613. Also see Thanos Veremis and Evangelos Kofos (eds), *Kosovo: Avoiding Another Balkan War* (Athens: ELIAMEP and University of Athens, 1998), pp. 164–5.
36. Ibid.
37. Ibid.
38. *BASIC Reports*, 32, 9 July 1993.
39. Author's interview with Lord Owen, 5 October 2001.
40. S/PV.3662. 9 August 1993.
41. UN Security Council Resolution 855 (1993).
42. *International Herald Tribune*, 3 March 1993.
43. Warren Christopher, transcript of 10 February 1993 news conference, European Wireless File News Alert, 11 February 1993. Emphasis added.
44. Statement by Warren Christopher to the North Atlantic Council, 11 June 1993. European Wireless File News Alert, 12 June 1993.
45. Testimony of Stephen Oxman at a CSCE Commission hearing on 21 July 1993. European Wireless File News Alter, 22 July 1993.
46. See Ivo Daalder, *Getting to Dayton* (Washington, DC: The Brookings Institution, 2000).

47. Robert D. Kaplan, *Balkan Ghosts: A Journey Through History* (New York: St. Martin's Press, 1993).
48. President Clinton remarks at a 'Town Meeting', Southfield, Michigan, 10 February 1993, in United States Information Centre: London, *Yugoslavia: A Document Collection*, 1993 (pages are unnumbered).
49. *Bosnet*, 18 November 1993.
50. David Warsawski, 'Will to Disaster: Interview with Tadeusz Mazowiecki', in *Index on Censorship*, 5, 1995.
51. Ibid.
52. Fabian Schmidt, 'Strategic Reconciliation in Kosovo', *Transitions*, 1(15), 1995.
53. *Guardian*, 1 June 1994.
54. Delegation of the CSCE Parliamentary Assembly Report to the Third Annual Session, Vienna, 5–8 June 1994, para. 1.3.1.
55. Report of the Special Rapporteurs and Representatives, UN General Assembly, A/49/641.S/1994/1252, 4 November 1994.
56. They were: United States, Russia, United Kingdom, France, Germany, and Italy. Italy was not an original member of the Group but successfully lobbied for inclusion in 1995. The Contact Group was formed at the beginning of the Bosnian war to provide a focal point for international peace efforts.
57. USIA, European Wireless File News Alert, 16 February 1995.
58. Bøgh was interviewed by the independent Pristina daily, *Koha Ditore*, 9 March 1995.
59. General Assembly Resolution 1994/204, A/RES/49/204, 23 December 1994.
60. Warsawski, 'Will to Disaster: Interview with Tadeusz Mazowiecki'.
61. See Alex J. Bellamy, 'Human Wrongs in Kosovo 1974–99', in Ken Booth (ed.), *The Kosovo Tragedy: The Human Rights Dimensions* (London: Frank Cass, 2000).
62. Letter from the Permanent Representative of Albania to the President of the United Nations Security Council, 15 August 1995. S/1995/700. Also see, *The Times*, 22 August 1995; *Independent*, 16 August 1995 and the *International Herald Tribune*, 12 August 1995.
63. Letter from the Permanent Mission of the FRY to the Chairman of the Commission on Human Rights, 19 April 1996. E/CN.4/1996/167 and Letter from the Ambassador of the FRY to the Chairman of the Commission on Human Rights, 9 March 1995. E/CN.4/1995/171.
64. Malcolm, *Kosovo*, p. 353.
65. Peter Koijmans, 'The Sole Solution' in Ger Duijzings, Dušan Janjić and Shkëlzen Maliqi (eds), *Kosovo–Kosova: Confrontation or Coexistence* (Nijmegen: University of Nijmegen, 1997), p. 212.
66. Judah, *Kosovo: War and Revenge*, p. 138.
67. Ibid., p. 124.
68. Ibid.
69. Holbrooke, *To End a War*, p. 234.
70. *The Financial Times*, 29 December 1995.
71. *Guardian*, 23 November 1995.
72. *International Herald Tribune*, 23 October 1995.
73. Recommendation 1288 of the Parliamentary Assembly of the Council of Europe, 24 January 1996.

74. Troebst, *Conflict in Kosovo*, p. 44.
75. *The Financial Times*, 15 March 1996; *Tanjug*, 6 March 1996; *Tanjug*, 14 July 1996.
76. *Tanjug*, 14 July 1996.
77. *Tanjug*, 13 July 1996.
78. *OMRI*, 1(6), 13 February 1996.
79. Ibid.
80. Author's interview with Geert Ahrens, 27 October 2001.
81. *Tanjug*, 5 March 1996.
82. Balkan Peace Team, *Kosovo after the Dayton Agreement*, April/May 1996, p. 1 (www.peacebridges.org).
83. Ibid.
84. International Helsinki Federation for Human Rights, *The Situation in the Federal Republic of Yugoslavia*, Vienna, 1996.
85. Shinasa A. Rama, 'The Serb–Albanian War and the Miscalculations of the International Community', *International Journal of Albanian Studies*, 2(1), 1998, p. 9.
86. Ibid.
87. Troebst, *Conflict in Kosovo*, p. 59.
88. *Tanjug*, 29 February 1996 and 9 July 1996.
89. Reported by *Politika Ekspress*, 16 July 1996. Similar views were expressed by Klaus Kinkel and Bill Clinton. See Ben Lombardi, 'Kosovo – Introduction to Yet Another Balkan Problem', *European Security* 5(2), 1996.
90. *OMRI*, 1(41), 15 October 1996.
91. Reported by *Reuters*, 6 June 1996.
92. The use of the centre for covert intelligence gathering was highlighted to the author in private conversation with undisclosable sources. Its use for open source information gathering is discussed by Vickers, *Between Serb and Albanian*, p. 297.
93. *OMRI*, Special Report, 3 September 1996.
94. The translation of the agreement can be found in Philip Auerswald and David Auerswald (eds), *The Kosovo Conflict*, p. 79.
95. *Independent*, 8 July 1996.
96. *AIM*, Belgrade, 11 October 1996.
97. United Nations General Assembly, Report of the Secretary-General, A/52/502, 12 December 1996.
98. Mr. Roseta, 'The Peace Process in the Balkans', report submitted to the Assembly of the Western European Union, 15 October 1996, Document 1540.
99. *Tanjug*, 15 January 1997.
100. Cited by Troebst, *Conflict in Kosovo*, p. 61.
101. Ibid.
102. Auerswald and Auerswald, *The Kosovo Conflict*, p. 85 and pp. 86–9.
103. *Tanjug*, 10 April 1997; Alex Heraclides, 'The Kosovo Conflict and its Resolution: In Pursuit of Ariadne's Thread', *Security Dialogue*, 28(3), 1998; European Action Council for Peace in the Balkans and Public International Law and Policy Group (of the Carnegie Endowment for International Peace), *Kosovo: From Crisis to a Permanent Solution*, 1997, p. 7.
104. This, and the following account of the descent into anarchy in Albania, is taken from Miranda Vickers, *The Albanians*, pp. 244–8.

105. Troebst, *Conflict in Kosovo*, p. 51.
106. Final Communiqué of the Ministerial Meeting of the North Atlantic Council, Brussels, 16 December 1997, para. 17.
107. *RFE/ERL*, 31 December 1997.
108. *Naša Borba*, 1 December 1997. The initiative is also discussed by Troebst, *Conflict in Kosovo*, p. 70.

Chapter 3: Towards Intervention

1. This argument was put forward throughout the BBC's landmark documentary on the Kosovo crisis, *Moral Combat*, first broadcast on 27 March 2000.
2. The dilemmas confronting international society with regards to Kosovo at the outset of 1998 are outlined in S. C. Chopra, 'Kosovo – Will NATO Intervene to Break Up Serbia', *USI Journal*, 533, 1998.
3. On the upsurge of violence in March 1998 see, 'A Balkan intifada in Kosovo?', *IISS Strategic Comments*, 4(2), 1998 and Jonathan Steele, 'Learning to Live with Milosevic', *Transitions*, 5, September 1998.
4. For an excellent history of the UÇK see Maj. Ben Farrell, *The UÇK: A Case for the Second Transformation*, Defence Research Paper, 2001, held at the Library of the Joint Services Command and Staff College. Also see, Robert Thomas, 'Choosing the Warpath', *The World Today*, May 1998. According to Veton Surroi, 'the Drenica uprising [1998] and the war that followed demonstrated two basic things to the Kosovar Albanians. It became clear, first, that the self-illusion of a state was not sufficient to create one, particularly since the Dayton agreement precluded any further advance without violence ...'. See Veton Surroi, 'Kosovo Political Life: Past as Prologue?', *The International Spectator*, 35(1), 2000, p. 30.
5. According to Bill Clinton, lessons were learned from Bosnia. 'We learned that if you don't stand up to brutality and the killing of innocent people, you invite the people who do it to do more of it. We learned that firmness can save lives and stop armies. Now we have a chance to take the lessons we learned in Bosnia and put them to work in Kosovo before it's too late ...' cited by Rhiannon Vickers, 'Blair's Kosovo Campaign: Political Communications, the Battle for Public Opinion and Foreign Policy', *Civil Wars*, 3(1), 2000, p. 56.
6. On the importance of containment for Western policy-makers see, R. Craig Nation, 'US Policy and the Kosovo Crisis', *The International Spectator*, 33(4), 1998; Alice Ackerman, 'Macedonia and the Kosovo Conflict', *The International Spectator*, 33(4), 1998.
7. Richard Caplan's 'International Diplomacy and the Crisis in Kosovo', *International Affairs*, 74(4), 1998, and Catherine Guicherd's, 'International Law and the War in Kosovo', *Survival*, 41(2), 1999, pp. 19–34 are two notable exceptions.
8. The massacre at Donji Prekaz and similar attacks in Likosane and Cirez are reported in detail by Human Rights Watch, *Humanitarian Law Violations in Kosovo* (London and New York: Human Rights Watch, 1999). The events at Racak will be discussed at greater length in Chapter 4.

9. See Thanos M. Veremis and Dimitrios Triantaphyllo (eds), *The South-East European Yearbook 1997–8* (Athens: Hellenic Foundation for European and Foreign Policy, 1998).

10. Statement by the Contact Group, 25 February 1998.

11. *The Times*, 1 March 1998.

12. Ivo H. Daalder and Michael E. O'Hanlon, *Winning Ugly: NATO's War to Save Kosovo* (New York: The Brookings Institution, 2000), p. 27.

13. Weller, *The Kosovo Crisis 1989–1999*, p. 21.

14. On Gelbard's statement in Pristina see Judah, *Kosovo: War and Revenge*, p. 138. The State Department reiterated Gelbard's argument in Department of State Press Statement, 2 March 1998.

15. Views privately expressed to the author.

16. Excerpts from Press Briefing by Secretary of State Albright and Italian Foreign Minister Dini, 7 March 1998.

17. *The Times*, 3 March 1998.

18. See James Pettifer in *The Times*, 3 March 1998. Pettifer is an internationally renowned authority on the southern Balkans. See James Pettifer (ed.), *The New Macedonian Question* (London: Macmillan, 1999) and James Pettifer, *The Southern Balkans* (London: Minority Rights Group, 1994).

19. On the problems confronting Macedonia see Pettifer, *The New Macedonian Question*, Lt Col. Martin Van de Lande, *The Macedonian Question*, dissertation for the degree of MPHIL, Cambridge University, 1999 and Gordana Icevska, 'Macedonia's Open Wounds', *Transitions*, 10(5), 1998.

20. UNPREDEP was the first preventive military mission undertaken by the UN. See Abiodun Williams, *Preventing War: UNPREDEP in Macedonia* (London: Rowman and Littlefield, 2000) and Alice Ackerman, *Making Peace Prevail: Preventing Violent Conflict in Macedonia* (Syracuse: Syracuse University Press, 2000).

21. See Chapter 1: Alex J. Bellamy, 'Human Wrongs in Kosovo 1974–99', in Ken Booth (ed.), *The Kosovo Tragedy*.

22. These reports are discussed in ibid. Also see Tim Judah, 'Kosovo's Road to War', *Survival*, 41(2), 1999.

23. *The Times*, 6 March 1998.

24. Ibid.

25. *Reuters*, 6 March 1998.

26. See Thomas W. Lippman, *Madeleine Albright and the New American Diplomacy* (Boulder: Westview, 2000), p. 214.

27. Press briefing by Secretary of State Madeleine K. Albright and Foreign Minister Lamberto Dini, Ministry of Foreign Affairs, Rome, 7 March 1998.

28. Albright in answer to questions, ibid.

29. Klaus Kinkel, German Foreign Minister, press briefing with Secretary of State Madeleine K. Albright, Bonn, 8 March 1998.

30. Statement by the Contact Group, London, 9 March 1998.

31. British Foreign Secretary Robin Cook in answer to Steve Erlanger from the New York Times, 9 March 1998.

32. See Lawrence Freedman and Efraim Karsh, *The Gulf Conflict* (London: Faber and Faber, 1993), pp. 52–4.

33. *The Times*, 11 March 1998.

34. Quoted by Judah, *Kosovo: War and Revenge*, p. 145.

35. Statement by the Contact Group, 25 March 1998, Bonn.
36. See S/PV 3868 and SC/6496, 31 March 1998. Also see *The Times*, 27 March 1998.
37. Statement by the Spokesman of the Ministry of Foreign Affairs of the Russian Federation, 2 April 1998.
38. United Nations Security Council Resolution 1160, 31 March 1998.
39. Statement by the Federal Ministry of Foreign Affairs of Yugoslavia, 1 April 1998.
40. See Statement by the Spokesman of the Ministry of Foreign Affairs of the Russian Federation, 2 April 1998 and Memorandum by the Russian Federation, 14 April 1998.
41. Report of the Organization for Security and Co-operation in Europe, 20 April 1998.
42. European Union Report, 21 April 1998. Annex to the United Nations Press Release [S/1998/361] 30 April 1998.
43. *RFE/ERL*, 24 April 1998.
44. *The Times*, 25 April 1998.
45. Judah, *Kosovo: War and Revenge*, p. 153.
46. For the best account of domestic politics in Serbia in the 1990s see Thomas, *Serbia under Milošević*.
47. *The Times*, 26 April 1998.
48. Report of the United Nations Secretary-General, Kofi Annan, to the Security Council, 30 April 1998.
49. *The Times*, 25 April 1998.
50. Holbrooke interviewed by Ivo H. Daalder and Michael E. O'Hanlon, *Winning Ugly*, pp. 38–9.
51. Ibid.
52. Comments taken from the Joint Press Conference by President Clinton and Italian Prime Minister Prodi, Washington, DC, 6 May 1998.
53. This story is recounted by Judah, *Kosovo: War and Revenge*, pp. 153–4.
54. See Richard Caplan, 'Christopher Hill's Road Show', *The World Today*, January 1999.
55. Jonathan Steele, 'Learning to Live with Milosevic', *Transitions*, 5(9), 1998 and Janusz Bugajski, 'Close to the Edge in Kosovo', *The Washington Quarterly*, 21(3), 1998.
56. This idea was expressed to the author by Gordana Ćirić from Novi Sad University.
57. Michael Ignatieff spent time travelling with Hill's diplomatic team. See Michael Ignatieff, *Virtual War: Kosovo and Beyond* (London: Chatto and Windus, 2000).
58. Weller, *The Crisis in Kosovo 1989–1999*, p. 348.
59. See Judah, *Kosovo: War and Revenge*, p. 171.
60. Opinions expressed to the author by UÇK regional commanders, Selimi, Remy, and Leka. Similar views were expressed to the author by Hydajet Hyseni, a former political prisoner and subsequent delegate at Rambouillet.
61. A more detailed analysis of the Hill plan can be found in Marc Weller, 'Legal Opinion on the Draft Proposal for a Settlement for Kosova', *Journal of Humanitarian Assistance*, October 1998.

62. Part II of the First [Hill] Draft Agreement for a Settlement of the Crisis in Kosovo, 1 October 1998.
63. Chapter III of ibid.
64. See chapter on Rambouillet.
65. On the need for an OSCE contribution see OSCE Report, Annexed to the UN Secretary-General's report, 3 October 1998. In Marc Weller, *The Crisis in Kosovo 1989–1999*, p. 350.
66. Figures taken from Briefing Notes provided for the Office of the UN High Commissioner for Refugees (UNHCR). Available at the UNHCR's website (www.unhcr.org).
67. Judah, *Kosovo: War and Revenge*.
68. Department of State Fact Sheet, 8 July 1998.
69. Report by the United Nations Secretary-General, Kofi Annan, to the Security Council, 4 June 1998.
70. Letter from the President of the United States of America to Congress, 10 June 1998.
71. Annex 5 to the Report by the United Nations Secretary-General, Kofi Annan, to the Security Council, 2 July 1998.
72. *The Times*, 4 June 1998.
73. Decision of the North Atlantic Council, 1 June 1998.
74. See Georgias Kostakos, 'The Southern Flank: Italy, Greece, Turkey', in Albrecht Schnabel and Ramesh Thakur (eds), *Kosovo and the Challenge of Humanitarian Intervention: Selective Indignation, Collective Action and International Citizenship* (Tokyo: United Nations University Press, 2000).
75. See David Haglund, 'Kosovo and the Case of the (not so) Free Riders: Portugal, Belgium, Canada and Spain', in Schnabel and Thakur (eds), *Kosovo and the Challenge of Humanitarian Intervention*.
76. Kostakos, 'The Southern Flank'.
77. *The Times*, 6 June 1998.
78. Private email to the author from a source in Whitehall.
79. *Washington Post*, 6 June 1998.
80. *New York Times*, 8 June 1998.
81. *New York Times*, 5 August 1998.
82. *The Times*, 8 June 1998.
83. *The Times*, 9 June 1998.
84. Ibid.
85. Preamble to Security Council Resolution 1199, 23 September 1998.
86. Statement by Secretary of State Albright, 23 September 1998.
87. Remarks to the Press by Secretary of State Albright and Secretary of Defense Cohen, Washington, DC, 1 October 1998.
88. Statement by Russian Ambassador to the United Nations, Sergei Lavrov, 23 September 1998.
89. Tim Youngs, 'Kosovo', *House of Commons Research Paper*, 98/73, 7 July 1998, p. 26.
90. *The Times*, 10 June 1998.
91. Richard Holbrooke emphasises this point throughout his account of the negotiations that brought about peace in Bosnia. See Richard Holbrooke, *To End a War*.
92. Ibid.

93. *The Times*, 11 June 1998.
94. *Guardian*, 12 June 1998.
95. *Independent*, 6 June 1998. Quoted by Youngs, 'Kosovo', p. 26. Editing is Youngs'.
96. *Independent*, 13 June 1998.
97. UN Press Release, SG/SM/6583, 5 June 1998.
98. Yurrii Davydov argues that Russian foreign policy is, 'made not for external but for internal use. In fact, it serves not the national interests of Russia on the world stage but the interests of various political groups within Russia's political elite'. The outburst of anti-NATO sentiment owed more to legitimising political elites than to genuine concern about either Kosovo or Russian–NATO relations. See Yurrii Davydov, 'The Kosovo Problem in the Russian Internal Political Context', in Dmitri Trenin and Yekaterina Stepanova (eds), *Kosovo: The International Aspects of the Crisis* (Moscow: Gandalf Press, 1999). Another account of Russia's internal dilemmas in regard to the Kosovo crisis can be found in, Pavel K. Baev, 'Russia's Stance Against Secessions: From Chechnya to Kosovo', *International Peacekeeping*, 6(3), 1999.
99. *The Times*, 9 June 1998 and *The Economist*, 13 June 1998.
100. *The Times*, 3 June 1998.
101. Ibid.
102. *RFE/ERL*, 18 June 1998
103. Ibid.
104. Youngs, 'Kosovo', p. 28.
105. *The Times*, 30 June 1998.
106. *The Times*, 23–27 September 1998.
107. According to Ted Galen Carpenter, 'The arrogance of the United States and its allies in bypassing the United Nations Security Council was especially infuriating to critics', in 'Introduction' to, Ted Galen Carpenter, *NATO's Empty Victory: A Postmortem on the Balkan War* (Washington, DC: The Cato Institute, 2000).
108. In a profile of Milošević, the Serbian writer Aleksa Djilas noted that, 'Milošević is now one of the most mistrusted politicians in the world'. Aleksa Djilas, 'A Profile of Slobodan Milošević', *Foreign Affairs*, summer 1993, p. 95.
109. Judah, *Kosovo: War and Revenge*, p. 182
110. Ibid.
111. Richard Holbrooke gave a similar account to the BBC documentary, *Moral Combat*. This version is taken from Judah, *Kosovo: War and Revenge*, p. 183.

Chapter 4: The Kosovo Verification Mission

1. *The Times*, 8 October 1998.
2. See Holbrooke, *To End a War*, pp. 101–8.
3. *Atlantic News*, 9 October 1998.
4. Quoted in ibid.
5. *The Times*, 8 and 9 October 1998.

6. *Washington Post*, 16 October 1998.
7. *Newsnight*, 22 August 1999. Background details are taken from interviews with Holbrooke and Short screened on the BBC's *Moral Combat*.
8. Ibid.
9. This discussion is reported by Judah, *Kosovo: War and Revenge*, p. 186.
10. Statement by the Secretary-General of NATO, Javier Solana, following the decision on the Activation Order, 13 October 1998.
11. *The Times*, 12 October 1998.
12. Richard Holbrooke in reply to questions, Department of State Press Release, 28 October 1998.
13. *Guardian*, 15 October 1998 and *Washington Post*, 15 October 1998.
14. President Milošević announces accord on peaceful solution, Belgrade, 13 October 1998. Marc Weller, *The Crisis in Kosovo*, p. 279.
15. Letter from the Ambassador of the Federal Republic of Yugoslavia to the Secretary-General of the United Nations, 23 October 1998.
16. Ibid. Also see 'Serbian Government Endorses Accord Reached by President Milosevic, Belgrade, 13 October 1998', in Weller, *The Crisis in Kosovo*, p. 279.
17. Massimo Calabresi, 'Third Time Lucky?', *Time*, 26 October 1998.
18. *Yugoslav Daily Survey*, 13 October 1998.
19. Press Points by the NATO Secretary-General, 15 October 1998.
20. NATO/FRY Kosovo Verification Mission Agreement, 15 October 1998.
21. Agreement between the Federal Republic of Yugoslavia and the Organization for Security and Cooperation in Europe, 16 October 1998.
22. These views were privately expressed to the author by British Foreign Office officials.
23. *OSCE Newsletter*, 5(10), October 1998.
24. William Walker, 'OSCE Verification Experiences in Kosovo', in Booth (ed.), *The Kosovo Tragedy*.
25. Weller, *The Kosovo Crisis*, p. 187, n. 16.
26. Paragraph 5, United Nations Security Council Resolution 1203, 24 October 1998.
27. Remarks by Ambassador Richard Holbrooke, State Department Press Release, 28 October 1998.
28. Ibid.
29. Transcript of William Walker interview, 8 January 1999. USIS Washington File.
30. Diana Johnstone, 'Humanitarian War: Making the Crime fit the Punishment', in Tariq Ali (ed.), *Masters of the Universe? NATO's Balkan Crusade* (London: Verso, 2000).
31. Walker, 'OSCE Verification Experiences', pp. 128–9.
32. Ibid.
33. Ibid., p. 117.
34. Walker, 'OSCE Verification Experiences in Kosovo', p. 131.
35. Hansard, 19 October 1998, Line 962.
36. *Electronic Telegraph*, 17 October 1998.
37. *Guardian*, 27 October 1998.
38. Tim Youngs, 'Kosovo: The Diplomatic and Military Options', *House of Commons Research Paper*, 98/93, 1998, p. 20.

39. *Electronic Telegraph*, 21 October 1998.
40. Ibid.
41. Ibid.
42. *Electronic Telegraph*, 29 October 1998.
43. 'War Suspended in Kosovo', *IISS Strategic Comments*, 4(9), November 1998.
44. James Gow, 'Kosovo after the Holbrooke–Milošević Agreement. What now?', *The International Spectator*, 33(4), 1998, pp. 21–2.
45. Ibid.
46. Brigadier General J. R. Michel Maisonneuve, 'The OSCE Kosovo Verification Mission', *Canadian Military Journal*, 1(1), 2000.
47. Ibid.
48. Weller, *The Crisis in Kosovo*, p. 350. Remember that the first draft had left Kosovo's status within Yugoslavia undefined, on the principle that an autonomous Kosovo would not need a strong presence in Belgrade.
49. Ibid.
50. Ibid.
51. Ibid.
52. Interview with President Slobodan Milošević, 13 December 1998. Text provided by Yugoslav Ministry of Foreign Affairs.
53. Ibid.
54. Kosova Press Release, 1 December 1998.
55. Kosova Press Release, 8 December 1998.
56. Kosova Press Release, 11 December 1998.
57. Ibid.
58. Gow, 'Kosovo after the Holbrooke–Milošević Agreement', p. 22.
59. Ibid.
60. *Electronic Telegraph*, 12 November 1998.
61. *Electronic Telegraph*, 10 November 1998.
62. KVM Report to the UN Secretary-General, 4 December 1998.
63. Ibid.
64. This story was reported by *Electronic Telegraph*, 11 December 1998.
65. *Electronic Telegraph*, 16 December 1998. These events were also reported in detail in the UN Inter-Agency Update on Kosovo Humanitarian Situation, 24 December 1998.
66. *Electronic Telegraph*, 25 December 1998.
67. Kosova Information Centre daily report, 25 December 1998.
68. *Guardian*, 5 January 1999.
69. Ibid.
70. Ibid.
71. *International Herald Tribune*, 6 January 1999.
72. *Guardian*, 7 January 1999.
73. Ibid.
74. Much of the following is derived from reports by the OSCE KVM, 'Massacre of Civilians in Racak' (www.osce.org), Helsinki Human Rights Watch (www.hrw.org), International Committee of the Red Cross (www.icrc.org), Society for Threatened Peoples, Amnesty International (www.amnesty.org) and the Finnish EU pathologists report written by Helena Ranta, the head of the team. The pathology report can be seen in Weller, *The Kosovo Crisis*,

p. 333. It is important to go into such detail because the incident at Racak has been the source of much debate in the West relating to the merits of Allied Force.

75. Walker, 'OSCE Verification Experiences in Kosovo', note 10, pp. 141–2.
76. *Washington Post*, 17 January 1999.
77. Report of the Independent Pathologists, in Weller, *The Kosovo Crisis*, p. 333.
78. It is interesting to note that the professional credibility of the Finnish pathologists has never been questioned by the Serbs.
79. This insights from various sources have been collated by the Society for Threatened Peoples at www.gfbv.de
80. See Johnstone, 'Humanitarian War', p. 163 and Edward Herman and David Peterson, 'CNN: Selling NATO's War Globally', in Philip Hammond and Edward S. Herman, *Degraded Capability: The Media and the Kosovo Crisis* (London: Pluto Press, 2000), pp. 117–19.

Chapter 5: From Rambouillet to Paris

1. Judah, *Kosovo: War and Revenge*, p. 197
2. UK House of Commons Defence Committee Report, para. 47.
3. *The Times*, 18 January 1998.
4. Briefing at NATO HQ, Brussels, 17 January 1998.
5. This insight comes from the author's discussions with KVM verifiers.
6. UK House of Commons Defence Committee report, para. 47.
7. Ibid.
8. Sandy Vershbow, BBC, *Today*, 19 January 1999. Transcript edited by author.
9. *The Times*, 20 January 1999.
10. Daalder and O'Hanlon, *Winning Ugly*, p. 70.
11. Ibid.
12. Ibid.
13. *Le Figaro*, 7 April 1999.
14. In *Le Monde*, 14 April 1999.
15. See Gunter Hofmann, 'Wie Deutschland in den Krieg geriet', *Die Zeit*, 20, 1999, pp. 17–21.
16. According to sources in the British Ministry of Defence.
17. UK House of Commons Defence Committee Report, para 40.
18. Excerpts from remarks by Secretary of State Albright, 4 February 1999.
19. Author's discussions with State Department official.
20. *The Times*, 25 January 1999.
21. See Barton Gellman, 'The Path to Crisis: How the United States and Its Allies went to War', *Washington Post*, 18 April 1999, A. 31.
22. See *Le Monde*, 31 January 1999.
23. These insights were provided in reports by the Carnegie Moscow Centre. See www.carnegie.ru. Also see Mark Smith and Henry Platter-Zyberg, *Kosovo: Russia's Response* (Camberley: Conflict Studies Resource Centre, 1999).
24. Statement by the Contact Group, 29 January 1999.
25. Quoted in *Guardian*, 29 January 1999.
26. United Nations Press Release (S/PRST/1999/5).

27. UK House of Commons Defence Committee Report, para 48.
28. See ibid. and para 49.
29. *Washington Post*, 1 February 1999.
30. *Danas*, 1 February 1999.
31. Letter from Yugoslav Foreign Minister Jovanović to the President of the United Nations Security Council, 1 February 1999.
32. *The Times*, 3 February 1999.
33. *Independent*, 3 February 1999.
34. *Tanjug*, 6 February 1999.
35. *Tanjug*, 5 February 1999.
36. Judah, *Kosovo: War and Revenge*, p. 199.
37. This story was widely recounted in the media, see *Guardian*, 7 February 1999 and *New York Times*, 7 February 1999.
38. Marc Weller, 'The Rambouillet Conference on Kosovo', *International Affairs*, 75(2), 1999, p. 228.
39. *International Herald Tribune*, 12 February 1999.
40. Robin Cook, press conference, Rambouillet, 11 February 1999.
41. The resident Serb delegation consisted of Cerim Abazi, Sokolj Cuse, Faik Jasari, Ljuan Koka, Zejnclabidin Kurejs, Vladin Kutlesić, Ratko Marković, Guljbehar Sabović, Nikola Sainović, Kefik Senadović, Vladimir Stambuk, Ihro Vait, and Vojislav Zivković. The Kosovar Albanian delegation consisted of Fehmi Agani, Idriz Ajeti, Ramë Buja, Bujar Bukoshi, Mehmet Hajriri, Xhavit Haliti, Hyadajet Hyseni, Bajram Kosumi, Jakup Krasniqi, Rexhep Qosja, Ibrahim Rugova, Blerim Shala, Veton Surroi, Azem Syla, Edita Tahiri, Hashim Thaçi. List taken from Weller, *The Crisis in Kosovo 1989–1999*.
42. Cited by ibid.
43. See Georgios Kostakis, 'The Southern Flank: Italy, Greece, Turkey', in Schnabel and Thakur (eds), *Kosovo and the Challenge of Humanitarian Intervention* (Tokyo: UN University Press, 2000).
44. UK House of Commons Defence Committee, para. 51.
45. Weller, 'The Rambouillet Conference', p. 228.
46. Author's interview with Hydajet Hyseni and Sulejman Selimi, Pristina, 4 and 5 January 2001. Also, *The Times*, 8 February 1999.
47. Judah, *Kosovo: War and Revenge*, p. 206.
48. Robin Cook on BBC Radio 4, 9 February 1999.
49. *RFE/ERL* 10 Feb 1999.
50. Albright in interview on *France 3*, 11 February.
51. Statement by the Serbian Delegation to Rambouillet, 11 February 1999.
52. Statement by Serbian President Milutinović, 12 February 1999.
53. *International Herald Tribune*, 13 February 1999.
54. *The Times*, 12–14 February 1999.
55. *Le Monde Diplomatique*, 16 February 1999.
56. *New York Times*, 9 and 11 February 1999.
57. *International Herald Tribune*, 16–17 February 1999.
58. Weller, 'The Rambouillet Conference', p. 229.
59. Authors interview with Hydajet Hyseni, Pristina, 4 January 2001.
60. Weller, 'The Rambouillet Conference', p. 230.
61. See Bellamy, 'Reconsidering Rambouillet'.
62. *The Times*, 19 February 1999.

63. Press Release Issued by the Co-Chairs to the Serbian Media, 18 February 1999.
64. Author's interview with Sulejman Selimi, 4 January 2001.
65. Judah, *Kosovo: War and Revenge*, p. 214.
66. See Weller, *The Kosovo Crisis*, p. 452. It was reported on the BBC's *Moral Combat* that Albright had personally delivered and signed the message. The author's interviews with delegates at Rambouillet suggests that this was not the case.
67. Judah, *Kosovo: War and Revenge*, p. 217.
68. Ibid.
69. Full text provided in Philip Auerswald and David Auerswald, *The Kosovo Conflict*, p. 592.
70. Federal Government of Yugoslavia Press Statement, 25 February 1999.
71. *The Washington Post*, 26 February 1999.
72. Ibid.
73. *Koha Ditore*, 25 February 1999.
74. *Politika*, 2 March 1999.
75. *The Times*, 3 March 1999.
76. Letter from the OSCE Chairman-in-Office to the Secretary-General of the UN, 20 March 1999. Reproduced in Weller, *The Crisis in Kosovo*, p. 338.
77. Ibid.
78. *Independent*, 11 March 1999.
79. Tony Blair lecture to the Royal United Service Institute, 3 March 1999. This speech was widely reported in the media. See for example, *Guardian*, 4 March 1999 and *New York Times*, 6 March 1999.
80. Ibid.
81. *Der Speigel*, 4 March 1999.
82. *The Times*, 5 March 1999.
83. Both quotes are taken from Daalder and O'Hanlon, *Winning Ugly*, p. 87.
84. *The Times*, 14 March 1999.
85. Quoted in *Evening Standard*, 16 March 1999.
86. *New York Times*, 15 March 1999.
87. Judah, *Kosovo: War and Revenge*, p. 223.
88. Ibid., p. 222.
89. Department of State Daily Press Briefing, Washington, DC, 18 March 1999. In Weller, *The Crisis in Kosovo*, p. 491.
90. *Reuters*, 18 March 1999.
91. Milan Milutinović Press Conference, Centre Kléber, Paris, 18 March 1999.
92. *Večernje Nevosti*, 17 March 1999.
93. Operation Horseshoe is discussed in greater length in the following chapter.
94. *The Times*, 21 March 1999.
95. *The Times*, 23 March 1999.
96. This interview was given to the BBC, for their documentary *Moral Combat*. It is also cited in Judah, *Kosovo: War and Revenge*, p. 227.
97. Judah, *Kosovo: War and Revenge*, p. 227.
98. General Wesley K. Clark, *Waging Modern War* (New York: Public Affairs, 2002), see ch. 6.
99. Barry R. Posen, 'The War for Kosovo: Serbia's Political–Military Strategy', *International Security* 24(4), 2000, p. 39.

Chapter 6: NATO Goes to War

1. For a good evaluation of the war see Daniel L. Byman and Matthew C. Waxman, 'Kosovo and the Great Air Power Debate', *International Security*, 24(4), 2000.
2. General Wesley K. Clark, *Waging Modern War* (New York: Public Affairs, 2001), p. 109.
3. Susan Woodward argues that it was the other way around. She argued that, 'the goal of the campaign seemed to narrow from forcing compliance with the Rambouillet accords ... to putting a stop to the "ethnic cleansing", "violence", and "repression"'. Once the campaign started very few leaders justified it in terms of the Rambouillet negotiations and NATO's five war aims lay ending the humanitarian catastrophe rather than enforcing a particular political settlement. Susan L. Woodward, 'Should We Think Before We Leap? A Rejoinder', *Security Dialogue*, 30(3), 1999, p. 278.
4. *Guardian*, 24 March 1999; *Independent*, 24 March 1999, *The Times*, 24 March 1999.
5. Cited by *The Times*, 25 March 1999.
6. Clark, *Waging Modern War*, p. 203.
7. *Der Speigel*, 4 May 1999.
8. Ibid.
9. Judah, *Kosovo: War and Revenge*, p. 266.
10. *Washington Post*, 21 September 1999.
11. *Washington Post*, 24 March 1999.
12. Judah, *Kosovo: War and Revenge*, p. 269.
13. Clark, *Waging Modern War*, p. 206.
14. See Ripley, *Operation Deliberate Force*.
15. Paraphrase of the five objectives. Objectives taken from the Statement of the North Atlantic Council, 12 April 1999 (NATO press release 99-51).
16. Clark, *Waging Modern War*, p. 183.The following quotes are also from this section, pp. 183–4.
17. Daalder and O'Hanlon, *Winning Ugly*, p. 103.
18. Ibid.
19. Author's conversation with a Royal Air Force pilot involved throughout Operation Allied Force.
20. Albright commented that, 'I don't see this as a long-term operation' while Solana predicted that the war would be over before the NATO summit at the end of April. See Sean Kay, 'After Kosovo: NATO's Credibility Dilemma', *Security Dialogue*, 31(1), 2000, pp. 72–3.
21. The British Harriers hit the same target on nights three and four, despite the fact that bomb damage assessment showed the target to have been destroyed. Over the duration of the campaign that same target was hit five times by the RAF. This shows that being seen to be participating was in many ways more important that what was actually being hit.
22. See Michael Ignatieff, *Virtual War: Kosovo and Beyond* (London: Chatto and Windus, 2000).
23. Daalder and O'Hanlon, *Winning Ugly*, p. 123.
24. See Dick Leurdijk and Dick Zandee, *Kosovo: From Crisis to Crisis* (Aldershot: Ashgate, 2001), p. 84.

25. Clark, *Waging Modern War*, p. 201.
26. *ABC News*, 7 April 1999.
27. *Libération*, 15 April 1999.
28. See Barry R. Posen, 'The War for Kosovo: Serbia's Political–Military Strategy', *International Security*, 24(4), 2000.
29. General Mike Willcocks recounted this episode to Judah, *Kosovo: War and Revenge*, p. 209.
30. The case was reported widely. See CNN, 26 March, *Tanjug* press release 26 March 1999 and *Guardian*, 27 March 1999.
31. The background to this move was covered in some detail by the Italian newspaper, *La Stampa*, 1 April 1999.
32. This information came from unnamed sources in the Croatian Ministry of Defence.
33. *BBC World Monitor*, 6 April 1999.
34. *RFE/RL*, 7 April 1999.
35. *Le Monde*, 8 April 1999.
36. Judah, *Kosovo: War and Revenge*, p. 240
37. Eric Herring, 'From Rambouillet to the Kosovo Accords: NATO's War Against Serbia and its Aftermath', in Booth (ed.), *The Kosovo Tragedy*.
38. See www.unhcr.ch/ – accessed on 14 May 1999.
39. Author's discussion with Violeta Hamidi, who was forced from her home in Pristina.
40. See Lenard J. Cohen, *Serpent in the Bosom: The Rise and Fall of Slobodan Milošević* (Boulder: Westview, 2001).
41. *Washington Post*, 1 April 1999, *New York Times*, 4 April 1999, and *International Herald Tribune*, 5 April 1999.
42. *The Times*, 5 April 1999.
43. *RFE/RL*, 25 March 1999.
44. *La Republica*, 26 March 1999.
45. *La Republica*, 12 April 1999.
46. *La Republica*, 24 March 1999; *La Gazzetta del Mezzogiorno*, 24 March 1999.
47. *The Times*, 26 March 1999.
48. Ibid.
49. *Institute of War and Peace Reporting (IWPR)*, 26 March 1999.
50. *Hindustan Times*, 25 March 1999. I am grateful to Maj. Rohit Sawhney of the Indian Army for bringing this passage to my attention.
51. This dilemma confronted many states and recurs throughout the excellent case studies contained in Schnabel and Thakur (eds), *Kosovo and the Challenge of Humanitarian Intervention*.
52. A good definition of the different phases of Allied Force is offered is offered by the official Dutch lessons learned report, *Kosovo evaluatie*, available at the website of the Dutch Ministry of Defence. Wesley Clark outlined his vision of phase one in *NRC Handelsblad*, 6 May 2000. NATO's operational plan consisted of five phases in total:

Phase 0: The deployment of air assets.
Phase 1: Establishment of air superiority over Kosovo and degrade air defence and command and control over the whole FRY.
Phase 2: Attack military targets inside Kosovo and military targets in Southern Serbia (south of 44 degrees latitude).

Phase 3: Expand air operations against military and security targets throughout the FRY.

Phase 4: Redeploy forces as required.

See, William Cohen and Harry Shelton, 'Joint Statement on the Kosovo After-Action Review', *Lessons Learned from the Military Operations Conducted as Part of Operation Allied Force*, Senate Armed Forces Committee, 106 Congress, I session (14 October 1999), pp. 7–8.

53. Clark, *Waging Modern War*, p. 211.
54. See *Guardian*, 28–29 March. The story was also covered in all major Western newspapers.
55. Clark, *Waging War*, p. 224.
56. Ibid.
57. See ibid and Leudijk and Zandee *Kosovo: From Crisis to Crisis*, p. 76, and Daalder and O'Hanlon, *Winning Ugly*, p. 118.
58. Daalder and O'Hanlon, *Winning Ugly*, p. 120.
59. *New York Times*, 17 April 1999.
60. See for example, *Washington Post*, 5 April 1999 and *The Times*, 15 April 1999.
61. Kenneth Bacon in answer to press questions in the Department of Defence daily briefing, 14 April 1999.
62. Interviewed in *Time*, 2 April 1999.
63. General Michael Rose writing in *The Sunday Times*, 11 April 1999.
64. *IWPR*, 17 April 1999.
65. These debates were captured well by *Le Monde*, which itself described Allied Force as a 'just war'. *Le Monde*, 7 April 1999.
66. *The Times*, 3 April 1999.
67. The extra troops were announced by Tony Blair to parliament on 13 April 1999.
68. *RFE/RL*, 13 April 1999.
69. See BBC Monitor of World News, 10 April 1999.
70. *The Times*, 13 April 1999.
71. Clark, *Waging Modern War*, pp. 299–301.
72. Ibid., p. 303.
73. *Washington Post*, 17 April 1999.
74. *Guardian*, 7 April 1999. This case was not investigated in depth by either Amnesty International or the ICTY, both of which conducted extensive investigations of the legality of Allied Force.
75. *Reuters*, 24 April 1999.
76. *RFE/RL*, 10 April 1999; and *IWPR*, 13 April 1999.
77. *RFE/RL*, 17 April 1999.
78. James Rubin confirmed in a press statement that satellite imaging had shown that Russia was not making shipments to Yugoslavia. State Department press conference, 15 April 1999.
79. *REF/RL*, 17 April 1999.
80. *Tanjug*, 6 April 1999.
81. See Thomas, *Serbia under Milošević*.
82. Accounts of the Oslo meeting can be found from the American perspective in the *Washington Post*, 14 April 1999.
83. Quoted in *The Times*, 15 April 1999.
84. Joe Lockhart in answer to questions at the White House press conference, 13 April 1999.

85. *Le Monde*, 14 April 1999.
86. Tony Blair speech to the Economic Club of Chicago, 22 April 1999. Text available from www.fco.gov.uk.
87. Remarks by Secretary of State for Defence Cohen and Chairman of the Joint Chiefs of Staff Shelton, 12 April 1999. White House Press Release.
88. *New York Times*, 25 April 1999.
89. Author's conversation with sources in the British Ministry of Defence. Also see *The Sunday Times*, 25 April 1999.
90. *Der Speigel*, 27 April 1999.
91. *Guardian*, 26 April 1999; *Independent*, 26 April 1999.
92. Daalder and O'Hanlon, *Winning Ugly*, p. 130.

Chapter 7: The Triumph of Diplomacy

1. NATO daily brief, 27 April 1999.
2. *Guardian*, 27 April 1999, *International Herald Tribune*, 27 April 1999.
3. *RFE/RL*, 27 April 1999.
4. *The Times*, 26 April 1999.
5. See www.carnegie.ru.
6. *Danas*, 26 April 1999.
7. *The Times*, 27 April 1999, *Independent*, 28 April 1999, and *Guardian*, 29 April 1999.
8. Foreign and Commonwealth Office statement, 27 April 1999. Accessed from www.fco.gov.uk on 23 September 1999.
9. Victor Gobarev, 'Kosovo Aftermath: Russia–NATO Relations after the Kosovo Crisis: Strategic Implications', *Journal of Slavic Military Studies*, 12(3), 1999.
10. Statement to the press by the office of the president of Yugoslavia, *Tanjug*, 30 April 1999.
11. *Washington Post*, 2 May 1999.
12. *RFE/RL*, 6 May 1999.
13. See Daalder and O'Hanlon, *Winning Ugly*, pp. 132–5.
14. House debate on H.R. 1569 (Military Operations in the Federal Republic of Yugoslavia Limitation Act of 1999), 28 April 1999.
15. This was the view of Representative Dick Gephart (Democrat leader), see ibid.
16. White House Press Release, 28 April 1999.
17. Senate Joint Resolution 20 (Deployment of US Armed Forces to the Kosovo region of Yugoslavia), 3–4 May, 1999.
18. *Washington Post*, 4 May 1999.
19. Cited by Judah, *Kosovo: War and Revenge*, p. 275.
20. Carl Bildt, *Veckobrev*, 22 March 1999.
21. Daalder and O'Hanlon, *Winning Ugly*, p. 169 and *Guardian*, 5 June 1999.
22. *The Times*, 6 May 1999.
23. See the Statement by the Chairman on the Conclusion of the Meeting of the G-8 Foreign Ministers, 6 May 1999. Paragraph 1 stated:

    'The G-8 Foreign Ministers adopted the following general principles on the political solution to the Kosovo crisis:
    • Immediate and verifiable end of violence and repression in Koaovo.
    • Withdrawal from Kosovo of military, police and paramilitary forces.

- Deployment in Kosovo of effective international civil and security presences, endorsed and adopted by the United Nations, capable of guaranteeing the achievement of the common objectives.
- Establishment of an interim administration for Kosovo to be decided by the Security Council of the United Nations to ensure conditions for a peaceful and normal life for all inhabitants in Kosovo.
- The safe and free return of all refugees and displaced persons and unimpeded access to Kosovo by humanitarian aid organisations.
- A political process towards the establishment of an interim political framework agreement providing for a substantial self-government for Kosovo, taking full account of the Rambouillet accords and the principles of sovereignty and territorial integrity of the Federal Republic of Yugoslavia and the other countries of the region and the demilitarisation of the KLA.
- Comprehensive approach to the economic development and stabilisation of the crisis region'.

24. *Washington Post*, 6 May 1999.
25. *The Times*, 11 May 1999.
26. Peter Gowan, 'From Rambouillet to the Chinese Embassy', from www.igc.apc.org accessed on 16 February 2000.
27. *Guardian*, 16 May 1999.
28. Leurdijk and Zandee, *Kosovo: From Crisis to Crisis*, p. 85.
29. Ibid., and see French Ministry of Defence, *Les Enseignements du Kosovo*, November 1999. Available in French only from the Ministry's website at www.defense.gouv.fr.
30. Clark, *Waging Modern War*, p. 291.
31. *The Times*, 13 May 1999.
32. Cited in *The Times*, 9 May 1999.
33. *RFE/RL*, 12 May 1999.
34. *Interfax*, 9 May 1999.
35. *Independent*, 11 May 1999.
36. Statement by the Supreme Command of the VJ, 10 May 1999. Text from the Ministry of Foreign Affairs of the Federal Republic of Yugoslavia, www.mfa.gov.yu accessed on 23 September 1999.
37. Sabrina P. Ramet and Phil Lyon, 'Germany: The Federal Republic, Loyal to NATO', in Tony Weymouth and Stanley Henig (eds), *The Kosovo Crisis: The Last American War in Europe?* (London: Pearson Education, 2001), p. 90.
38. *RFE/RL*, 12 May 1999.
39. *Bild*, 11 May 1999. Quote edited by the author.
40. See Leurdijk and Zandee, *Kosovo: From Crisis to Crisis*, p. 87.
41. *International Herald Tribune*, 14 May 1999.
42. *La Republica*, 15 May 1999.
43. Remarks by Italian Prime Minister Massimo D'Alema, 20 May 1999, NATO press release.
44. Clark, *Waging Modern War*, p. 266.
45. *Newsweek*, 16 May 1999.
46. Remarks by Tony Blair to the press in Sofia, 17 May 1999. Accessed from www.fco.gov.uk on 23 September 1999.

47. See Judah, *Kosovo: War and Revenge*, pp. 270 and Daalder and O'Hanlon, *Winning Ugly*, p. 169. The broad outline of the plan was gathered from informal sources.

48. The British Ministry of Defence conducted several planning exercises and the Pentagon began administrative preparations for a ground operation.

49. Posen, 'The War for Kosovo', p. 71.

50. Clark, *Waging Modern War*, p. 337.

51. Judah, *Kosovo: War and Revenge*, p. 284.

52. General Mike Short interviewed on the BBC's, *Moral Combat* documentary.

53. Louise Richardson, 'Britain's Role in the Kosovo Crisis', in Pierre Martin and Mark R. Brawley (eds), *Alliance Politics, Kosovo, and NATO's War: Allied Force or Forced Allies?* (London: Palgrave, 2001), p. 151.

54. Ibid.

55. Though there has never been official confirmation of this, the existence of such plans is widely known. Also see, *New York Times*, 7 November 1999.

56. See Daalder and O'Hanlon, *Winning Ugly*, p. 158.

57. *Tanjug*, 27 March 1999.

58. Marc Weller, 'The Kosovo Indictment of the International Criminal Tribunal of Yugoslavia', in Ken Booth (ed.), *The Kosovo Tragedy*, p. 209. Also see Indictment by the International Criminal Tribunal for the Former Yugoslavia Against Yugoslav Leaders, 22 May 1999. Accessed from www.balkanaction.org and also available along with trial proceedings from www.icty.org

59. For more on the ICTY, and competing views about it see Geoffrey Robertson, *Crimes Against Humanity: The Struggle for Global Justice* (London: Penguin, 1999).

60. *Washington Post*, 27 May 1999. Also see, *International Herald Tribune*, 28 May 1999.

61. Daalder and O'Hanlon, *Winning Ugly*, p. 171.

62. Kosovo Peace Plan, 3 June 1999. United Nations Press Release (S/1999/649, Annex), 7 June 1999.

63. Clark, *Waging Modern War*, p. 354.

64. See Noel Malcolm, 'Yes there were Mass Killings', *Spectator*, 283 (8939), 1999.

65. UN Security Council Resolution 1244, 10 June 1999.

66. Though monumental obstacles remained. See David Rohde, 'Kosovo Seething', *Foreign Affairs*, 79(3), 2000.

67. This argument was put forward by Michael Mandelbaum, 'A Perfect Failure: NATO's War Against Yugoslavia', *Foreign Affairs*, 78(5), 1999.

68. On the security challenges confronting KFOR see Espen Barth Eide, 'The Internal Security Challenge in Kosovo', *The International Spectator*, 35(1), 2000; Susan L. Woodward, 'Kosovo and the Region: Consequences of the Waiting Game', *The International Spectator*, 35(1), 2000; Mike Jackson, 'KFOR: The Inside Story', *RUSI Journal*, February 2000.

69. Javier Solana, 'NATO's Success in Kosovo', *Foreign Affairs*, November/December 1999, p. 12.

70. I share Daalder and O'Hanlon's view that there were two wars but disagree that NATO 'lost' the war against Serb forces on the ground in Kosovo for reasons that I outline in the conclusion. See Ivo Daalder and Michael E. O'Hanlon, 'Unlearning the Lessons of Kosovo', *Foreign Policy*, 116, 1999.

Conclusion

1. See Roland Bleiker, *Dissent, Human Agency and Global Politics* (Cambridge: Cambridge University Press, 2000).
2. Author's interview with Lord Owen, London, 5 October 2001.
3. Wheeler, *Saving Strangers*, p. 284.
4. Ibid.
5. Ibid.
6. Karl W. Deutsch *et al.*, *Political Community in the North Atlantic Area: International Organization in the Light of Historical Experience* (Princeton: Princeton University Press, 1957), p. 5.
7. Emanuel Adler and Michael Barnett, 'Security Communities in Theoretical Perspective', in Emanuel Adler and Michael Barnett (eds), *Security Communities* (Cambridge: Cambridge University Press, 1998), p. 17.
8. Ibid., p. 50.
9. Ibid., p. 56.
10. Ibid.
11. Stephen Walt, 'NATO's Future (In Theory), in Martin and Brawley, *Alliance Politics, Kosovo, and NATO's War*, p. 15.
12. See Chapter 4.
13. Justin Morris, 'Force and Democracy: UN/US Intervention in Haiti', *International Peacekeeping*, 2(3), 1995.
14. Such arguments can be found throughout books such as N. W. Hutchings and Larry Spargimino, *Where Leads the Road to Kosovo?* (Oklahoma: Heatherstone, 1999); Michael Parenti, *To Kill a Nation: The Attack on Yugoslavia* (London: Verso, 2000), and throughout Tariq Ali (ed.), *Masters of the Universe*.
15. Jim Whitman, 'The Kosovo Refugee Crisis: NATO's Humanitarianism versus Human Rights', in Ken Booth (ed.), *The Kosovo Tragedy*, p. 164.
16. Cited by Wheeler, *Saving Strangers*, p. 267.

Index